BOULDER CITY LIBRARY

3 1432 00186

658   Dreeke, Rob
.4092
DRE   Code of trust
        American
        counterintelligence
        expert's five rules to lead
        and succeed

D0389479

Boulder City Library
701 Adams Boulevard
Boulder City, NV 89005

DISCARD

The
CODE
of
TRUST

Boulder City Library
701 Adams Boulevard
Boulder City, NV 89005
JAN 2018

DISCARD

The
CODE
— *of* —
TRUST

AN AMERICAN
COUNTERINTELLIGENCE
EXPERT'S FIVE RULES TO
LEAD AND SUCCEED

ROBIN DREEKE

and CAMERON STAUTH

Foreword by Joe Navarro

St. Martin's Press ⚓ New York

THE CODE OF TRUST. Copyright © 2017 by Robin Dreeke. Foreword © 2017
by Joe Navarro. All rights reserved. Printed in the United States of
America. For information, address St. Martin's Press, 175 Fifth Avenue,
New York, N.Y. 10010.

www.stmartins.com

The Library of Congress Cataloging-in-Publication Data is available
upon request.

ISBN 978-1-250-09346-2 (hardcover)
ISBN 978-1-250-09347-9 (ebook)

Our books may be purchased in bulk for promotional, educational,
or business use. Please contact your local bookseller or the Macmillan
Corporate and Premium Sales Department at 1-800-221-7945, extension
5442, or by email at MacmillanSpecialMarkets@macmillan.com.

First Edition: August 2017

10 9 8 7 6 5 4 3 2 1

For Kim, Katelyn, and Kevin with endless gratitude for helping me hone my trust-building skills every day of my life through their great tolerance and patience with me.

—Robin Dreeke

For Lori Brockman, with deep appreciation and everlasting love for sharing her life with me, and making it the best part of mine.

—Cameron Stauth

CONTENTS

FOREWORD

IMAGINE A WORLD WHERE THERE is no trust. Our lives would be hell, since there would be no one, and nothing, that we could rely on—not our parents, our institutions, our organizations, or even our friends. Life would be bleak.

Food would be unsafe, cars would be dangerous, the firefighters and paramedics might not respond, and depending upon a pilot to safely fly us where we wanted to go would be a coin toss.

Trust—one concept—underpins virtually everything we value. Without trust, we would be merely surviving, not thriving.

Fortunately for us, trust is a universal attribute. It is something we all want.

It is trust that allows us to establish relationships quickly. Lack of trust, though, is what ruins many relationships, at home and at work.

But as important as trust is, how do we establish it? How do we keep trust? How do we fix trust issues? How do we better imbue trust? How can we gain someone's trust in a few hours, minutes, or even seconds? How do we know when others are not worthy of our trust?

Perhaps you have never thought about this. Most of us don't. In previous generations, when most of us lived in small towns and villages, trust was easy to establish. Everyone knew whom to trust. But now most of us don't live in small towns, where our parents' pedigree is well known, and where we also have been a known commodity since birth. Most of us live and work nowhere near where we were born. You may be living in Miami one morning, and the next week you are working in Phoenix, where no one knows you—and yet, within a short time, you must establish trust.

We live in a world where trust is required, although you may not always see it. Trust is the social tissue that binds us together, so that we can get things done, work together more effectively, and grow our relationships.

Trust must be established not over a lifetime, but, more often than not, in minutes, if not seconds. Yes, seconds—that is how quickly our fast-paced, interconnected, transient e-reality world works.

So, how do we do it? How do we garner and establish trust? This is where this book and Robin Dreeke come in.

Robin and I share a few things. We are both pilots, we both worked for the FBI as Special Agents, and we were both in the FBI's elite National Security Branch Behavioral Analysis Program. More important, we are both in the people business.

That's right, the people business. I hear this all the time: "I sell appliances," or, "I work in real estate," or, "I work for a financial institution," or, "I do landscaping," or, "I am a stay-at-home dad." What they are really saying is, "I am in the people business," and in that business I sell refrigerators, sell houses, invest people's money, make someone's yard look nice, or I am rearing the most precious thing in this world: a child. They always put their occupation first, but what they forget is that, first and foremost, they are in the people business. Most of us are in the people business, and if you are not, you are the rare exception.

In the people business, how we interact with each other is anchored in trust.

There have been books in the past about the importance of trust, but when Robin told me he was going to write one about how to create and nourish trust, I immediately thanked him, because this is something we can all use. A guide to understanding trust, how to exercise it, and how to make it work for us is so important and so needed.

Robin is a master of looking at human behavior, and simplifying our understanding of others. Using those skills—developed in the FBI, where matters of life and death are a daily challenge, and everything happens in seconds rather than days—Robin gives us insight into how to assess others, and determine their needs, wants, desires, intentions, and fears. Once you understand that, and establish trust, all else follows.

People want to be appreciated, cared for, loved, trusted, and respected. But they also want to be understood, and if you master the skills to achieve that, you truly become exceptional. You become one of those people we often read about—someone who is well respected, well liked, and sought after. That is the power of trust.

With trust, true relationships are possible, and become a source of comfort and happiness. Realistically, with trust, almost anything is possible. Without trust, knowing what's in the mind of others becomes a mere exercise in futility.

The tools, strategies, and secrets to working with others, and to establishing trust, are well known to Robin, because he has dedicated himself to studying this subject as a Naval Academy graduate, a lieutenant in the United States Marines, as an FBI Special Agent, and as manager of the FBI's most prestigious behavioral program. When your job is commanding others, or catching criminals and spies, you can't help but master the art and science of what works—and nothing works faster than trust. In those high-stakes situations, trust is critical.

If the skills practiced by the knowledgeable few who work in those high-stakes positions are effective for them, they will certainly be effective for you, in your daily life.

Written in a very practical style, full of examples and anecdotes, this book is for anyone interested in understanding themselves, and more important, understanding others.

—Joe Navarro, former FBI Special Agent,
author of *Three Minutes to Doomsday*
and *What Every BODY Is Saying*

PART I

THE LEADERSHIP
POWER OF TRUST

— 1 —

BEYOND MANIPULATION:
THE CODE OF TRUST

Trust in the Streets of New York

I AM GOING TO TELL YOU how to inspire trust, and rise to the rare level of leadership that only trust can confer. It's a simple lesson, but not an easy one.

Here it is, fully revealed, in all its simplicity. First: Be eminently worthy of trust. Second: Prove you are.

Could anything be harder than that?

The first part is hard, and the second is even harder.

How many people in your life—and even in history—do you consider worthy of absolute trust?

Who would you trust with your life? The lives of your family? Your life savings? Your deepest secrets? Your career? Your reputation?

Would you trust your best friend? Would you place your full trust in our current president, a past president, or any current office holder? What about your doctor or attorney? Your boss? Your business partner? Your brother or sister? Your spouse?

Would you follow that person's lead implicitly, and do whatever you possibly could for them, with minimal questioning?

You probably *would* do that for some of these people. That's common—especially if they're family—and it's healthy.

Some of that trust may rest upon universal social agreements: "You're my mother, so I trust you." Even more commonly, though, your trust may stem in part from contractual agreements that imply at least a minor degree of uncertainty: a business contract, a confidentiality agreement, a prenuptial agreement, a living will that governs the treatment of your loved ones, or your citizen's right to remove untrustworthy people from power.

There's no shame in that degree of uncertainty. It's not easy to grant someone your trust, especially when it concerns things you can't afford to lose, such as your marriage, the well-being of your children, your job, your assets, your professional reputation, or your personal honor.

Often, it's even harder to trust people than it is to love them.

That said: it's just as hard for people to trust you.

I'm going to tell you how to make it easier for them.

When you do learn how—and you will—you'll have the central quality of character that defines all great leaders. People are happy to follow those they trust, and rarely follow those that they don't trust. That's a wise and deeply embedded element of human nature.

Of course, from time to time, people that you don't trust may temporarily have power over you. They might be bullies, or people who gambled, lied, or manipulated their way into power.

That kind of power doesn't last, and the influence of those people fades fast. Bullies are overthrown, liars are exposed, gamblers lose, manipulators make mistakes—and trustworthy people inevitably take their place. The world isn't perfect, but it does reward and empower those who have earned the honor of being trusted.

Those who inspire trust are the only people who can retain the power of personal influence for a lifetime, and wield it without revolt or resentment. They are the great people in history, and the great people in your own life: strong, humble, and dedicated to your own best interests.

Some people are natural born leaders who can inspire trust without even trying. But most people who inspire trust need to be taught, and they often learn the lessons through pain, failure, and humbling moments. If you're lucky and smart, though, you can learn it from a good teacher.

I'm in a good position to teach you how to inspire trust, because I had to learn it myself. I'm not a born leader. I thought I was, until I finally looked at myself with unblinking honesty. Like most people who long to be great leaders but have to learn the art, I paid dearly for the lessons.

The only way for me to become the man that people now trust was to analyze every hard lesson I learned from the fine leaders around me, and characterize it, categorize it, prioritize it, test it, tweak it, and integrate it into a system.

I'll teach you that system, and make the lessons easier for you than they were for me.

As I said, it won't be easy, but I have to assume that you're intelligent enough to grasp hard lessons, or you wouldn't even be looking at a serious book like this. You're probably also someone who sincerely yearns to inspire genuine, *well-placed* trust—or you'd be looking at books with a quick fix, full of tricks: *Trust for Dummies.* There definitely are books about how to manipulate people into trusting you, but this isn't one of them. Manipulation is about pushing people. Trust is about leading them.

How do you achieve that lofty goal? Again, I can give you a simple answer that's hard to do.

To inspire trust, put others first.

That single, central action empowers all legendary leaders.

It is so grounded in common sense that—like other self-evident truths—it is often overlooked.

It's *easy* to lead people when you put their needs first—but it's almost impossible when you're only serving yourself.

If you adopt another person's goal as part of your goal, why *shouldn't* they follow your lead? If you don't, why should they?

This philosophy, to some extent, goes against the grain of popular business and social culture, in which creating trust is often reduced to various forms of manipulation, and is typically referred to as "winning" trust, as if that sacred goal were a game.

Many books teach the dubious arts of manipulation—but there are *no other books* that offer the lessons in this one. Trust me. I looked for one before I started writing.

It's also widely believed that the fast track to success is to carefully narrow your focus to your own goals. But that's one of those lazy shortcuts that just slows you down. Success comes far faster when you inspire others to merge their goals with yours, and forge ahead with you, in unison.

For many people, therefore, this book offers a new outlook, and a new set of lessons.

We'll start your lessons where I started mine: in the streets of New York City, among spies and counterspies.

If you can learn trust there, you can learn it anywhere.

It was 1997: a pivotal time in foreign affairs. The Cold War had ended, but it still had the potential, as simmering conflicts always do, to rage again—probably not as a military march toward mutually assured destruction, but as a battle for the true power of the twenty-first century: economic domination, backed by the dark swagger of limited but deadly engagements.

The new world order of that era had created both chaos and unlimited opportunity, and there was even less trust among the world's superpowers at that time than there is now. No one knew where the countries of the newly disintegrated Soviet bloc were headed: to democracy, to dictatorship, to prosperity, to ruin, or to war. For America, it was a delicate tipping point in history, and it needed to be handled just right.

If, at that time, the direction of American foreign affairs had been up to me—a fledgling FBI Case Agent working boots-on-the-ground in national security—things probably would *not* have been handled right.

I had a lot to learn.

I didn't know it then, but I would learn a great deal of what I needed to know on the first day of my first important assignment in the field.

I learned so much that at the end of that day, as you'll soon see,

I didn't even know how much I'd learned. It took me years to break down the basics of what happened, and use that knowledge to develop my comprehensive system for inspiring trust.

When I eventually became the head of the Counterintelligence Division's Behavioral Analysis Program, I presented this system to thousands of FBI agents and other law enforcement officials. I've also taught it to hundreds of military groups, corporate groups, law firms, financial institutions, and universities. In addition, I've counseled a select group of CEOs, academicians, public servants, and think-tank analysts.

My system is based on two straightforward, tightly linked components:

(1) **The Code of Trust:** a set of five rules of engagement that must be embraced by all who wish to inspire legitimate, lasting trust.

(2) **The Four Steps to Inspiring Trust:** an action plan that implements the Code of Trust. The Steps make the Code work in the real world. This world, however, is rightly skeptical—but the Four Steps also *demonstrate* your mastery of trustworthiness—to your family, your friends, your coworkers, and your supervisors. It shows people that you are a person to be trusted with the fates of others, and the responsibility of leadership.

Most people can master this system, but it presents a steep learning curve for those who are still trapped in the outdated but still common attitude that the best way to achieve compliance with one's wishes is through crafty manipulation, appeals to emotion, velvet-glove coercion, and by outmaneuvering and out-thinking others. If some elements of that approach apply to you, you're probably looking for a better way to lead: one that's more effective, simpler, and more equitable and attractive to others. You want *leadership that lasts a lifetime*. We all do.

When you unlock the secrets of this fine form of leadership, you will naturally amass a group of people who trust you—a veritable tribe of trust—and they'll all know other people who trust them. At that point, your reach and influence will expand exponentially, with leadership flourishing in its wake.

If you're truly conscientious and self-aware, you may be questioning, at this point in your journey to leadership, if you really *do* deserve the full trust of others.

It's very possible that, yes, you *do* deserve trust—but just haven't yet mastered the ability to inspire it in everyone around you.

Or maybe, like many people, you're still struggling, as a student of trust, to learn how to be 100 percent worthy of it. Perhaps you haven't yet achieved the ability—or understood the power—of putting the needs of other people first.

Both of these challenges can be met.

If you're worthy of trust but aren't sure how to convey this to others, this book will help show you how.

If you really aren't, at this point, fully worthy of everyone's trust, you can learn to be. Character is never a constant in a world governed by change.

Inspiring trust is truly an interpersonal art form. But even in its complexity, it is—as you'll see—the kind of art that can be achieved through the paint-by-numbers techniques that comprise my system. The techniques are derived from social psychology, evolutionary psychology, neurobiology, classic codes of morality, business tradition, historical fact, and common sense.

Most of the people who have learned my system have been professionals who apply it in their jobs, but the lessons of this system are not solely applicable at work. Even people who aren't very career oriented still want to be trusted. We all want to be the type of person who makes friends easily, and keeps them. We all want other people to trust us enough to share their secrets. We want to be the type of adult that children naturally gravitate toward. We want to be trusted by our wives or husbands: in our relationships, and our partnerships. We want to lead our families without rancor, and show our children how to lead. And we want to be the person who gets treated in an equally friendly way by supervisors, subordinates, strangers, store clerks, and old friends.

None of this is possible if you don't exude authentic trust. By the time you have internalized the five rules of the Code of Trust, and mastered the actions of the Four Steps, you will be the person that others naturally turn to for direction.

In this chapter, we'll jump straight into the Code and the Steps. I'll teach you the lessons of trust through stories about my career as an agent and program director at the Federal Bureau of Investigation, where I learned most of what I know about trust. Other examples of the power of trust will come from my days as a midshipman at the U.S. Naval Academy, an officer in the U.S. Marines, and also from my personal life, and my work as a business consultant.

All of the FBI stories are set in the arena of intelligence and counterintelligence, where I worked for about twenty years. In the profession of spies and counterspies, trust is a scarce commodity, even though it's the currency of the trade.

This isn't a spy novel—it's about the qualities and techniques that will make you a better person, and a trusted leader. Even so, there's a strong element of entertainment in it, because lessons don't need to be boring. In these lessons, you'll probably see yourself, partly because the favorite topic of most of us is—no surprise—*us*. A tenet of behavioral science is that approximately 40 percent of what we say every day is about ourselves. That's natural and normal, and is absolutely necessary for the introspection that creates self-knowledge and growth. So to have fun, and get the most from this first chapter and all the others, look for yourself.

Here's the first of many drills for you: as you read the story in the first chapter, try to figure out the five rules of the Code, and the actions of the Four Steps, before I spell them out at the end of the chapter.

While you do it, make a mental note of how many of them you

already knew. If you recognize several of them as old friends that are part of your existing character, it's a good sign. If you don't, it means you're learning, and that's good, too. I'll be brief. Your time is valuable, I'm grateful for it, and I promise to finish as quickly as possible. This book is about you, not me.

New York City, 1997

Jesse Thorne, my mentor on my first important day in the field, said, "When our guy gets here, I'm going to promise him that we'll finish this as quickly as possible."

"Why?"

"Because his time's valuable, and I'm grateful for it. This is about him, not us.

"If he thinks we'll drag this out, he'll pull away. If we get to the point, it shows that we respect him—as a professional and as a person—and nothing opens the door to trust better than plain-old respect. So talk nice to him, and make a connection."

"But we don't *know* him, so we have no *reason* to respect him. Especially under our current, uh . . ."—I tried to remember some good spy lingo, but couldn't—"circumstance."

The circumstance was that we were tasked with uncovering espionage, and we were hoping that this guy would give us insight into a known spy.

"We'll *find* a reason. There's always a good reason to respect someone, and there's never a good reason to judge them. But that doesn't mean we have to be friends."

"Then what?"

"Then we'll ask him about himself, and figure out his context."

"Context?"

"Spy talk: It means, what kind of guy he is, where he's from, what he likes. We'll ascertain his context. Learn *important* stuff. We don't make small talk."

"And?"

"And then we make small talk: *all* of it about him."

"Why?"

"To make friends." The bewildered look on my face made him smile. Jesse loved to play the Jedi Master, and enlighten poor, dumb me with his paradoxical Zen insights. "You can never have too many friends," he said.

When we walked into the restaurant to meet our Access Agent—the guy who knew the spy we wanted to expose—Jesse nodded slightly at some of the staff and they nodded slightly back. He often did business here because it was a controlled environment, owned by a former FBI agent, with a staff that knew not to ask too many questions, or come around too often. Choosing the right place for a meeting is part of an investigative technique called crafting your encounters.

The restaurant had an upscale Irish-pub atmosphere, and exuded comfort and security, with plush booths and soft lighting that was coupled with the inviting smells of well-oiled leather, polished oak, sizzling steak, and baking bread. It was the kind of place that made you want to stay, and it was out of the way, where our contact wouldn't have to worry about getting spotted with FBI: a strong concern to some.

At the open grill, behind a bar as smooth and slick as a bowling lane, juicy top sirloins dripped onto charcoal and kicked up yellow spires of fire that lent further to the atmosphere of contentment. The creature comforts were critically important, because in a first encounter—or any other in which you're trying to inspire trust—it's important to treat people well.

That especially applied to Access Agents—another term for confidential human sources of information. Intelligence gained directly from a human being, referred to as HUMINT, is often considered more valuable in clandestine operations than information from any other source—such as imagery intelligence, called IMINT, or public knowledge, known as open-source intelligence: OSINT. In the final analysis, the perspective and experience of a person is the gold standard of information. That's another reason why trust is so important.

This guy was not the subject of our investigation—but just an entry point to the spy—so he had nothing to fear from us. But he didn't know that. He'd never heard of us until we'd called, might reasonably think we were trying to trick him, and owed us nothing: including his trust. Why should he trust us? He knew we wanted something, but didn't know what it was, or who it might help—or hurt. And he wasn't expecting us to give him anything in return.

In spite of that, most people—even total strangers—are cooperative: if you give them a good reason to be. In FBI investigations, this is especially true in the realm of national security, rather than crime. One of the nice things about working in national security was that we were usually dealing with highly intelligent people: diplomats, attachés, foreign policy experts, and business executives.

As a rule, these intelligent people were quite rational, and that's always helpful in building trust. Rationality is the brick and mortar that creates a firm foundation of trust. It keeps things real, reflects only honesty, and helps you determine who people actually are, and what they really want. Emotion builds a foundation of sand, evershifting as moods change, creating sinkholes of confusion, doubt, and dishonesty.

Not that I knew even these simple things back then. I was a young buck fresh out of the Marines, thinking that I already knew what it took to inspire trust, and lead others. In actuality, all I knew was the tip of the iceberg.

In fact, I was such a newly minted, immature leader that I didn't even know back then that leadership was my ultimate goal. And I *absolutely* did not know that the grand key to leadership is as simple as: it's all about them.

(*We interrupt this narrative to inform the reader that all five rules of the Code and all Four Steps have been revealed. Now back to our regularly scheduled reading!*)

On this life-changing day in New York, I thought my ultimate goal was to have a good lunch, get some information, and go home to my wife and newborn daughter feeling like I'd done something important that would impress other people. That's not even *close* to being an ultimate goal, or even a good one.

You don't *need* to impress people—I later learned—if you put their needs ahead of your own. They'll naturally trust you—and like you, too—because when trust comes first, people will feel good, and light up every time you walk through the door.

Getting people to like you is not how you make them feel about you, it's how you make them feel about themselves.

We were there early, well before noon, in accord with Jesse's plan, and his eyes darted around the room obsessively, seeming to note details, as he made minor adjustments to where we sat, who could see us, who our waiter would be, and what we were wearing. He wanted my sport coat off, and my tie in my pocket. He said that a more casual look provoked less defensiveness. He told me to keep my watch visible, though, because it was a Darth Vader watch that my daughter had given me for Father's Day. Can't beat that for casual. Jesse liked props. There was always a chance, he thought, that some prop, even if only used subliminally, could bring people together, on common ground.

"When he gets here, try to find something that we can do for him—some favor—anything that makes him feel appreciated. If he says something you disagree with, keep it to yourself. Because this is *his* meeting, let him take the lead, and don't try to force any agenda. We'll see what his interests and needs are, and then find goals we have in common. We don't need to be manipulative, or even want to be."

"Uh, isn't *all* of that kind of manipulative, Jesse?"

"Bite your tongue!" he said. Or words to that effect. "It's just good manners. We don't judge people. We accept them. We validate them—for who they are, not for who we want 'em to be. That's how everybody wants to be treated. Besides, this meeting is too important to be manipulative. That never works."

"Why?"

"Cuz people aren't stupid. You play them and they'll play you."

Jesse was a born leader, and didn't need to systematize the art and science of trust, as I later did.

These days, I think of him as a Beacon: the type of person who's a shining light of safety. Beacons are humble and accepting, and inspire trust as naturally as sunlight signals each new day.

By the end of this book, you can be a Beacon—unless you're one already, who needs only to learn how best to show it.

Jesse Thorne came up in the Bureau with the esteemed Joe Navarro—who graciously wrote the foreword to this book, and pioneered the application of behaviorism to espionage, as a cofounder of the Behavioral Analysis Program. Joe and Jesse were part of a tribe of trust that had an indelible influence on the Bureau, and I flatter myself to think that I eventually earned the honor of standing among their ranks.

Jesse was one of the most successful agents in the Bureau's modern era, but one of the most humble. He'd received the FBI's highest honor, the Director's Award, but the only ornamentation in his office was a pen holder made out of a Tropicana orange juice can.

Jesse could tell that I was totally befuddled. "Just watch," he said, making a hand movement like the Jedi mind trick, "and learn."

He became quiet, still surveying the room, and I asked him what he was thinking. "I'm just smelling the room," he said.

"You mean, like, casing the joint?"

"No, like, smelling. I love the smell of steak in the morning. Smells like . . . victory." I looked blank—because he was usually too humble to even think in terms of victory—so he said, "That's a joke. It's from a war movie." Jesse loved humor. It's one of those universal things that brings people together.

Jesse was an ex-serviceman, like me. Lot of FBI guys are. It's a natural progression for people who are serious about serving their country in national security, and it's one of the American government's greatest teaching and training institutions. Theoretically, a guy like me had already been fully trained in leadership—by the Marines. But that assumption was quickly becoming *very* theoretical.

As we waited for the Access Agent, I was thinking about this same early stage of my U.S. Naval Academy career, and my military career.

In my first semester at the Naval Academy, I became very adept at following orders—earning the ranking of #1 in my company—and became the Fourth Class Company Commander, the guy in charge of the other plebes. I became very full of myself. My second semester, when leadership became the determining factor in my ranking, I plummeted to number thirty. What's that tell you? To me, it says: good followers aren't always good leaders, even though they're often promoted to leadership—and they're *never* good leaders when they let it go to their heads.

I worked on leadership, and learned to get things done by enforcing my will. By graduation, I thought I'd learned everything there was to know about leadership. I had a rank sufficient to lead men into battle, and assumed that if I had the rank, I had the ability.

As a young Marine, my perception of the world was that I had finally become a fantastic, charismatic guy, a hardcore officer, a great friend to everyone, and a real solid professional.

As you may have noted, all of those perceptions about the "world" were really about me, with the blithe assumption that the world and I were one in the same. I still had a lot to learn.

I was an Air Support Control Officer—basically a combat air-traffic controller—at Camp Lejeune, North Carolina, a humid coastal training center you've probably seen in some movies. At Lejeune, there was about as much water in the air as in the bay, and there were mosquitoes that rivaled the size and maneuverability of Harrier fighter jets. Both of these burdens created the level of esprit de corps that comes only from shared suffering.

One night—a night I'll never forget—we we're getting ready for a bombing run early the next morning. We were out in the middle of nowhere—to enable us to sharpen our bombing skills without blowing up anything valuable—and the air out there was heavy enough to deliver not only all the oxygen we needed, but the water, too.

Depending upon the air to keep you hydrated is not a great thing, especially when the temperature range swings from *way*-too-hot to just-*shoot*-me.

Our unit was junior-officer-heavy, with about a dozen first- and second-lieutenants: all skilled Marines—in the rear with the gear—and we were all racking in one big tent. I was lucky enough at this time to have an actual cot—or manipulative enough, to be honest—so I went to bed early, with my head burrowed into my sleeping bag to escape the mosquitoes, listening to the quiet camaraderie of my buddies around me.

Half asleep, I heard shuffling feet, then I felt hands all over me, and realized I was getting duct-taped into my bag, and tied to the cot. I wasn't fighting it, because: (1) nobody was beating on me, and (2) I couldn't. I was lifted up, and all of a sudden I was going for a ride, hearing only the muffled chuckles of Marines and the engine of what sounded like an old Desert Storm dune buggy. About thirty minutes later I was lowered back onto mother earth, hearing only the hungry buzz of the plane-size flying vampires. I had the feeling I was facing a long walk back to the barracks.

I heard a huge blast from overhead, and someone cried, "Ohhhh, the *humidity*!"

At least somebody was having fun. Things grew quiet quickly.

Luckily, I had gone to sleep that night, for no good reason, with my Leatherman multi-tool in my pocket. So I hacked my through the sleeping bag, stuck my head out, and couldn't help but notice that I was in the Gulf-Ten Impact Zone: the site of our morning bombing exercises.

A moment of clarity! I had been graced with a friendly Communications Exercise by my fellow Marines!

In short: as a newbie looie, I'd screwed up, and they'd sent me a message.

With what content? I had no idea.

It was another humbling moment: the priceless moments that teach humility. They're best learned in books. In real life, you pay retail.

Back in the barracks, I learned fast. Turns out, one of the guys wasn't happy with me, and that meant that his friends weren't, either. And this guy was far more aware than me that you can never have too many friends.

The guy in question was the same rank as me, a personal friend, a comrade in arms: *an equal*—who was newly married, like me, and had taken a brief, proactive, self-selected leave to see his wife for a few hours. I, in contrast, had played by the rules, sucked it up, stayed where I was supposed to be—and in the interests of keeping the Corps strong and true—dropped a dime on my buddy to a superior officer, who reprimanded the good-husband, bad-boy Marine.

As night became day, I was informed that an officer does *not* build esprit de corps by diming-out a buddy. I learned that I was *not* a better officer than him, and that the title of our deployment was not *Legend of Robin: The War Years*.

The men told me that I hadn't thought about the needs of my fellow married officer, and that if I thought that the ultimate goal of our training was to be Playground Leader, I was not the type of officer that Marines would follow into peril.

Thus endeth the lesson. I got it. Or thought I did. Let's just say I got some of it.

Daydream over: as Jesse continued to scan the room, I had the distinct feeling that I was getting a refresher course on leadership, at a pace I could barely follow.

"Here's our guy," Jesse said.

I felt a surge of nerves. The stage was set and the curtain rose on my new life as a recruiter of spies!

The Access Agent, Steve—not his real name, but better for our purposes here than Boris, Yao, or Shirazi—was walking toward us. "So what's my role?" I asked Jesse—perhaps a bit late.

"Your role is to listen to him. That's my role, too. We'll try to find a way to help him, and we'll let him know what we need—but in a subtle way, without demanding anything. Then we'll hope he helps us. So just be yourself. Don't say anything that's not true," Jesse said. "Don't put on a *show*. And don't *show off*."

Jesse stood. "It's showtime!" he said.

As Steve arrived, Jesse held out his hand and said, "Thanks for coming on such short notice. I appreciate the favor."

Even that was a lesson. One law of behavioral psychology is that if somebody has done you a favor, it makes them more willing to do you another favor. They're even more likely to do it than someone who *owes* you a favor. The theory is that if they've done you a favor, they assume that surely they must like you. Otherwise, it makes their brain tense with contradiction—the fancy label: *cognitive dissonance*. It's called the "Ben Franklin effect," after the famous American who figured it out, without applying the fancy label.

Steve stood by the booth with a telltale demeanor of what-am-I-doing-here? Jesse—an expert in nonverbal communication, like Joe Navarro—defused the awkwardness by tilting his head slightly and flashing a shy grin as he shook hands.

Steve was a senior executive at a major New York think tank: one of the companies that offers research and advice on military and other issues to the government, and to private industry. Among the most famous of the think tanks are the RAND Corporation and the Brookings Institution, but there are about five thousand of them around the world. Steve's company specialized in European matters, so its services were in high demand in the years after the collapse of the Soviet Union. Nobody knew who to trust in Eastern Europe, and it was even hard to tell who was in power—or would stay there.

Steve focused mostly on military trends, and his area of particular expertise was the intersection between the American defense industry and the armies of the Eastern European countries. The governments and defense companies in the emerging nations, after years of being pawns in the Soviet's game, couldn't possibly build all of the military products they needed. So they bought many of them from America—or stole the secrets about how to build them. The thefts were usually achieved in the classic criminal manner: by an inside man—most commonly a defense industry executive, or government employee, usually for money.

For example, an Army officer named Clyde Lee Conrad earned more than a million dollars funneling military secrets to the Soviet bloc—before he met my friend Joe Navarro, and spent the rest of his life in prison, as a convicted traitor. Joe later wrote a book about it, *Three Minutes to Doomsday,* which at this time is being developed as a movie.

Conrad was one of the major spies Americans hear about, but an even bigger problem for America is the damage done by hundreds of minor spies—people who don't steal very much, for very long, but who commit crimes that accumulate by the thousands. Not all of them get caught, even when they're suspected—and *many* people are suspected.

Most of the thefts don't even involve classified material, but just proprietary information that's worth a lot of money—and could eventually be used by an unfriendly force.

Relatively less valuable is open-source material that anyone with enough expertise can access. This OSINT is often information that soon fades from relevance.

As a rule, the nexus of a large number of minor spies is one person: a recruiter, who's working for another country. The primary recruiting tactic of these people is to build trust among the spies who steal for them.

It's true that shady people can build trust—but it's a weak, fake type of trust, built on lies, manipulation, and coercion, and it can topple overnight.

Most commonly, the spies that are recruited befriend people who have access only to open-source information, but who understand the OSINT so well that their perspective is very valuable. Because these well-informed people are quite innocent, and have nothing to hide, they're often good Access Agents. Steve was one of those people. That's why we were buying his lunch.

Steve knew a person that we suspected of being a recruiter and a spy. This person had become the subject of our investigation. He was therefore referred to, in spy lingo as—guess what?—the subject. Steve probably liked the subject, and had a certain degree of trust in him. But when I say a certain degree, I mean trust that was a mile wide and an inch deep.

I can't give you any of the details that are classified, but I can tell you, without violating Bureau policy, that our subject was an ambassador for a former Soviet bloc nation that was scrambling to buy all the armaments it could, as were most of those suddenly independent countries.

Before the day was over, we wanted to leverage the mutual trust that Steve shared with our subject, and get a better idea of exactly what the subject was up to, and what his priorities were. Then, with enough patience and work, we could make sure our subject was out of business, and facing the appropriate consequences of his actions.

After Jesse finished shaking hands with Steve, he introduced me. "This is Robin," Jesse said—no title, no last name—as if I were just a buddy. Casual in the extreme. "Robin's gotta go pick up his daughter in about an hour, so we'll wrap this thing up before you even finish your steak."

We made small talk for about ninety seconds and then our waiter magically appeared, quickly took our order, and vanished just as magically.

"So," Jesse said to Steve, "I've heard that you're an expert on Eastern Europe. I'm really interested in that, too. I was hoping you could give us some insights and opinions on what's happening over there these days."

"I'm happy to," Steve said. People love to talk about their own area of expertise: It makes the conversation about them.

As Steve outlined the issues and major players of Eastern Europe, Jesse seemed genuinely impressed, and gradually steered the conversation to the country that our subject worked for.

Jesse's questions about the country were very nonjudgmental and open-ended—the verbal equivalent of an ink-blot test. He wanted Steve to feel free to speak his mind.

That's not just common courtesy, but the only way to find out what people really think. If they censor themselves, you get pablum. It also prevents you from putting your foot in your mouth with a remark that someone finds offensive. Even in a casual conversation, a judgmental remark like "I love Kobe Bryant but hate the Lakers" can be a nonstarter. Especially in L.A.—even if you're talking to Kobe.

"Do you know any other people who know the inside stuff on that country?" Jesse asked.

Steve rattled off a few names—including the name of our subject: Terrence Bonney.

"I've heard of Bonney," Jesse said. "He's one their diplomats, right?"

Steve said that, yes, Bonney was a diplomat, assigned to the United Nations—and Jesse dropped the subject.

The pivotal point is that Jesse acted as if Terrence Bonney and the other people that Steve mentioned were just names on a list that we had been tasked to compile.

Bonney was a military attaché, meaning that he was attached to an embassy, but worked outside of its standard diplomatic ranks. That gave him a bit more flexibility for the job that we suspected him of doing: recruiting, or co-opting, Americans who had inside information about U.S. military industries, or about government military operations, State Department policy, or executive branch intentions. These Americans are known in the coin of the spy-bureaucracy realm as not only sources, but also operatives, and co-optees. They are most likely to be employed by private industry—mostly manufacturers of military equipment or armaments, or by subsidiaries of those companies. Some of them, though, are government bureaucrats—or work for think tanks.

Their inside information can be something as mundane as the proposed completion-date for a project, or which products a certain country just bought.

To a busy defense-industry executive with a million things on his mind—much of it classified, or restricted for international export—the information in question often seems like just another factoid. It might be a piece of seeming trivia that he's already knowingly or inadvertently leaked to one of his professional contacts—such as a buddy from his previous job, who'd picked the exec's brain at a lunch just like this one.

In our current multinational society, corporations can be just as powerful as countries, and intellectual property—piling up piece by piece, as it forms a grand puzzle—is often the primary weaponry of domination that's used by companies and governments.

Every bit of it is up for grabs, and—in the general spy world, but not my world—nobody *really* trusts anybody.

Sometimes it's not even possible in these scenarios to know who's the thief and who's the victim, because a number of companies are usually pursuing the same essential goal. Not only that, trade journals and foreign policy organizations publish vast volumes of information. And forget about always being able to distinguish good guys from bad guys. If you're Microsoft and I'm Apple, who's the good guy? Often as not, the good guy is just whoever you happen to work for—or (more or less) trust.

So the job of superspy Terrence Bonney was to approach some executive or bored bureaucrat, buy him lunch or a few drinks, talk shop, share gossip, maybe mention a company that's looking for somebody with his skills, and develop a relationship—of trust, naturally.

Mr. Bonney positions himself as simply an honest person who's worked in the private and public sectors, and is now patriotically serving his country, free from the Soviet yoke, as a military attaché. His dream in life, of course, is to make his nation strong enough and safe enough to be a valuable ally to America, because he *loves* America.

Everything may feel quite innocent to the business executive until a particular, very specific favor is requested, and a consultancy fee is offered. Then that exec feels either one of two ways: repelled, because he has no intention of sharing proprietary information with a foreign nation—or excited, and feeling no more traitorous than he would for jumping ship to another company, and bringing along some facts and figures that are already indelibly embedded in his big, overworked, underpaid brain.

In reality, Bonney's government is mostly just trying to save its own corporations—and thereby spare its own military budget—

from the onerous burden of research and development. America leads the world in R&D, and America leads the world in getting its R&D ripped off.

Then another reality arises, and things get uglier. The foreign company that rips off America's industrial information may well use it to build military products not only for itself, but to sell to other countries. Some of those countries may not like America. Those nations may wish to use these products to harm the American nation, Americans abroad, innocent people who support America, or people who are just in the way. The identity of those countries shifts from era to era, so it would be pointless and inflammatory to name names. Just use your imagination.

Bottom line: An American company suffers, and so do the people who work for that company, as well as those who invest their 401(k)'s in it. Innocent people in other countries suffer. And the United States ultimately faces an extra, unnecessary threat: militarily, and economically.

That's why we were interested in Bonney.

We hoped that Steve would give us enough information about Bonney to enable us to know who he was trying to help in his own country, who he was trying to recruit in this country, who his American friends were, and what his primary focus of interest was. Some of those questions could be answered indirectly, by knowing what cities Bonney visited, who he saw, who his wife was, where she worked, and—if this was a spy novel—who his girlfriend was, and who his wife's boyfriend was.

But it's not a spy novel, and I, for one, am always more fascinated by reality than make-believe. Make-believe is always set *in a world* of strange new rules, but in real life, the rules remain the same, and a smart person can eventually learn all of them.

The rules of real life aren't the only thing that's constant and universal. People are, too. I've worked closely for many years with people from all over the world—primarily from the Middle East, Asia, and Eastern Europe—and we are all, at our core, essentially the same. We all long to be appreciated and respected, and we all want people to understand our motives and goals, even if they don't always approve of them.

If you accept that as a reasonable perception, good for you! Not everyone wants to hear it. Millions of people need to feel superior—usually because they have an inferiority complex.

It's hard for these people to resist putting themselves above others, on a separate plane. Unfortunately, it prohibits them from getting what they need from others, including love, support, and community. As the saying goes, it's lonely at the top—but it's lonely at the bottom, too. The only place where it's not lonely is on the same plane as other people: in the everlasting, unchanging nest of human connection, where all people—identified without regard to wealth, power, or beauty—truly are equal.

This plane of equality is the proving ground for trust. It's the place where people who meet as equals break down barriers, build bridges, and make connections.

It's Action Central in this world, because nothing ever really gets done without trust. When trust is absent, people are stuck with carving out their own little niches, and fighting for the scraps of what already exists.

Trust changes everything, directing teamwork toward a common cause, and sparking the creativity of all involved.

When the power of many people is focused on a single challenge, anything can happen. Companies are created, fortunes are made, families grow strong and happy, and groups of friends build relationships that last for lifetimes.

Most important: when people work in tribes of trust, they make the dreams of *those they care about* come true, and achieve a feeling that transcends even personal glory.

As this occurs, one thing that's certain to happen is the emergence of a few people, and sometimes just one, who are trusted above all. As a young man, that was the person that I wanted to be: *the leader*.

In my early years at the Bureau, I didn't really succeed at this, and feared that maybe I was in the wrong business. Finally I realized that in this life there is only one business: the business of trust.

That's the business I'm in now.

It's the business you're in, too, even though you might not yet know it.

In the business of trust, you'll find the finest people you've ever met, and together you'll create things that will last forever.

But you'll also find manipulators who mimic the words and acts of trust, to subdue other people and build themselves up. You *can* do that, if you want. It's your life, and it's a short one. The choice is yours.

I can tell you on good authority, though, that if you make the mistake of cherry-picking the techniques of trust to serve selfish and manipulative needs, they will eventually backfire on you. People will sense your hypocrisy, turn away, do their business elsewhere, and fulfill their personal needs with other people.

That was the mistake that Mr. Bonney had made, as people like him always do. He wasn't working for his country. He was, we'd learned, working for himself: skimming some of the money that his country was giving him to recruit spies.

You don't work for your country by being greedy and playing dirty, day after day. That's what brings countries down. You work for your country by playing fair, and letting this increasingly skeptical, cynical world see that your country wishes only the best for the rest of the world. That's trust.

I took a stab at uncovering who Bonney was trying to ingratiate himself with.

"Has Bonney," I asked Steve, "ever consulted with your division on an issue?"

"Not that I know of," Steve said. Jesse shot me a look. "But it's possible, I suppose."

"He must be more valuable than ever to his country these days, since he's got an American degree," I said.

"I *guess*," Steve said. He seemed uncomfortable. Another look from Jesse—more pointed. Brows pointing down. I was in my earliest days of decoding nonverbal language.

Steve stayed silent. It was possible that he didn't trust us, and was suspicious about the sudden shift of attention to his friend, Terrence Bonney. It was even more possible, though, that he just had other things on his mind. Everyone has their own agenda. You can't get to know them if you don't acknowledge that, and if you can't get to know them, they'll never trust you.

Steve looked like he wanted to change the subject. "Did you guys get to fly here in a private plane?" he asked. "Like in the movies?"

"Jetpack," Jesse said. "Actually, an Apache helicopter from the White House lawn to the top of the Empire State Building—then a jetpack from there."

Steve smiled. The little joke, implying that Jesse and I were just regular guys, made him feel included.

"Robin," Jesse said, "what time do you have? Your daughter okay?"

I pulled my shirtsleeve away from my Darth Vader watch, and Steve noticed it. "I got this for Father's Day," I told him. "My wife lets my daughter get me whatever she wants. So I've got three Frisbees, a sled, and two pogo sticks."

"Do you have kids?" Jesse asked Steve.

"Yeah." His distracted look came back. "Actually, I don't *know*. Things are weird. I'm in the middle of a divorce."

"Oh, man, that's tough," I said. I meant it.

"After twenty *years*," Steve said.

"Oh Lord," I said. "Kids okay?" For a second, I'd put myself in his shoes, and if I was him, that's what I'd be most worried about.

"They don't know what to think. I don't either. I thought we were fine, except for an old argument about spending instead of saving. Then, *boom*. It's a nuclear issue."

"Were you the spender or the saver?" Jesse asked.

"The spender."

"I thought so," Jesse said. "My motto is, you can't take it with you, and it's easier to be happy when you're young than when you're old." I wondered if that was really how Jesse felt.

Steve looked better. It didn't matter if that was how Jesse really felt. When somebody is hurting and reaching out, you help. We owe that to everybody: friends, strangers, whomever. If that person is someone who can do something for you, fine—and if it's not: fine.

"I feel for you," Jesse said, simply and quietly. I knew he meant it. Sometimes, he'd tell a little white lie, to make somebody feel better—but he never said a false word about anything remotely important. Honesty and trust are married.

Steve gave Jesse a look of gratitude, took a breath, and for the first time that day he looked like he was really present. "Thanks," Steve said. He started talking about how his wife had never really seemed to love him as much as he loved her.

Jesse and I listened carefully, and I'll always remember what Steve said next: "I don't think two people ever love each other in exactly the same amount. But I know this. The one who loves most is the winner."

"So true," I said. I gave Jesse a fist bump, and he passed it on to Steve. At that moment, Steve, Jesse, and I were a tribe. Maybe it was the tribe of men—or the tribe of married men, or fathers. Maybe it was the tribe of people who'd been hurt. Didn't matter. What mattered was that we were all linked by something bigger than the business at hand.

"Maybe I *changed*," Steve said. "She said I did."

"Nothing wrong with that," Jesse said. "The people who don't change are the ones that scare me."

"Amen," Steve said. "But maybe some good will come from this. My wife loved me for who I was. The next woman I'm with is going to love me for who I am."

Another round of fist-bumps. Steve was finding his own path out of the darkness.

For each of us, there is only one path: our own. That path was made for our steps alone.

We talked for over an hour about women, love, kids, work, and family, with two digressions about how bad the Knicks sucked, with Patrick Ewing injured.

Toward the end, Jesse said, "I only have one piece of advice. Don't put anything in an email that you don't want read in Family Court. And if you get tempted to email her after you've had a couple of drinks, install a Breathalyzer stop-lock on your computer."

Steve laughed. His mood was far lighter.

Jesse often used humor at the most important moments. He said it put everybody on the same level, and made all of us smarter and softer at the same time.

As Steve was rising to leave, he said, "Thanks, guys—I'm sorry I kept you so long. Keep in touch. Let me know what you need. I'll do everything I can."

He was gone. I didn't feel good about it. Jesse did.

"You said some good things," Jesse said, finishing his coffee. "It was like they were meant just for me. That's how I can tell they're good."

"I think I spooked him," I said. "It's my fault we didn't have a more productive meeting,"

Jesse seemed a little insulted. "It was *very* productive."

"What did it produce?"

"*Trust*. That *was* our goal, wasn't it? Getting the *next* meeting? It's the *second* one that counts. You seemed to learn so much today that I thought you knew that."

"I did learn a lot. I just don't know what it was."

Again, the Jedi mind-trick motion. "Good! That means you'll keep guessing."

"At least I'll feel good the day I figure it out."

"Nah. By then you'll know it."

"Yes, Obi-Wan."

My Other Jedi Master

When I got home, my wife and I talked for a long time about my first day on a major assignment in the field. I couldn't help but feel that I'd failed, but she saw that I hadn't. She told me she was proud of me. She said it exactly as a loving wife should, and if I'd been wiser then, I would have been thrilled.

Not me. I wanted her to say it more like a Bond Girl: "Oh, James, your daring stories are so *exciting!*"

As I say: lot to learn.

In many ways, my wife is more perceptive than me. When people talk, she listens. That's a great trait in a wife—in anyone—and a rare one. Most people, while you're talking, are thinking about what they'll say next, and how they can say it in the most interesting possible way. They consider that the art of conversation. It's not.

On this night, she listened very carefully to my career concerns, but did exactly the right thing: She downplayed the importance of my growing pains in the FBI, and focused on who I was as a person, and how I treated others. At that time, years ago, I thought that her focus on my growth as a human being was a good balance for my focus on my career goals. Now I regard a focus on growth in the same way she did back then—as the *only thing* that really matters.

When you develop character, your career takes care of itself.

By the end of the evening, I had learned at least bits and pieces of everything I am about to show you. (Assuming that you didn't figure it all out in the clues in the first few pages—which was, by the way, the hardest drill in this book.)

It took me the next twenty years to get the Code and Steps into this format:

The Code of Trust
Five Rules to Gain Trust and Be a Leader

1. **Suspend your ego.** Each of us, by the very nature of our existence, is and must remain the focus of our own life. To gain the gift of another's trust, you must grant them that natural, normal focus. Their life, regardless of all the people they're responsible for, is all about them. Not you. If you accept that, they will open the door of their trust to you. The single most compelling trait of trust is simple humility.

2. **Be nonjudgmental.** Respect the opinions, attitudes, ideas, and perspectives of all people—no matter how foreign, or even opposed to your own. No one trusts people who look down on them, and no one trusts people who don't understand them. Not being judgmental is the greatest invitation to trust that you can possibly offer.

3. **Validate others.** There is common decency in every person—regardless of their opinions—and to be worthy of their trust, you must recognize their common decency, show them your own, and join them in that shared respect. All of us are born with the sacred right to our own ideas, and not one of us was born with the desire to destroy or alienate others. Common decency is the common ground of humankind.

4. **Honor reason.** Resist every temptation to personalize, emotionalize, debate, exaggerate, manipulate, or coerce. Stick to the facts, and be honest. Only those who rely on reason, reflected by honesty, can create the foundation of rational, shared self-interest that all enduring trust rests upon. Trust inspired by mere emotionalism lasts only as long as the next emotion. Leadership inspired by fear is simply fear. Give people a good reason to trust you, and they will.

5. **Be generous.** Don't expect to receive the gift of trust unless you offer a gift of your own. People do not allow themselves to trust those who create one-sided relationships. Selfishness repels. Generosity attracts. The most generous gift you can offer is your own trust. The most lasting gift you can offer is the loyalty of enduring trust.

The Four Steps
The Action Plan for Inspiring Trust

1. **Align Your Goals! First:** Determine your own ultimate goal: the prize that justifies your sacrifices. Choose it carefully, and follow it faithfully. Don't get distracted by lesser goals, no matter how pivotal they may appear at the time. Second: Learn the goals of others, and find valid, honest reasons to respect those goals. Third: Seek ways to align your goals with theirs. As you begin this process, look for ways to make their goals part of your goal, and your goal part of their's. If you're successful, you'll achieve the power that only combined forces can attain.

2. **Apply the Power of Context!** To successfully align yourself with others, you need to discover their desires, beliefs, personality traits, behaviors, and demographic characteristics: the central features that define their context. When you know where they're coming from, you'll be able to know them inside and out. You'll know who they are behind the personality that they're trying to project—or, possibly, the person that you fear they may be. Knowing others includes knowing how they see you. If they get the wrong impression, show them the real you. Because people are who they are, approach them on that level, without trying to make them into something they're not. In short: never argue context.

3. **Craft Your Encounters!** When you meet with potential allies, plan the meeting meticulously: *especially the first one*. Create the perfect environment for it. Know—before the meeting begins—its proper mood, the special nature of the occasion, the perfect time and place, your opening remark, your goal, and your gift: what you have to offer. With well-crafted encounters, you'll be able to travel toward trust with the force of a river to the sea, carrying everyone present on the same current.

4. **Connect!** To successfully align your goals—and *maintain* the alignment—speak the same language: figuratively, and literally. Words—and the character traits they reveal—are the primary tools that build trust. To create strong, lasting relationships that fulfill goals, speak the language of reason, respect, and consideration. The language of trust—verbal and nonverbal—does not express egotism, judgment, irrationality, or selfishness. It is a language—and a lifestyle—of understanding, validation, and help. *It's about them, not you.* Even when relationships change, and goals are forgotten, words and the sentiments they convey can remain in the brain forever.

South Beach
The End of the Beginning

"Robin!"

"Cliff! My friend with one of the best jobs in the world!"

I wasn't exaggerating. Cliff rented a fleet of kayaks in one of America's most gorgeous spots, the sugary sands of Miami's South Beach.

(Not incidentally, exaggerating is one of the no-no's in the language of trust, because when you break it down, it's another word for lying. Exaggerations are usually noticed, and not only brand you as a liar, but invite people to launch a flank attack on your central point by quibbling with your exaggeration: "South Beach isn't *the* most gorgeous spot—it's just *one* of them—so you obviously don't know what you're talking about!)

I knew Cliff from a previous trip, and we had a relationship of trust—which can be just as important with a supposedly powerless person as anyone else. You never know whom you might need a favor from, or who might punish you for disrespecting them. Besides, it's common decency.

The last time I was here, I'd tried to rent a kayak for my son and me, but Cliff was out of them. Some people, in those situations, take out their frustrations on the rental person, but that never solves anything. So out of habit I stayed friendly, and helped him move some rented kayaks down to the beach. While we did it, I asked him about himself, showed approval for his goals and plans, and introduced him to my son.

The next day, we came back, and same story: nothing available. But one of Cliff's customers was a no-show, and Cliff said—in a quiet voice that indicated he was tweaking the rules—that we could have the kayak: for free. I offered him a twenty—and more important, a sincere thank-you. He refused the tip, but I stuck the bill in his shirt pocket.

He shook my hand, and I felt that unique mind/body surge of it's-a-wonderful-life that you get when a stranger is suddenly a friend, and you join a new tribe: in this case, the Tribe of Beach-Loving Good Guys.

This time around, Cliff and I caught up on what we'd been doing. Like a lot of people, he was interested in my job, and probably assumed it was more glamorous than working on South Beach—which is arguable.

I told him there was someone I wanted to meet. The person was attending a convention at the resort, and I knew that all the attendees got a few free perks, including a kayak rental. "Can you see if he's scheduled for one?" I asked.

"Absolutely. Let me check the Guest Services site. It's strictly in-house confidential, but . . . ." He winked, then made a few clicks and said, "He signed up, but didn't specify when."

"When he does, can you call me—and let me surprise him?"

"Absolutely, my friend."

(Another lesson, this one from Cliff: If you're going to say "yes," say "absolutely." And "my friend" never hurts, either. As Shakespeare said, "Thinking doth make it so." And as Shakespeare would say, if he were alive today, "And saying doth make it *way* so.")

The next day, as I lounged by the pool, my phone rang. "Robin, this is Sea Base. The eagle has landed."

"Roger that, Sea Base. Out." Now we were in the tribe of Junior G-Men.

I wandered down to the kayaks, crafting the encounter as I walked. The guy I wanted to meet was there, so I used some of my techniques for striking up a conversation with a stranger, which I'll tell you about later. The first technique I used is called "third-party reference," in which you don't invade someone's space, but simply comment upon something in your mutual environment. In this case, I used the kayaks.

I eyed them skeptically as I stood near the guy. "Are those things safe?" I smiled and turned my head only halfway toward him, a non-verbal technique that helps people feel at ease.

"They better be," he said.

I laughed. Who can resist somebody who laughs at their jokes?

"They offered me a free session," I said, "but I the took mani-pedi instead." How nonthreatening is that?

"You're at the convention?" he asked. I nodded.

"Really? What do you do?"

"I'm a beach bum. But I support my habit as a contractor." I paused, as if my occupation was too boring for words. "Aerospace."

"I think that's fascinating," he said. "It's what modern defense is all about. I can't get enough of that subject. After I'm done with this, can I buy you a drink at the pool cabana?"

"Only if it's got an umbrella."

"I'm Terrence Bonney," he said, holding out his hand.

"T-Bone! I'm Robin Dark."

That was the beginning of the end of Terrence Bonney's exploitation of the American defense industry, his use of his country's security budget as his own ATM, and his day job as a military attaché.

And this is the end of the beginning of this book.

I told you you'd understand it. And if you're as smart as I know you are, within about three chapters you'll understand it better than I do.

— 2 —

THE FIVE RULES OF ENGAGEMENT

If I Knew Then

Me: young Marine officer, home on leave from the Basic School at Quantico, working recruitment and looking sharp and salty at the local mall.

A subject-of-interest appeared: tall, well-dressed, fit—probably the hottest girl in the mall! My recruitment radar went nuts.

I was single. Painfully single. I kept striking out with women, and had no idea why. I'd soon find out.

My mission at the mall was simple, and in accord with a Marine slogan that emphasizes determination over rumination in the pursuit of a mission: see the hill, take the hill!

My mission: find woman, get woman.

My primary rule of engagement: confine all actions to raw displays of ego. Back then, I had a word for that: *charm.*

I now realize that I had the wrong concept of my mission, and the wrong rule of engagement. My mission should have been to achieve my *ultimate goal:* finding a woman to love. My sole rule of engagement should have been to focus on *her* greatness, not mine.

Even so, I was confident about my mission, as you probably are about yours, which is, I assume, to achieve success in all aspects of your life. But if your concept of success is the common one of attaining the respect and affection of others, gaining power and influence, and achieving wealth, you're still probably not pursuing your *ultimate* goal.

Material, external goals often feel like ultimate goals—especially when they're just distant dreams—but you'll probably discover at some point that they're not. Unfortunately, you might not realize this until you actually achieve your external goals, and find yourself still struggling for more. Hopefully, reading this book will prevent that from happening.

Ultimate goals—the ones that never fail to satisfy—almost always consist of achieving *internal* qualities—such as unshakable optimism, complete self-confidence, sublime peace of mind, a deep sense of security, abundant self-esteem, and true love.

When you have those qualities, you really don't need much from other people. Instead, they need you.

These goals are definitely the most difficult to achieve, but once you've got them, they usually last a lifetime.

Completing these majestic missions requires the single most demanding rule of engagement: to methodically achieve your goals by helping others achieve theirs. Although difficult, it's by far the best rule for creating ultimate empowerment.

If you're still focused on the wrong goals and wrong rules, you probably bounce between brilliant success and breathtaking failure, and often end up humbled.

When hard-chargers are humiliated, they frequently blame others, blame fate, summon their perseverance, stick with the same strategies, and focus on fighting another day.

In reality, though, most people create their own humbling moments, and keep failing until they change.

That was my problem, and it may be yours.

That was definitely what I was doing wrong back in the day, as I cruised the mall. Full of vim and vigor, I focused on Woman and moved in. *Friendly smile?* Yes sir! *Back ramrod straight?* Roger that! *Ego locked and loaded?* Affirmative! The plan is in place!

"*Marine!*" screamed my alter-ego drill instructor. "This little ego trip of yours is not a *plan*! It's a game, and you will *lose*!"

I didn't let that distract me, because I had no comprehension of the power of a great plan. Lacking methodology, I resorted to a full-frontal charge: I preened until I caught her eye, then preened some more. She was into me!

Until I started talking. It made no sense, because I maintained full focus on the most interesting subject on earth: *The True Story of Me*.

Woman not responding! Eyebrows compressed! Lips pursed! Arms crossed! I called in my secondary forces: Me, *me*, MEEE!

She lapsed into a standing coma. Code blue! Lost her.

Poor kid. She can't handle the truth.

I solemnly escorted her to her final resting place—the food court—and reconnoitered.

Twelve o'clock high! A girl from my high school!

I engaged, and discovered that she was hosting a party that evening with some of our classmates. Mostly females!

That night at the party, I popped a beer and launched surveillance. Tough environment: too many civilians, unaccustomed to desperate measures. I engaged with another girl, who again withered under my firepower.

Back to spotting mode. Kim! She was supercute, and we'd been drawn together since fifth grade by a power far greater than ourselves: the alphabet, which had put us at adjacent desks.

We'd never gotten boy-girl, though, mostly because she'd always been—I hate to admit it—smarter than me. I'd sacrificed academics back then for football and pole vaulting.

My glory days ended, though, when I ripped up my knee at a track meet. Successful pole vaulting is more a matter of system than strength, but my methodology was to charge the crossbar at the maximum velocity, grit my teeth, and . . . well, that was it: see the crossbar, clear the crossbar! I'd stride down the ramp, spear the pole into the box, and often as not it would explode out of my hands and fly across the field like a javelin jumping out of hell. When my coach saw me striding, he just ducked and covered.

Even when I cleared the height, I had no idea why.

I began reminiscing with Kim about school and vaulting, sticking as closely as I could to *The True Story of Me*, but this time something was *different*. She listened.

People had often allowed me to talk, but as soon as I'd pause, they'd have a story of their own, so I knew they weren't listening. When I paused with Kim, though, she asked questions—about what *I* was saying.

I suddenly felt as if I didn't have to try so hard. That unusual occasion felt absolutely natural, though, as if I'd been given an answer to a question I hadn't even asked.

I changed the subject—to her. Then it happened: the head tilt and smile!

Now that I understand the science of nonverbal cues, I recognize this gesture as a signal of nonjudgmental acceptance—but even back then, I knew something good was happening.

I'm also aware now that Kim's personality type—according to a system I'll soon teach you—made her an ideal match for me.

Bottom line: It was the luckiest day of my life. It was the day I learned that the secret of being liked is not how you make people feel about you, but how you make them feel about themselves.

We were married three months later.

The beautiful marriage that emerged from that evening made me start to doubt that achievements can come from nothing more than charging forward with high hopes, ambition, courage, and energy.

In almost every situation, there's one drawback to that approach. You usually fall flat on your ass.

These days, I rely on the Code of Trust to guide me, and achieve far better results, much more easily. Each day it brings me closer to one of my own most important goals: teaching others how to be trustworthy, and project it.

Trust me on this: The lessons I'll teach you won't be painful.

Several years ago, when I finally comprehended the power of the lessons I'm offering you, I experienced a palpable pleasure—a weight off my back—just from realizing the world didn't revolve around me.

My eyes were suddenly opened to the joy, wisdom, and potential for leadership in a life led by the principle of putting others first.

It was my first glimpse of the central theme of this book: *to inspire trust, put others first*. If somebody sees you reading it and asks you what the key to inspiring trust is, just tell them, "Put others first."

Couldn't be simpler. That single rule is the foundation of the Code of Trust, and the Code is the foundation of the Four Steps to Trust.

It is the one inviolable rule of engagement, and leads you to everything else—starting with validating people, and not judging them. Making it all about them is the greatest validation of all, and if it *is* all about them, your judgment is irrelevant.

But you saw that lesson coming, too, didn't you? That's why you're going to like this book. I'm going to tell you what you already know, and you're going to realize how close you already are to achieving sustained, predictable success, by systematically building and communicating your trustworthiness.

But at least you got a refresher course on How to Pick Up Girls. (Or how *not* to—same difference. I think.) Believe it or not, that type of book—the *Idiot's Guide to Manipulating Women*—long dominated the niche of books about how to win trust in romance. I know. I read them.

The same glorification of manipulation was also rampant until very recently in a great many business books, some by America's most popular management gurus. I read those, too. They all acknowledged the power of trustworthiness, but didn't train people how to attain it. It was taken for granted that almost everybody was innately trustworthy, and only needed to show it to others.

Things have changed, haven't they?

The shift away from admiring skillful manipulators hit high gear during the Great Recession.

It was preceded, quite naturally, by a tsunami of manipulation. Banks wrote billions of dollars of funny-money loans; accounting firms acted criminally; companies looted their treasuries for C-suite bonuses; billions of dollars in cash disappeared from pallets in Iraq; and the wealthy morphed into the One Percenters, an echelon once admired, and now often despised.

According to social satirist Tom Wolfe, the 1970s were the Me Decade—but the trend of that decade seemed as if it would never end, didn't it? It just shifted from psychological self-absorption in the '70s, to obsession with money in the '80s. Remember "greed is good?" Then the economy hit ramming-speed in the '90s and early 2000s, and the celebration of selfishness hardened into narcissistic status seeking. The new elite thought that mini-mansions were starter homes, and that Hummers were practical transportation.

Millions of people drank the Kool-Aid of: *to hell with the future and everybody in it.*

Millions more resisted that nonsense, but it was contagious enough to become an epidemic, and it almost crippled this country.

The business principle of blunt-force self-aggrandizement—and its attendant personal philosophies—went down to defeat in that economic war, and we're lucky that there's still enough left of our country, economy, and personal lives to start over, and build a better way.

Our present epoch is the start of a new era, even though the profound significance of this watershed moment is often overlooked in the lingering fog of war. We've entered a promising but painful age in which people no longer have faith in the power of manipulation of markets, people, nations, and ideals. That faith was replaced by fear, with distrust now reigning as the new norm.

Quite naturally, though, our new era of wariness is lit by a dim but ever-growing dawn of respect for the authentic trust that long made America strong, prosperous, and proud—until it slipped away, almost unnoticed, when the roof caved in.

Here's how much things have changed, based on recent polls:

- Since the Great Recession, trust in America's most fundamental institutions—business, government, and media—dropped by a combined average of approximately 60 percent.
- Only 20 percent of all Americans now trust the federal government, after highs in the relatively recent past of 80 percent.
- Only 19 percent of all Americans now trust big business.
- Only 33 percent trust now trust America's most prominent banks.
- Only 57 percent of us currently have one very trusted friend, after a high of 80 percent about twenty years ago.
- Trust in religion fell from 60 percent in 2001 to 40 percent in 2015.
- Only 33 percent of all people trust the store clerks who take their credit cards.
- By 2016, 45 percent of all American households distrusted the Internet so much that they had stopped using even basic services, including posting to social networks or making online purchases.
- Only 18 percent of the Millennials who are still in high school trust most people, making them America's least trusting age group ever.

We can't let this continue. If we do, we will fade forever from our former glory—not just as a country, or an economy, but as a culture.

Trust is something that human beings cannot adequately live without, because it is so absolutely primal. Trust is the touch you felt from your mother's hand, and the warmth you felt from your father's smile. It's the trait that all of us yearn to inspire in our children and our friends. It was, and forever will be, the feeling that there is always a bridge from every island.

We all have fears. We all want to be loved. And since we were children, we knew that there was only one feeling we could count on to overcome the cold and sometimes almost constant specter of fear, and make the safety of love and reason once again appear: *trust*.

Spycraft

"Count me in, Robin!" said the man on the phone who was going to help me catch my spy. "Tell me very specifically how I can help you."

It was music to my ears! No HUMINT on earth is safe from my charms!

HUMINT, as you may recall, is spy talk for a human source of information: from a spy, counterspy, an expert in a field, or an eyewitness. You may also remember that it's the source that's most valued by those of us who work in the trade of spycraft. This is partly because human sources are very observant, and also because they're scarce, since it's not the kind of business most people want to get involved in.

The HUMINT source in question had first come to our attention because he'd known Terrence Bonney, the Eastern European spy I told you about in the last chapter.

Bonney, by this time—after I'd neutralized him—had been called back home. Word was, his skimming had been exposed, and he was working in some very cold and dreary environs.

At this point in my career, I took a certain pleasure in his downfall. Later on, after I'd created the Code of Trust—and with it, a new way for me to look at the world—I took no pleasure in the suffering of anyone. That includes people who create their own downfall. They deserve empathy, too, because—let's face it—we all take ourselves down from time to time.

The same source who'd known Bonney, as so often happens in the small world of international intelligence, had also been observed in the company of a military operative for one of the old Soviet Republics that no longer wanted to *be* a Republic. It wanted to be a nation. I can't offer details that might interfere with ongoing foreign affairs, but I can tell you that this was all happening at the tail-end of the last century, so you can reasonably assume the Republic in question was Chechnya, Dagestan, Abkhazia, or Tajikistan.

If you prefer, you could call it Erehwon—one of the FBI's favorite nicknames for unnamed countries, since it's *Nowhere* spelled backward. The other favorite is Centralia, which has a nice, homey ring to it. Take your pick.

The country's identity doesn't matter for our purposes here, but it certainly mattered to the people who were there at that time. Bombs were falling, little kids were getting blown up in their beds, and soldiers—either "freedom fighters," or "bandits," depending on your point of view—were being abused and murdered as opposing soldiers made home movies, available these days on YouTube.

Russian president Boris Yeltsin—either a freedom fighter or a fascist—was limping along the razor's edge between chaos and brutality, and President Clinton was following Yeltsin's lead, such as it was. Vladimir Putin was waiting in the wings, as was the burgeoning Russian mafia, as well as another largely unknown group of self-described freedom fighters, Al-Qaeda, which was in the early stages of manipulating the Russian revolts.

The operative in question worked for—again: take your pick. It was either the Republic, which he claimed to represent; or for his former Soviet bosses at the Russian KGB; or for Putin, who was already the real power in Russia; or for a crime consortium; or maybe for one of the even darker splinter forces.

The world, seemingly so close to utopia at the end of the Cold War, teetered on the brink of dystopia.

In short, it was not a good time to screw the pooch. So I was overjoyed when my HUMINT source vowed, during my first phone call with him, to help.

I'm going to tell you what happened with my source, "Best Friend," and I've got another drill for you. I want you to figure out, on your own, whether my mission was fated to succeed, or to fail.

Make no mistake—our own fate is neither meant to be, nor made to be, but is a single thread in a fabric of manifest destiny that cloaks us all, governed—if governed at all—only by happenstance steered by systems and codes, tested and true. In this case, the relevant operating system was the Code of Trust.

You've already had your introductory briefing on the Code, so we're coming up on your final in assimilating it before we move out, break down its biochemistry, and learn to deploy it with the Four Steps.

Here's a last-minute review of the five rules of the Code of Trust, before you read the Russian story, and go into action: the Code of Trust requires that you: (1) suspend your ego, (2) be nonjudgmental, (3) validate others, (4) honor reason, and (5) be generous.

To put it another way, to inspire trust, treat people with: (1) humility, (2) nonjudgmental acceptance, (3) validation, (4) reason, and (5) generosity.

You may be new to these groundbreaking rules of engagement, so I'm going to cover them in detail in the next chapter, and at the end of that chapter I'll tell you how the Russian tale turned out.

By the time you've absorbed the details, you should know how I'd sealed my fate.

Spy vs. Spy

The Setting: the restaurant in *Seinfeld*—Tom's Restaurant, identified on TV by the sign that says only: RESTAURANT. It was just off-campus from New York's Columbia University, where my source went to school. I assumed it would not only be convenient for him, but fun—a little like being in the show. Remember: It's All About Them. In every mission, you've got to take care of your people, and try to offer them something before you ask for something.

The Confidential Human Source: a mid-20s PhD candidate in mathematics, specializing in cryptography. According to a communications system I created—the Communications Style Inventory—the source was a Task-Oriented, Thought-Based, Process-and-Procedure guy.

I was hoping that I would be a good fit for him, because at the Naval Academy, my poly-sci degree was bolstered by a core curriculum of engineering: thermodynamics, systems engineering, naval architecture, and computer-aided system dynamics.

Even so, he was a tech *pro*, laser-focused on detail, and I'm mostly a big-picture, theme-based guy.

Also, he was more Millennial than Gen-X, and that put him on a wavelength that was a little foreign to me. A potential clash of personalities was possible, and I still wasn't adept at instant course correction—despite my exposure to the ethic of Semper Gumby!—a principle equally espoused by the spy branch of the FBI, which operated in vagaries that made even the military's fog of war seem manageable.

The Target: This is where it gets interesting: Who Knew? We knew the target's name, and his presumed employer—the rebelling Republic—but odds favored duplicity. Because his former employer was the KGB, he was probably still with them, counter-spying on the Republic.

Another strong possibility was that he worked for Putin, who was months away from his becoming one of the most powerful people in the world—and, unbeknownst to most, one of the richest, due to his veiled, majority stake in Russia's two largest corporations.

Or maybe the subject was freelancing—for private industry, a terrorist group, or: Who Knew? I was hoping my confidential human source would help me *know* who.

The Agent: Me, working alone, in recognition of my growing reputation as a guy who could get people to talk. I was finally starting to realize that at the absolute core of everything is: It's all about them. I had a strong base of confidential human sources—thanks to my growing, gut-level familiarity with the five rules of trust—though I was still far from codifying them.

The Mission: To determine the target's employer. If, as I suspected, the target was really working for Russia, it helped to indicate not only where Russia was headed, but also, to some degree, history itself. It seemed painfully possible at that time that Russia was reviving its desire to control the world. Partly because of that, Clinton wanted to help the Republic—and thought he could, based on his recent success the Yugoslav Wars. But when he'd pushed Russia about the

Republic, Yeltsin had issued the chilling warning that: "Russia has a full arsenal of nuclear weapons."

Just bluster? No easy way to find out. Maybe it was, though, if the target felt safe enough to go against his old bosses, and work for the Republic. He knew those people better than we did.

My guess? He was too smart to go against Russia.

Russia was still the Big Danger, and it seemed as if it was bent on becoming even more dangerous.

"Hi, I'm Robin," I said, as my subject walked in. He offered me a warm handshake, but a look that drilled right through me. "I got us the table where Jerry, George, and Kramer used to sit."

"Cool."

Visualize him as a carelessly rumpled techie—the kind of character in a romantic comedy who's never the leading man, but the dorky Best Friend. Even so, he was a Best Friend with an IQ approaching 160: pudgy and squishy in the middle, and wearing khakis—but topped by eyes so sharp they seemed to shoot bullets.

"So. What do you need?" he said. "I've got seventy-five minutes between classes."

That's what I wanted to hear, but it was discordant, coming so early in the relationship.

"We should order then. Do you know what's good here?"

"Not much."

I laughed. He was funny. I liked him.

"It's usually easier to start a case like this with general stuff," I said, "but we can do this however you want. Basically, I'm curious about what a military consultant for a Russian republic could learn from you. If we can figure that out, it might give us a better idea about what's going on over there."

"He could learn a lot from me." I waited for him to continue. He didn't. I was concerned he might feel slighted.

"Right," I said, "I'm sure he could learn *everything* from you about this." Maybe the comeback was too much. Probably not.

There's no such thing as too much validation. "I meant, what do you think he was *most* interested in?"

"About sending secure messages. And breaking secure messages. That's what I do."

"That's fascinating stuff. Tell me about it." I wanted to make this about him as fast as I possibly could, and assure him that I respected his intelligence.

"I do RSA encryption. Familiar with it?"

"No, but I'd love to hear about it."

"RSA stands for the guys who created it—Rivest, Shamir, and Adleman. Like anything that's coded, you need a key, but in RSA there's like crazy math, with quadratic residues," he said—or something to that effect. His eyes still looked like they could pierce body armor, but now they were directed at a waitress in a short skirt.

I apparently looked lost. He slowed down. "It's like, as you square things in a field, you find special types of numbers that are rare, but exist infinitely." He was off and running again. Great! As long as he was happy talking, it didn't matter if I could keep up. My job was to make him feel good when he was with me, not to learn about quadratic residues.

"Britain came up with RSA a couple of years ago," he said.

Aha! Something I could respond to! "The UK," I interjected, "has been pivotal in helping us with the Russian republics."

"Yeah. They declassified RSA last year, but people still can't figure it out." His order came, and broke his train of thought. "What kind of stuff are you interested in?" he asked. Good sign. Bonding.

"This time of year, the Yankees. You're lucky, having the Stadium so close to campus."

"I'm more into hockey."

"Rangers fan?" He nodded. I knew all of one thing about the New York team: Wayne Gretzky was on it.

"Gretzky's incredible," I said. "He'll go down in history as the Babe Ruth of hockey."

"Gonna miss him," he said. I didn't respond. He looked up from a sandwich he was dissecting, seeming to search for something edible. "He's retiring."

Ouch! Bad move, acting like I knew about Gretzky. A guy as smart as him would wonder what else I was fudging on, but he let it slide, and shot straight back into cryptography, and the significance of RSA as a code-breaking tool.

It was hard to follow, but in any investigation, if you're not in over your head, you're not in deep enough. Then—bing-bing-bing!—it came together.

Remember: The national security details have been changed to protect the innocent—and to not piss off the guilty—but my take on it was: a spy *working for Russia* might not *need* to learn about RSA, because Russia probably already had it.

Nor would the spy probably be working for somebody in deep left field—such as Al-Qaeda, or a crime consortium—because they probably wouldn't know what to do with it. I was was starting to think the target was on the up-and-up: a true patriot to his republic, who wanted to break Russian codes.

Couldn't rule out Putin, though.

This would take time. But I had time.

So far, it seemed to me, I'd made this about him. I hadn't judged him, I'd validated him, and I'd kept the discussion well within the frame of reason.

I'd done everything on my evolving trust-inspiring checklist except to offer him something—an inducement, or at least a motivator. My read on this guy was that playing up the emotional aspects of helping people in need, or doing something for America, wouldn't have much impact.

I settled on the classic motivator. "I don't want to make you late for class," I said, "so we can finish this later, but I do want to mention that we have a budget for confidential sources, and you've already helped me enough to qualify."

"Cool."

I smiled at him, and he smiled back. Of course, "cool": he was a kid struggling to finish school.

He looked at his watch. "Gee, where'd the time go?" he said.

"Your lunch okay?" I asked.

He said it was good, without much conviction. By then I knew that being in the setting of a sitcom wasn't the same as being in one.

"I'll be in touch," I said.

"Anytime!" He gave me a big grin. "It was interesting!"

He was gone.

I felt good. Not perfect. I'd screwed up a couple of things—Gretzky, and maybe the choice of restaurants. But the science of social engineering is the science of people, and that makes perfection impossible. It's not even desirable. People can tell when you think you've handled them perfectly—and it leads to distrust. Ironic, yes—but nothing is ever as it seems in spycraft.

So: how do you think I did?

Your Final Briefing

Read the next chapter before you decide. The Code holds the answer.

Some people at my seminars wonder if it's too pedantic to reduce a fluid, nuanced concept like trust to a five-point code. I remind them that as a pilot, I fly with a set of laminated procedural checklists: personal preflight; aircraft preflight; warm-up; run-up; take-off; climbing; cruise; and descent. It's in my lap at all times. As my instructor has long drilled into me: it is not a to-do list—waiting for you to get around to it.

I may be a good pilot—I may not be. Hopefully, I'll never know, because the codified process takes care of me.

My son often flies with me. That's an important enough reason to honor the process, isn't it?

Is the trust of your family, colleagues, and friends less important?

— 3 —

BREAKING THE CODE

BEFORE YOU DEPLOY THE CODE in the field, I'm going to break it down into concepts that even cats and dogs can understand. That's not condescension: it's respect. *The most important lessons are always the simplest, and only the smartest people know that—and understand the lessons.*

The simplest rules are the ones that save lives, save careers, save relationships, and save self-respect.

They are *deceptively* simple. That's why they're easy to forget.

Your final briefing: the five rules of engagement are (1) suspend your ego, (2) be nonjudgmental, (3) validate others, (4) honor reason, (5) be generous.

Your assignment: by the end of this chapter, be able to recite the five rules in fifteen seconds.

Code Rule 1: Suspend Your Ego

There's one more pivotal principle in this part of the book that I learned from a sitcom—so you know it must be important.

My resource material was another episode of *Seinfeld,* the sitcom characterized by legend as "the show about nothing." That's a clever description, but totally untrue. Even a cursory understanding of *Quantum Physics for Dummies* proves that *nothing* can be about *nothing*. That's metaphysically absurd.

A friend of mine knows one of *Seinfeld*'s producers, and shortly before the show aired, the producer described it to him as, "A show about life's *little moments*"—which is exactly what it is. That's why it's aged so well. Contemporary humor comes and goes, but life's little moments are a constant, that seem insignificant only in isolation.

They create the patterns of behavior that define us: as leaders, followers, or nothing more than clowns. That's why you need to know the Code. It's your default mechanism for governing the moments that only seem trivial at the time.

You already discovered—from our first lesson in Seinfeldian thought—that being at the set of a sitcom isn't the same as being in one, but the second lesson is even more critical.

According to Seinfeldianism: *suspending your ego can save your life*—figuratively, and sometimes even literally.

I learned that in the episode in which Jerry cuts off somebody in traffic, and the guy gives him the finger. Jerry's foil, George—famous for putting the "id" in *idiot*—urges Jerry to return fire, but Kramer, the Jedi superego who is disguised as the court jester, tells Jerry to control the situation with an I'm-sorry-wave: "You raise the hand, lower the head—'I'm sorry, I'm sorry. The buttons are really big on the car! I don't understand it! I haven't read the manual. *Ohh!*'"

Jerry took Kramer's advice, and kept his ego on ice. Jerry invariably created his own humbling moments, but always survived to live another episode.

The wisdom of the I'm-sorry-wave may have saved my *own* life, or at least my career, during one of my very first days in the FBI, shortly after I met my mentor, Jesse. I was still twenty-nine, and feeling very much the ex-Marine who was holding the world by the tail, working national security in New York City, with a gun on my hip.

If you know the city, you know rush hour traffic is like maximum-security lockdown in certain areas, including Broadway & Worth, near the FBI headquarters, just north of the Brooklyn Bridge. A certain degree of ruthlessness is needed to just run with the pack and not get trampled, but even within this context of survivalism, I was unprepared for a bike messenger to blur past me so fast that all I could see was the afterimage of his giant, gnarled index finger.

I, the victim, flipped back a quick double-salute—one for the Corps, and one for the Bureau—proud to do the right thing for God, country, and myself (not in that order).

Next thing I knew, though, I came up on this guy at a stop sign and saw that he was an unholy mix of Paul Bunyan and King Kong, hardened by unmistakable notes of Lance Armstrong with roid rage. His cold stare said: "I *know* you. Punk." I kept eye contact just long enough to prove my manhood—to myself, but apparently not him. He grabbed his five-pound bike-chain and ten-pound padlock (for a $10 bike), swinging it in circles like he was up for a little David and Goliath role play, unless I wanted to wuss-out.

Which I did, mashing down on the accelerator like a little girl running for Mommy.

Problem solved. Dignity more or less intact. Until I hit a stop light. And waited. Sure enough, King-David-Kong grew ever-larger in my rearview mirror.

What was on my mind? The Bureau's deadly force policy.

If I was genuinely threatened with a potentially deadly weapon, and could not defuse the situation, I had the right to invoke the policy, and endure the predictable *New York Post* headline: Newbie FBI Agent Guns Down Bicyclist—subhead: Killer Says: He Looked Scary! And Had a Padlock! I also had the privilege to *not* invoke it, and have my survivors endure the headline of: Dumb-Ass New Agent Gets Killed by Bike Messenger—subhead: Survivors Claim Dufus Was an Former Marine.

In a moment of clarity, I asked myself, "What would Jerry do?" and the answer was: Offer the I'm-Sorry Wave. My ego would hate me, but my far more reflective superego, in the Freudian schemata, would love me forever for realizing that my ultimate goal was not to win a battle of egos with a bicycle messenger, but to become a successful architect of the New World Order—which required being alive, as well as out of prison.

I swiveled in my seat, made eye contact, raised my hands, lowered my head, and tilted it, offering the proper exposure of my carotid artery. I could literally see the fire in his eyes go out, and he stood above his saddle and coasted. The light changed. I gunned it, and was gone.

My advice to you: Don't wait for a scenario as dire as road rage to sharpen your skills at ego sublimation. Swallowing your pride may be a bitter medicine, but take a little every day and the bad taste goes away.

Sublimation of ego gives you the power to steer clear of conflict, stay focused, move forward, win friends, and influence people.

Suspending your ego is the single most important element of being trustworthy, and enlisting others in the pursuit of your goal.

It's the central action that animates the four other rules of the Code.

Mastering this counterintuitive but all-powerful principle takes you so deep into the mission of being trustworthy that the rest becomes second nature. To use the analogy of peeling an onion, you'll always find ego suspension at the core of the Code.

The harder somebody comes at you, the better it works, because people are particularly impressed when you meet their aggression with humility. Arrogant people (meaning: insecure people) might think you're just a coward, but almost anyone whose allegiance matters will know that capitulation by a powerful person is invariably an act of courage.

When you give in on a second-tier goal, people see that you have a wider worldview than they do—unfettered by the debris of minutiae—and they usually want to know what *else* you know that they don't. They're happy to follow your lead, because they know that you won't crush them, just to throw your weight around.

Ego suspension gives you the freedom to laser-in on your ultimate goal, without needing to convince everybody that you're always right about everything. It makes it easy for you to align your goals with those of others, and thereby make the goals that you're trying to reach part of their own set of goals.

It also gives you the super power of X-ray vision into other people, allowing you to see things from their point of view.

It makes you lovable to many, and likable to almost everybody.

Confrontation disappears and divisions fade.

Your concentric circles of influence expand. Your tribe of trust grows.

Things get done.

And suddenly you're flying at falcon speed toward your ultimate goal.

Take this principle for a test run the next time you're in a business meeting where people start ragging on you or your product.

The knee-jerk reaction is to say, in effect: You're an idiot to think that. People rarely use those exact words—but that's how they come across when they get defensive.

When you do that, do you really think that somebody will patiently argue with you that they're not, in effect, an idiot?

When that kind of discussion turns into an argument—and it will—do you think there's any chance of a win/win ending?

We all have egos. We all want respect. That won't change. But other people don't have to lose for you to win.

The conventional wisdom is that winners impose their egos, and losers go along. When you think it through, the opposite is true.

When somebody dumps on you, don't take it as an assault on your ego, or a threat to your survival, and try to talk them out of it. Assume that they feel the way they do for for a reason. Find out the reason. Do it the easy way: ask.

If their complaint sounds reasonable—even if only from their perspective—tell them you'll try to fix it.

If you can't fix it—or don't think their view is valid—at least tell them that you understand. You'll be amazed at how fast resistance will fade.

When you stop playing defense, they'll stop playing offense. It's really that simple.

Before you know it, the people around you will be doing the same thing: Cordially and rationally searching for ways to solve problems. When you don't force people to change their minds, you make it easy for them.

We all want to be in a tribe, so to speak, and we all want our tribe to be righteous, constructive, and—to be quite honest—better than the other tribes.

Accept that in others. You have never met a person who wants to be *almost* as good as you. That's human nature, and if you want to be successful among humans, you need to honor their nature.

That's not too much to ask, because your nature is just the same.

When you suspend your ego to focus on your endgame, you'll feel fine about absorbing a loss here or there. You might even welcome it, because a favor granted becomes a favor owed.

When you stop playing King Kong, conversations change. Rancor recedes, humor and goodwill rise to the surface, commonalities emerge, and bonds are created.

People put down their shields.

An axiom I now live by is: *Shields Down, Information In.*

Treasure every bit of this information, even if it's not what you want to hear. Some of it will lead to your goal. *All* of it will bring you closer to reality—and reality is the sole environment of all lasting success.

Differences of opinion will never go away. So what? Do you really want all of your colleagues to be yes-men, your customers to be passive, your friends to be sycophants, and your spouse to be a doormat?

Some people do.

But people don't trust them.

There's a better way, and a better world, and it's right in front of us, right now.

Code Rule 2: Be Nonjudgmental

By now I'm sure you see that the segue from suspending your ego to being nonjudgmental is absolutely natural—hardly a segue at all, but a mere continuation.

That natural flow will continue throughout your final briefing on the Code. *You've already got the core concept.*

It's surprisingly simple, isn't it? (I know: Simple to understand, hard to do. You'll get there.)

It took me ages to figure out how to lead people, and even how to be liked. When I first started working for the FBI, the only people who really seemed to like me were my espionage sources. Didn't make sense. I was putting them at risk, with little to return.

I finally figured out why: I wasn't judging them. I was just grateful for their help, and knew their own agendas were different from mine. I was in no position to judge them. I had to assume that they had their reasons for everything they did.

That doesn't mean I approved. Being nonjudgmental doesn't mean that you judge people favorably. It means that you do *not* judge them—one way or the other. Even judging people favorably can make them uncomfortable, because they know you might reverse course.

Even though I initially adopted this mode because my approval or disapproval was irrelevant, I later realized that this was a trait that people loved, and wanted to be around. It let them open up and be themselves, which is one of life's great luxuries.

I often ask the cops in my seminars if they've ever gotten a confession from a suspect. Every hand in the room goes up.

I ask them how they got the confession. Was it by forcing perpetrators to see that they were a bad person who'd done a bad thing? Or was it by not judging their actions, and trying to understand *why* they'd committed a crime.

Perpetrators rarely expect acceptance of their criminality, but they're invariably grateful for simple, human understanding—especially if you understand their darkest side. If a cop offers that understanding, criminals are far less likely to be defensive, and to deny what they did.

No matter the cause of any crime, confessions typically come—according to detectives inside the Bureau and outside it—from empathy, sympathy, compassion, and understanding.

In the crime dramas with good-cop-bad-cop scenarios, the good cop usually gets the confession, and in real life, the phenomenon is even more pronounced.

That doesn't mean the good cop pretends to approve. It means he or she inspires enough trust for a criminal to stop denying responsibility, and transfers some of that trust to the criminal justice system. With the right approach, most perps pragmatically recognize that, contrary to their long-standing beliefs, their own best interests can be achieved by working *with* the system, instead of against it.

Quite often, their decision to confess isn't even based on this pragmatism. They simply see a nonjudgmental face in front of them, feel a moment of release from fear, and conform to the natural human desire to unburden themselves of lies, guilt, remorse, and tension.

I assure you that it's hard for law enforcement officers—and everyone else—to refrain from judging people, especially if they've done something heinous.

Aside from our unavoidable repugnance to a terrible crime, much of the difficulty of suspending judgment, on a day-to-day basis, comes from our own insecurities and fears. The desire to feel superior to others is always tempting, and is sometimes almost irresistible. It gives us a sense of safety and status to think that we're better than others, and to let them know it—subtly, or not.

It's even hard to suspend your sense of superiority over people who are in the modern version of your tribe: your family, friends, coworkers, and community members. Everybody at one time or another has wanted to be their parent's favorite child, or the smartest kid in class, or most popular, or richest, or best looking.

When you think about it, though, the value that our tribe places upon us is rarely based on our relative rank in the hierarchy, or on the performance of our *own* goals, but on what we bring *to the tribe*, in the pursuit of *its* goals.

The surest way to be valued by your tribe is to combine your own goals with your tribe's goals. That's also, of course, the best way to meet your own goals.

To be the leader of your tribe, be the person who sets a goal that's so good that everyone wants to achieve it. There's a saying in the Marines that's become one of my guiding lights: any time two or more Marines are together, one becomes the leader—*and the leader is the one who sets the goal.*

Leadership is almost never a reward for reaching a goal. It's a reflection of your actions in the *pursuit* of a goal.

Leadership is all about doing, not being.

It's easy to call yourself a leader, but it's never easy to lead. Leading is based on inspiring others to follow, and the only way to do that is to construct a mission that it's all about your followers, not you.

Once you've got that mission in place, and the action starts, your first job as a leader is not to judge. You can evaluate proper performance, and eliminate ineffective practices, but the second you start judging people—even if they're not performing well or being effective—you lose them.

For example, neurosurgeon James Doty, MD, of Stanford University, made an insignificant mistake during his first brain operation that triggered such an outburst of blame and judgment by the surgeon that it damaged not only Doty, but the entire attending staff, eroding their creativity, clarity, teamwork, and trust. Doty later dedicated much of his career to teaching physicians that judgmentalism is dangerous. Even brain surgeons do best, he says, "when you're kind to them."

Some people, though, are afraid to suspend their judgments. Attendees of my seminars sometimes say, "Robin, you sound like an accommodating guy with nice ideas—but don't you end up getting *walked all over, like a carpet?*"

No, because I've got a goal—to be a leader—and every action I take is toward the furtherance of that goal.

If I judged the people around me, and always put my own needs first, no one would *want* me to lead, and it would create one humbling moment after another. But if my goal is to help everyone around me achieve their *own* goals—without judging them—people are *happy* to have me leading them, and the path to my goal is wide open.

That's logical, but hard. I'm as vulnerable to anxiety and anger as anyone else, and it's not hard for me to get emotionally highjacked. When I allow that to happen, though, emotion clouds my judgment, and humbling moments arise.

Every day I reevaluate my behavior, and make sure it leads to my goals. If I start to get arrogant, or complacent, or rebellious, I know I'm headed toward the danger zone. Then it's time to correct my course—Semper Gumby!—and move forward.

Course correction is something that people have to do themselves. If you try to impose it on someone else, they'll think you're judging them. The best way to help people see their shortcomings without feeling judged is to just ask them questions about their ultimate goal.

People are smart. When you prompt them to refocus on their priorities, instead of taking a side trip to their insecurities, they go back to work at improving themselves. They usually do this with the resolve of a bird flying home to its nest.

Leadership is an eternal journey toward self-discovery. It isn't a prize. If anything, it's a burden, because you have people depending upon you. Even so, if you bear the burden well, it can bring great joy and satisfaction.

Leadership is power, but the type of leadership that is most brilliant, and most effective, is soft power: humble, nonjudgmental, validating, reasonable, and generous.

Code Rule 3: Validate Others

You just saw that the segue from suspending your ego to being non-judgmental is an organic, almost seamless progression, and now you'll see that the same straight path leads from being nonjudgmental to validating others.

Refraining from judgment is clearly not an end point, but a transition to the higher goal of helping others feel good about themselves.

Let's face it: We all judge ourselves—that's why we're so touchy about others judging us. If you can help somebody feel good about themselves, they'll feel good about you, too, and their trust for you will grow ever greater.

Validating someone else doesn't mean approving of them, since the goal is to not judge people *at all:* with approval, or disapproval. Validation is far less complicated: no moral inventory is needed. It just means knowing who people are, what they're doing, and why you think that what they're doing is valid—not good or bad, just valid: something *you* might do if *you* were them.

That's all people need from you, or want. They can decide for themselves if they're doing something good or bad.

To me, validating somebody is the greatest gift you can give. Validation isn't flattery—because that's making a judgment, and carries all the burdens and baggage of judgment. Leave flattery to manipulative people—or more specifically, inept manipulative people, because flattery is usually obvious, and raises red flags.

Validation means seeing someone as a whole: their wants, needs, pressures, history, goals, beliefs, and whatever else might matter to them. When you offer that level of insight into a person, their brain lights up with the neurochemicals associated with safety, security, acceptance, and trust.

With this one action, people won't feel threatened by you, even though they know you're different. They might even be tempted to drop their perspective in favor of yours: shields down, information in.

As always, make your feelings clear the easy way: Just show them. Last week, FBI Director James Comey—a master of social engineering—sent me a certificate of commendation for a tough project I'd completed. It was beautifully designed and presented on rich parchment, personally signed, and accompanied by a note that said, "Great job, hero!" His effort showed that he understood the difficulty of the project, and appreciated my work—whether it was perfect, or not.

The certificate is a memento I'll keep forever, not out of ego, but as a remembrance that someone I respect saw a situation from my perspective, thought it through, and realized that my actions were valid. Not flawless. Just valid: reasonable and understandable.

You may be thinking: fine, but what if you'd really screwed up?

If I had, Director Comey would probably have done the same thing that I advise my students to do. He'd validate the effort I made, and help me figure out what went wrong. He'd tell me I was still a valued member of our tribe of federal agents, and he'd guide me through my *own* critique, until I figured out my mistakes by myself.

Shields down! People are almost always honest with themselves when they're not forced to be defensive. Nobody wants to make the same mistake twice, and the more you force them to admit a mistake, the more their shields will go up.

There's a hilarious depiction of the value of validation in a classic, 11-million-view YouTube video: "It's Not About the Nail." This guy and his girlfriend are sitting on a couch as she earnestly tries to describe her headache. "There's all this pressure . . . and sometimes it feels like it's right up on me, and I can just feel it—like literally feel it, in my head, and it's relentless . . . I don't know if it's ever gonna stop." The camera pulls back. She's got a huge nail in her forehead.

Her boyfriend, brow furrowed, says very sincerely, "You do have . . . a *nail* . . . in your head." She sighs and looks away: "It is *not* about the nail."

He's very conciliatory: "Are you sure? Because I'll just bet, if we got that outta there. . . ."

She gets pissed: "Stop trying to *fix it*!" He tries again—gets nowhere. She's fed up: "You always *do* this! You always try to *fix* things. When all I really need is for you to just *listen*!"

So he just listens, and she tells him how she can't sleep, and how all of her sweaters are snagged—all of them.

He's struggling, but says, "That sounds really hard."

He gets it! Her tone softens: "Thank you." She touches his hand, leans forward to kiss him.

His forehead drives it deeper. She cries out.

He loses it: "If you'd *just*. . . ."

Her finger is in his face, like: "*Don't!*"

Ignition! Blast off! By this time, it's *not* about the nail. It's about *him*.

The credits roll, to the sounds of the key lyric in the Beatles' "We Can Work It Out": "Try to see it my way. . . ."

Moral of the story: When you hear "Thank you," *quit*. No matter *what*. Bite your tongue. Whoever you're talking to feels validated. That's good enough. You'll receive your reward later, even if it's just the reward of knowing you controlled yourself in a difficult situation.

If you want to achieve your ultimate goal, and lead others in the quest of that goal, get ready for a lot of tongue biting.

If it's not worth it to you, don't. Saying whatever you think is very gratifying. It's just not a leadership trait.

In Beverly Hills, where parking fees require a small mortgage unless you visit someone who validates your parking, Hollywood legend Bernie Brillstein—who managed the careers of everybody on *Saturday Night Live* from Lorne Michaels to all the wild and crazy guys, and who said his most valuable advice to John Belushi was "to write thank-you notes"—had only one piece of art in his palatial corner office: a wooden sculpture that said, "*We validate.*"

It wasn't about the parking.

Brillstein was famous for rarely having written contracts with his clients. His motto was, "My wink is my bond." At the time of his retirement, he was known as the most trusted man in Hollywood.

Code Rule 4: Honor Reason

The only two species that engage in organized warfare are human beings, and ants. Let's start with that.

It tells us, from the perspective of evolutionary psychology, that we've got a lot of growing up to do. Most people aspire to that. Some obviously don't.

Our ascendance to the peak of the animal kingdom did not change the fact that humans still have beastly tendencies, devoid of all logic. Blame the brain for most of that. After all, the brain is just flesh and blood.

Only *one* of the three primary parts of the human brain has risen above our irrational, animalistic instincts: the forebrain. The forebrain's outer layers—most notably the frontal lobe, near the forehead—are our focal point of reasoning. As we move closer to the center of the brain, though, we take a veritable journey to the heart of human darkness. After a long trip through the midbrain, or mammalian brain—capable of love, but limited in intelligence— we end up in the hindbrain—also known as the reptilian brain.

It's the reptilian brain that gets us into trouble.

The reptilian brain knows only fear, and controls basic physical housekeeping, such as heartbeat. It is not prime real estate for leaders—or even lovers. Our mission, as trusted leaders, is to transcend the reptilian brain, care about others, and learn to think things through.

That *does* take learning. Hence: the Code. You were born with the ability to fear, but not to trust. Your early (easy) lessons on that probably came from your mother, and they've been coming at you ever since, through one humbling moment after another. Even after a life of learning, though, it's still hard to get something so rare and wondrous as trust through our thick skulls.

The moment a primal instinct surfaces—danger! reward! sex! chocolate!—your reptilian brain kicks into high gear, and says: Seize! But evolution has been kind to humans, and has given us a quarter-second head start on seizing everything in sight that we covet, or fear. That's the time it takes for your midbrain to use a shortcut to the forebrain, and offer you a reasonable analysis of your environment. That common act is, in effect, your brain's way of "counting to ten" before reacting.

When you're done counting, though, you still need to honor reason, instead of being defensive, deceptive, sly, coercive, and overly emotional. That's the hardest part of this process.

As your initial animalistic instincts cool off, you're still vulnerable to brain hijacking by the dark and often seemingly irresistible force of manipulation.

Here's the shortcut honoring reason:

1. Immediately thrust yourself into the protective pocket of your *ultimate goal.* If you can focus on that, you automatically become reasonable, because achieving the lofty ambition of your life's dream absolutely *demands* reason.

2. Stick to words and actions that will help you reach your ultimate goal. There's no room for quick venting, to get the steam of your emotions out of your system. Keep your emotions *in* your system. Or don't—if you'd rather be emotionally relieved than perceived as a leader.

Here's a painfully personal example:

I was at my father-in-law's wake, grieving a great man, but feeling glad I'd known him, and that I'd become part of his family. We were celebrating his life with an appropriate level of high-decibel revelry, in a private room of an Italian restaurant, when: *Whap!*—somebody hammered the hell out of my shoulder. I sprang around, already so into the war zone of slow motion that I saw a couple of cousins whose faces seemed to say: "Wow! I've always wanted to see a former Marine break a man's body with his pinky!"

The perpetrator started unloading: "What in the name of *Christ* makes you think you *own* this place, you noisy son of a bitch!" By this time, I'd been working in the Behavioral Analysis program for so long that I automatically went into instant Science Experiment mode: What's my goal here? Is it to please my cousins—which would feel pretty good? Or to de-escalate, and honor my wife's father—as a real man would?

Tough choice! Love those cousins!

I analyzed the mutual context of the possible combatants. I thought he was an ass. He thought I was an ass. As usual, it was a wash. But that didn't matter. *Never argue context,* right?

Who did he think this was about? Him, of course!

Behind him I saw his date—with big hair and a mane of curls, seated in what I'd thought was our private room—wearing an expression of: *my hero!*

What's his *goal*? Obviously, it's to show his date a good time, even if he has to kick ass (or *especially* if he has to kick ass).

By the time I'd slithered all the way out of my reptilian brain to the warmer regions of reason, I saw that he had a valid beef, and would probably listen to reason—*if* it was a reason that centered around what *he* wanted. "I'm sorry," I said. "You're completely right."

The tension broke. I didn't offer the obvious excuse—death in the family—because that would just make it about me, and not him. Very possible response: "Not my problem, buddy! You oughta know better!"

"I'll talk to my family," I said—palms up—"and tell them to save the rowdy stuff for tomorrow, after my father-in-law's funeral." That, of course, was my excuse for my behavior—but I didn't deliver it as an excuse. I just framed it as my context. The rest was up to him.

His shoulders suddenly sagged, the fire went out of his eyes, and his girlfriend's expression suddenly flipped to: *"Honey, please set your trouble-making ass back down! For me?"*

I walked over to the manager, told him his staff was great, and mentioned that my group had inadvertently annoyed another guest. He said he'd comp them a bottle of wine. My people gradually got loud again, but I wasn't going to tell them to stop. They needed it, and the guy at the other table didn't seem to mind anymore. At this point, he was rising in his date's esteem by *matching* my rationality.

As we were leaving, the guy stood up, held out his hand, and said, "Tell your wife I'm sorry for her loss." For a moment, he was part of our tribe—the tribe of American families, or maybe just the tribe of two guys who didn't throw down and become unforgettable asses.

He knew my misery, and I knew his: It was just a difficult moment during a date, but those little moments matter at the time, and a little understanding goes a long way. The old saying is: Misery loves company. The truth is: Misery loves empathy.

He stayed on his feet and shook a couple of hands as we all filed out—now ready to face a harder day than this one—and the warm feeling in the room was palpable.

In the movies, the heroes are the warriors. In real life, the heroes are the peacemakers.

Try to imagine this same scenario with the absence of reason. It would be a great movie scene: People crashing through breakaway tables and smashing each other with breakaway beer bottles, accompanied by lively background music. In real life: a disastrous and haunting episode that would linger forever with an entire family—and with a guy who would wish for a long time that he'd just kept his mouth shut.

Honor reason.

In reason, there always lies at least a little love.

Code Rule 5: Be Generous

The first part of the brain to develop during human evolution was the reptilian brain—aka the reptilian complex, the R-complex, and the croc-brain (mostly in Australia and Florida). It's also the first part of the brain to sprout in a human fetus. Because it's only good at two things—heartbeat and fear—think of the croc-brain as survivalism in the flesh. Its overriding urge is territoriality—as demonstrated by the initial acts of the guy in the restaurant whose space we invaded—and it's bereft of the ability to love. That's why lizards are less cuddly than kittens: It's *not about the fur* (so don't try to *fix* it). Your lizard will never love you back, even if you nurture it and name it Fluffy.

We are without doubt, therefore, hardwired for hard times.

Thank God for the mammalian brain, though, which adds the element of love, and a moderate level of reasoning. Even more valuable is the forebrain, which endows humans alone with high-level reasoning. It is nature's single greatest gift (although it's apparently returnable, judging by the behavior of some, for a gift card of equal value.)

The two advanced regions of our tripartite brain are, in effect, the software of survivalism. Long before the advent of agriculture—during the hunter-gather days of about 80,000 years ago—it was obvious to people that sharing food and shelter helped everyone survive. That stark reality, recognizable by the reasoning of that epoch, superseded even the fact that it *feels good* to give something to someone.

The irrefutable value of generosity was categorized by early social scientists as a variation of survival of the fittest. Among humans, fitness includes the social value of reciprocal altruism.

The practical value of generosity is obvious. As in:

- **One hand washes the other.**
- **To have a friend, be a friend.**
- **What goes around comes around.**
- **Two can live cheaper than one.**

(I could go on, but I won't. So you owe me one. *That's* reciprocal altruism.)

It's hard to comprehend how deeply generosity is embedded in the human heart until you see little kids get more excited about giving gifts than getting them. When that beautiful act happens, there's probably not a parent alive who hasn't gotten tears in his or her eyes.

Sadly, we only regress as we grow. Hurt sets in, it hardens the heart, and our selfishness begins. We tell ourselves that selfishness is survival. We try to rationalize that it's us or them, that if we don't grab first we'll get nothing, and that if we don't play dirty and pull strings, someone else will.

And we wonder why it doesn't work.

It doesn't work because it's been unnatural since the dawn of civilization, as well as the earliest days of your own life.

Being generous is one of only five inviolable rules of the Code of Trust because it is *intrinsic to human nature.*

The Code of Trust isn't built on fairy tales. It's built on the facts of life. Fairy tales collapse under the weight of wishful thinking, but the facts of life are constant, universal, eternal, and inescapable.

No matter how often you've been betrayed and manipulated, you'll never be able to inspire trust if you let yourself get stuck in the pain of your past, and learn to love only what's yours.

You need to rise above that—if only for the sake of the survival of your soul—and create your life in the image of your childhood generosity.

If you hold back, and wait for love to come to you, it probably never will. And even if it does, then what? Feeling *loved* is fine. It gives you a nice sense of security. Feeling *love* is rapturous. It transports you through time and space.

The only love you can truly, viscerally feel is your own.

It's already in your heart, and no pain can drive it all the way out.

Probably the most terrible but beautiful paradox of life—the only true alchemy of emotion—is that your need to give is even stronger than your need to get.

One of my more successful buddies—a typical Type-A guy—had to be dragged kicking and screaming to fatherhood, because he thought it would screw up his career, and then he'd screw up his kid. The day his son was born he held the baby in his arms while his wife was sleeping—and felt *nothing.* Just overwhelmed, and already a little resentful. But he's a stand-up guy who'll give you the shirt off his back, and he said to his little boy, "I'm gonna take care of you all your life, just like my dad did me." Then: *Whoosh!* A blast of love swept through him—"so hard" he later said, "that it damn near knocked me off my feet. I never felt anything *like* it."

He was one of the best dads I ever knew, and loved every second of it.

Your generous heart is the real you.

It's the key to your power, and your peace.

When you're generous with others you get paid back in ways that have nothing to do with them at all.

Endgame: How the Russian Tale Turned Out

I called back the math student—the pudgy, wrinkled guy that I nicknamed Best Friend. It was two days after I met him, and I wanted to schedule our next appointment. He wasn't in, so I left a message.

When a week went by and he didn't call back, I started to get a little nervous. The Russian crackdown on its wayward republics was moving in fast-forward, and no one knew what to expect. Any HUMINT at all would help.

Trying not to get too paranoid, I made a quick mental inventory of the meeting with the math wizard—limited to *what I knew then.*

What I did "right": I made it about him. I showed interest in his work. I was deferential and considerate. I took him to an interesting place. I overlooked any flaws he might have that would have made him feel judged. I didn't tell him any of my own stories. I offered him a fee for helping. I stayed very rational, and didn't try to manipulate him with emotion. I thought that was enough—*though now I know it's not.*

I called again. Two more times. Nothing. Sent an email. No response. I was starting to feel like a jilted boyfriend, so I did what any logical (pathetic) guy would do. I called on a phone he wouldn't recognize.

He picked up. "Hey, it's Robin Dreeke!" I said. "How are you *doing?*"

"I'm fine, Robin, but. . . ."

"I'd really like to get together and have another chat."

For an ominous moment, he said nothing. Then, cheerfully and kindly, he delivered his message. It was, in so many words:

"I don't think I can help you. I can't seem to figure out exactly what you want, and I'm only good at very specific things. I wish I could help, because it's obvious you're passionate about your work, and are great at it. But I'm struggling to keep up with classes, so I don't think it's a good idea for me to schedule more time with you."

He wished me the best of luck, said he would try to stay in touch, and thanked me again for lunch. Click.

Basically: it's not you, it's me—but can we still be friends?

I went straight to my boss with my hat in my hand. He was like: You? The guy who gets people to talk? I can't believe it! You're so *good*! That guy's *crazy*!

Wow, killed with kindness twice in one hour—a double-murder of my suddenly delicate psyche!

But facts were facts, and I knew I'd get nowhere if I didn't face them. I'd blown this right out of the water.

I thought about it: every day, for a long time. I knew I had to find a way to keep it from happening again. I was *good* at what I did, but *not* great. I was still playing see-the-hill-take-the-hill. To be great, I needed a system.

What *exactly* did I do wrong?

I don't know what your assessment of my behavior was in this drill, but I hope you had a better sense of how doomed I was than I did.

In one of those if-I-knew-then-what-I-know-now scenarios, here's what I know now:

It's not *enough* to keep from doing things wrong. You've got to do them right. And by right, I mean very, *very* right. Human beings are extraordinarily sensitive creatures. Fact of life.

Therefore, a better question: what did I do that was not right *enough*?

For starters, I didn't make it completely about him. I chose a restaurant that I thought would be fun to tell my family and friends about. He'd obviously been there before, and would have probably preferred a nice steak house, or a cool sushi place—anywhere but a local diner with only one claim to fame. How could I miss something so obvious? Simple: not giving it much thought.

I didn't even suspend my ego enough to pay attention to his preferred style of communication. I was all over the board with the Yankees, foreign affairs, generalities, and whatever else made *me* feel comfortable. He, on the other hand, was an uber-logical, left-brained, compartmentalized mathematician, working in a field of absolutes and specifics. What part of "Tell me exactly what you need" didn't I get?

And do you remember me asking him, "What can a military consulate learn from you?" And him saying: "A lot." Yikes! That's not validation. I made an okay comeback, but is a comeback ever *really* okay?

He clearly saw that I was exaggerating my knowledge about hockey. So why should he trust me *more* about something *important*?

Did I even respect his time limitation? Not really. I wasn't paying much attention to time. These days, I know that when somebody says to you: "Gee, where'd the time go?" that they usually *know*.

And let's consider the nickname: Best Friend, due to how I saw him back then: as a second banana, somebody who was socially insecure, just because he was nerdy and geeky. You think he missed that? People have a sixth sense about your opinion of them— especially their areas of vulnerability—and you can betray condescension without saying a word. It'll emerge as a gesture, a tone, or a subject you *don't* bring up. *They'll* know when you do it. You won't.

When you spot someone's weakness—and you will, if you make

the effort to truly know them—you've got to use that knowledge to *protect* them from their fears and doubts. Build them up a little in those areas. *That's* validation.

He knew that some people judged him, but he didn't see himself as inadequate. He saw himself as brilliant. If you really want people to trust you, don't listen to them with your ears, or see them with your eyes: listen with *their* ears, and see with *their* eyes.

I thought I was being generous when I offered him money. I was being an idiot. When I actually got interested in the guy—*after* it was too late—I discovered that he's from a wealthy family. I should have offered him something more personal and less material, like walking with him to his class, to save him time.

It was even naive of me to think that everything was fine, just because he said and did all the right things. That's how nice people blow you off. They say, "You're great, but we're not the right fit." Or: "We're going in a different direction." Or: "I'd love to, but can't right now."

Assessing my failure was all in a day's work of creating humbling moments. A *long* day.

How did *your* assessment go? Probably better than mine. It's usually easier for us to spot other people's flaws than it is our own. Keep that in mind, as your own humbling moments beckon with their siren's song.

One other thing: I could have told myself it didn't matter at *all*, as we so often do when reality slaps us around. In real life, though, Best Friend became the new best friend of another FBI agent, and helped on several critical cases, including the one that I had blown all to hell. On that case, our subject *was* working for his own republic, and later became its secretary of defense. Best Friend's connection with him was worth its weight in spy satellites.

Despite all this, it would be twenty years before I talked to Best Friend again.

It was a long twenty years, filled with learning, but this day was my turning point—because I got the most important lesson of all that very evening, on the ride home from work, from an important mentor.

The lesson came from a man who was emerging as my other Jedi master, in addition to Jesse Thorne. His name was Vern Schrader, and I commuted each day with him from Upstate New York, where I could afford to live, and where Vern preferred to live, as a great place to raise his kids.

On the long daily drives, he offered me priceless advice, while I pumped him for war stories about his combat duty in Vietnam—which was extra-hairy, because he was a combat photographer who had to run into the fire zones that others were running out of.

He'd transferred those crisis skills into forensic, crime-scene photography for the FBI, and became hugely successful, leading large teams of investigators into situations that were sometimes still treacherous. He was one of those humble, ultra-effective Bureau guys who became a legend, almost against his will.

Vern had a passion for leadership strategies, and was ahead of his time in glimpsing the power of trust. He introduced me to some of the lessons that I'm teaching you, including the theme of this book: *to inspire trust, put others first.*

Driving home that day, I gave Vern the pity-party version of my hard day at the office, ending with: "What did I do *wrong,* Vern?"

"Nothing out of the ordinary. You just focused on yourself instead of him. So as far as he was concerned, what you were proposing would work for you, but not necessarily him. So he bailed."

I waited for him to address the career ramifications of my flame-out, with strategies to win back the math wizard.

He didn't. "So what's my next step?" I prompted.

"There isn't one. He doesn't trust you. If you start sucking up, he'll know you're just blowing smoke."

"It's not that simple," I said.

He shrugged and gave me a half smile that said: yes, it is.

"Next time," Vern said, "just put the other guy first, and see what happens. And don't beat yourself up over this. That's just more of the same problem—thinking that it's all about you."

"Okay. That's good advice." I didn't really mean it.

But I never forgot it.

Truth is funny that way. Even when you don't believe it, you don't forget it. And if you're lucky, you'll finally grow enough to get it.

— 4 —

THE CHEMISTRY OF TRUST:
IT'S ALL ABOUT US

Boot Camp
Parris Island, South Carolina

WHEN I WAS A SERIES Commander of Drill Instructors, one of my recruits was a twenty-year old kid with a tough background who didn't seem to trust anybody—a dangerous trait for a man on a team—and one sticky-hot afternoon he trudged to his footlocker after a guts-out inspection and sifted through his meager belongings, in a moment that changed three lives. He was slow and deliberate, keeping his locker as squared away as possible, to avoid a thrashing from his Senior Drill Instructor with the dreaded exercises that we called Incentive Training.

His Senior DI, in charge of four other Assistant DIs, was the kind of seasoned Marine who saw everything, and he watched the recruit's movements accelerate into a frenzy. *Not* acceptable.

Frenzy gets Marines killed. Panic assaults mental clarity, incinerates blood sugar, robs the lungs of oxygen, turns motor control into quivers and shivers, and narrows sight down to tunnel vision. These physical responses to fear then feed-forward into more fear, as the body develops a mind of its own.

That material mind—operating beyond the constraints of reason—is the human twilight zone of free-floating fear.

In battle, it's literally lethal. Even in a boardroom, unchecked fear can kill a career.

The DI stomped toward the recruit, and the kid didn't even hear. He wasn't a Marine yet. A Marine would have put a lid on his panic, and kept his eyes and ears open.

The pivotal objective in Recruit Training is teaching civilians how to replace instinct with systematic reactions: standard operating procedures.

The SOPs apply to everybody in the chain of command. When you see a DI in a movie with dog tags dangling from his neck, those aren't for identification—they're abbreviated SOPs for various situations. Think of them as a miniature version of the lapboard I carry when I fly—or as the Code of Trust, and the Four Steps.

"What *is* your major *malfunction*, Recruit?"

The recruit bolted upright so fast that his head almost hit the brim of the sergeant's Campaign Cover—also known as a Smokey the Bear hat. He didn't even notice that his buddy was already at attention.

"Sir, this Recruit cannot find all of his belongings!"

"And that gives you the right to dirty up my deck?"

"No sir!"

"Take a *breath*!" The Drill Instructor liked this kid. They were both brick-solid, small guys from the hardscrabble mid-South—one from Kentucky, one from Tennessee—and neither had come from money, nor had any now. The DI, Staff Sgt. Conrad Howell, was already a lifer with infantry-combat experience—which is as hairy as it gets in the service of your country—but he and his family of four still qualified for food stamps. Nobody serves for the money. "You *will* square away this locker, Recruit!"

"Sir, permission to help the recruit!" said his buddy, a slightly older kid with three years of college.

"Granted! Then you two clean the head."

Staff Sergeant Howell pivoted and marched off in a stride as smooth as a glide, with his Smiley Bear seeming to float in the air.

"What the hell, Shane?" said the panicked kid's buddy, who'd been nurse-maiding his fellow recruit through the training.

"Somebody took my jing!" His money. "It was my whole bank!"

"Tell Senior."

"What could Staff Sergeant Howell do?" The recruit was not accustomed to help.

"Uh . . . I dunno, Shane. I guess that's just what a Marine would do."

"I seen enough of what a Marine would do."

"If you don't, I will."

"Go for it, Joe" the recruit said glumly.

They trudged off to clean the bathroom.

The punishment was actually a reprieve, far milder than getting smoked with thirty push-ups—the maximum allowed in this weather, according to the tags that Howell kept under his Smiley Bear Cover, with sundry other paperwork. The arm busters were followed by the maximum flutter kicks, mountain climbers, rifle drills, and a foul variety of other IT. By the end of it, the recruit would have been soaked and gasping.

Howell—a starter-level sarge, or E5—had a soft spot for the way the recruit, Shane Frink, busted his hump every day without complaint, just as the sarge had done, years before. Another thing they had in common was a gift for kinetic learning—and difficulty with written material. The kid's instinctive wariness also reminded Howell of his own younger days. They had good chemistry.

The recruit was in awe of the DIs fairness—he treated *all* the recruits like crap, even Shane's quick-witted buddy that everybody called Joe College, due to the fact that he'd dropped out of the University of Virginia six months before graduation, in a moment of patriotism piqued by the liberating blitzkrieg of Desert Storm.

Shane was totally in sync with his DI's hard-boiled take on the bitter reality of peacekeeping, and the far more cruel actuality of battle, which he'd already seen, in microcosm, on the streets of his own city. In the movies, the recruit hates the DI until he finally realizes that the Old Man is trying to keep him on the oxygenated side of the ground—but in real life, thank God, most Marines are smart enough to see that from the get-go.

Turns out, the recruit had been robbed of the $800 he'd just gotten from cashing his final basic-training check at the Navy Federal Credit Union—where my wife, by the way, worked. (Irrelevant to the story? Not if the story's about teamwork: A Marine's wife is in the Corps. She is the soldier's single closest comrade.)

(Also seemingly off the subject, but not: I had Kim's personal number at work, and once when she spotted my phone on her caller-ID she answered, "Hey handsome, any plans tonight? To which one of my DIs, who'd borrowed the phone, answered, "Be happy to, ma'am, but I don't think my boss would approve." Humor bonds, and esprit d'corps is as effective as anything else at keeping soldiers alive.)

At this time, we were in the pivotal eleventh week of training, just before a final hellish test of worthiness called The Crucible. At the eleven-week review, one platoon goes outside its squad bay for scrutiny by the battalion commander, while another platoon prepares that bay for inspection—then the platoons switch jobs. The tradition teaches trust, and exemplifies the exponential power of shared goals.

This time it backfired. A Marine had stolen from another Marine.

Does that mean it's foolish to trust unsparingly, even in a brotherhood?

No: In all honesty, you *can*—with reasonable cause, and rational limits—trust almost all people, almost all the time. Trust is much like hope, or faith—in the secular sense as well, as well the spiritual. You can have an abundance of it, throughout life, with no absolute certainty of its fulfillment.

When you take the leap of trust, though, it will be rewarded far more often than thwarted, and will consistently inspire others to be more trusting in you.

But if you do trust most people, someday you will be betrayed. That is virtually inevitable.

All betrayal hurts, and a bad enough betrayal will break your heart. When that day arrives, it will become *your* Crucible. You will be compelled to examine the power and the pain of freely offering trust in a world of imperfect people.

I believe you'll decide that trust is worth the risk, and worth the reward.

When people with a wholehearted commitment to trust are betrayed, they almost always find a way to summon the resilient, ever-blooming courage of youth, when a heart can be broken and still remain open, and new trust dawns with each day.

Not everyone, though, has this strength. Some people let even a single betrayal kill their trust, and with it the power that flowers when "you and I" becomes "us."

That's what happened to the recruit. He was now convinced that the gift of trust is wasted on the people of this world. As far as he was concerned, the bad ones hurt you, and the good ones can't help.

In the sergeant's sparse quarters at the end of the bay, Joe College, still wet with sweat from the humid head, told Sergeant Howell what had happened.

"Do *not* give this another thought!" the sergeant said. "It's *my* problem now, not yours. That boy *will* be a fine Marine! *Some* day. Tell him to keep his head up. If he helps his people, they'll help him!"

"Sir, I don't see how they can help with this. Shane's pretty down. Sir."

"Your buddy will *live*," Howell snapped. "Trust me! Dismissed!"

Joe went to his buddy and tried to tell Shane that he was in one of our culture's fairest institutions, and that things would somehow be fine.

Shane, hardened too young by a hard world, said the whole thing reminded him of the life he'd left behind, when he'd been punished for things that weren't his fault at all, like being poor, and short, and dyslexic—and that was just the start of a long story.

But for the first time, he had a friend who really cared—not just out of emotion, but as a standard way of operating.

Even more important, he had a guardian angel, cloaked in the least angelic demeanor imaginable.

We all have one, though for many of us, it's merely the better angels of our nature.

As the recruits talked, Howell set in motion a plan that would change the young recruit's life.

The plan also changed Howell' life.

And it changed mine.

It became the quintessential act that led me to realize what leadership really is.

Doughnut Diplomacy

Do you remember when Krispy Kremes became a national phenomenon in the early 2000s? It was practically a cult. Even before that, Krispy Kremes were available locally in the Carolinas, where the company started, and when I was at Parris Island, the never-before-seen doughnuts were like a cult within a cult: so rare and steeped in desirability that they manifest near-mystical qualities.

When I tapped into their mojo, my life was granted new powers.

Those irresistible amulets of sugar and fat led me to the life-changing event that culminated with the DI's plan.

Our base was so close to the Krispy Kreme bakery that I could—if my timing was immaculate—pick them up at a 7–Eleven and get them to my Drill Instructors while the bag still steamed with the aroma of doughnuts still in the oven, glistening with chocolate glaze, almost too hot to handle.

I brought them to my men twice a week, and doughnut days produced some of those golden moments of camaraderie that stay in your mind long after memories of far greater glories and losses ebb into the unknown.

Offering the doughnuts fulfilled all five rules of the Code of Trust. At the time, though, all I knew was that I was getting doughnuts for the guys. The clarity of classification, as in most moments of action, came later.

By Code categorization, the doughnuts were all about the men, not me, nor my reflected glory in their procurement (Rule #1, as always), and they carried a message of nonjudgmental acceptance that was delivered equally to everyone, since I bought only one basic variety. The Krispy Kremes cost enough to convey generosity, and taking the trouble to deliver them piping hot held the same substance as offering the men at least a part of my heart.

The doughnuts also conveyed an inarguable respect for reason: *the men were hungry!* And therein lies the lesson of our last chapter about the Code of Trust: *The body has a mind of its own*—ruled by material needs as mundane as hunger—and this mind has its own way of reasoning. The material mind of every person on earth—the flesh and blood of the brain—can be programmed for trust, or for distrust.

This physical phenomenon is universal, and it can either work for you, or against you. Your choice.

As my guys chowed-down on sugary carbs, and fueled-up on coffee, they were rewarding their brains with the earth's own chemicals of energy and contentment, and it invariably made them more open and relaxed.

Whenever the smell of the Krispy Kremes hit our office and mingled with the dark fragrance of fresh coffee, the men instinctively gathered, let down their guard, and shared information about our recruits and superior officers. Shields Down, Information In!

It was our own variation of one of humankind's oldest communal rituals: gathering to share food—from which people have historically derived equal value from the sharing, and from the food: the behavior, and the biochemistry. In civilization's earliest millennia, when a small group of hunters brought home enough food for a large tribe, it was not just the first application of universal health care, nor even mutual survival through altruism. It was a flat-out chemistry experiment, in which nature's sweetness and ripeness was transformed into the human brain's molecules of contentment.

This custom, carried to us today through evolutionary psychology, is as common as ever, and in this era of greater ease, it's often centered around foods that are the direct nutritional precursors of the brain chemicals of pleasure and camaraderie, sometimes categorized as comfort foods: high-carb sweets and starches, caffeine, chocolate (with traces of the intoxicating aphrodisiac phenethylamine), and the blunt gastronomic instrument of alcohol.

After all, people tend to meet over coffee, cocktails, or dessert—not spinach—due to the symbiotic confluence of the evocative chemicals and the behaviors of bonding, both of which reward the brain similarly.

On doughnut day, the chemical elements primed the pump for actions of sharing, and the sharing then heightened our sense of tribal commonality, encouraging thoughts and feelings to emerge untrammeled.

I maximized my Doughnut Diplomacy back then, because I needed all the information I could get to lead the sixteen DIs under my command, and the eighty-eight recruits they had in every platoon. I regularly reminded my DIs that the only way I could protect their careers was by having my commanders trust me. And I warned them that the protection that our superior officers provided us—our Top Cover, in Marine-speak—was based on the brass knowing about every issue before it became a problem, and every problem before it became a disaster.

I kept the lines of communication open, above me and below me, so that everybody up and down the chain of command would know every action I was taking, and why. If they understood, they would help, as people generally do. It was a classic case of invoking the power of survival through mutual, reciprocating trust—and not just my people's survival, but mine.

If somebody under my command screwed up, they were not the first person the Commander called in. I was. I had to be able to explain why my Marine had messed up, and why it wouldn't happen again—and that meant knowing, to the best of my ability, everything about everybody. If there was no reasonable explanation, it might ruin the offender's career—and probably mine, too.

Of course, there was even greater value in knowing about the lives of my men than just reinforcing our mutual protection. My collection of knowledge was the core of our camaraderie: the glue that held us together. Everywhere I went, I carried a platoon commander's notebook to jot down birthdays, anniversaries, reenlistments, and achievements: all the stuff that mattered to my men as individuals. On each man's own special days, I gave him a pat on the back, a good word, or a doughnut: unsolicited and unexpected, with no reciprocity required. The men's appreciation of these minor acts of kindness was so visceral you could almost see a light shine on them.

I thought I was just being a nice guy, but I was being a leader. I was making *my* life about the lives of my *men*.

In Recruit Training—as in so many situations—it would have been crazy to do otherwise. I was surrounded by men I was completely dependent upon. In war years, our very existence would depend upon one another.

The DIs—seasoned men who'd seen life and death from every angle and at least a couple of continents—were the real leaders at Parris Island, regardless of rank. I was technically the boss, but my main job was to lead by learning.

As I passed around the doughnuts on this ultra-important week, I was surrounded by the body language of distress: compressed lips, elevated eyebrows, chins angling downward, and arms crossed.

Sergeant Howell looked especially troubled. He was trying to settle into his chair, but he was so tense that he teetered on the edge of it, his arms clamped to his sides. He was a block of rigid muscles and right angles, with his shoulders clenched so tightly that they seemed to be crawling up his neck. Several of the guys cast glances at Howell, then me, that said: time to be the boss, Lieutenant!

I took Howell aside.

"Something bothering you?"

"Hell yes." Howell didn't mince words or mask feelings. I liked that, and so did his recruits, because they always knew where they stood. There's no better conduit for trust than plain speaking.

Our Company Commander, though, thought Howell was a pain in the ass: a loose cannon, who was noncompliant with some of the new politically correct etiquette of the postwar Corps. Howell and the captain had bad chemistry, and it came to a head in front of a squad of men one day when the captain chided Howell for using profanity with a recruit—a no-no, believe it or not—and Howell responded, in effect: "Are you effing *defecating* me, sir?"

Howell told me about the theft. So far, he'd kept it under his Smokey Bear.

This was bad. No-win. If we could sweat the offending platoon into offering up the thief—which wasn't likely—the whole platoon would feel betrayed, either by one of their own, or by us, or by both parties.

The thief, of course, would be out on his butt with a dishonorable discharge—one that might forever haunt a kid who in all probability had just committed the first felony of his life, in a moment of temptation and stupidity.

If we didn't make it right with the recruit, though, he would never have the faith in his comrades that keeps Marines safe in situations of peril. It could result in harm to him, or to somebody that he didn't totally dedicate himself to, as if his own life and limbs were on the line.

The only way we could keep it in-house, among the recruit and his platoon, would be to pass the hat. That would restore the kid's trust in an organization that might some day ask him to lay down his life. It would also bond the platoon.

It would, furthermore, be *completely* illegal. Officers and noncommissioned officers are strictly prohibited from instigating any type of fund-raising among people under their command, due to the presumed pressure on the troops to comply.

Staff Sergeant Conrad Howell, however, was a man who placed far greater value on the spirit of Marine brotherhood than the letter of its laws.

"I can *handle* this, sir," Howell told me. I knew what he meant, and he knew that I knew. He was offering to pass the hat, and save the kid's sense of trust at the possible expense of his own career. Years before, in Asia, his superior officer had overridden orders that had literally saved his life, and that was a debt he didn't take lightly. It was one that he tried to repay, symbolically and in small, undramatic acts, every day of his career.

"Sergeant," I said, "this is *not* a problem. I've got an idea, and I'll take care of it myself."

"*Thank* you, sir!" His shoulders wilted in relief. He finished his doughnut with gusto.

I finished mine, too, asking myself: well, Lieutenant, what *is* this plan of yours?

There was an extra doughnut left, and for once, I took it myself. I needed a little bit of biochemical backup.

The Krispy Kreme, washed down with sweet-creamy coffee, gave me that little jolt of confidence that sugar and caffeine so adroitly confer.

I was glad this was a doughnut day, and thankful for the ones that had come before, because I had a gut feeling that without all my prior Doughnut Diplomacy, I wouldn't be enjoying the wide-open door of communication that I had. The ritualistic recognition of my men had gradually built a bond of trust that granted me the extra flexibility that now represented my best hope for solving this seemingly insoluble problem without killing somebody's career: with mine first in line. Semper Gumby.

The Chemistry of Trust, 101

Trust is a feeling. Feelings are carried by chemicals—primarily neurotransmitters and hormones. Positive feelings like trust are transported mostly by dopamine, serotonin, GABA, adrenaline, endorphins, and several other mind-body messengers.

These messengers travel from brain to body and back again, in constant loops of feedback and feed-forward that harmonize mental and physical function.

When you help people open their hearts to trust, it sets off an explosion of biochemical fireworks that rewards their brains, warms their hearts, and makes them want to see you again.

But when you make people think they should close themselves off from you, they feel only the coldness of disconnection—reinforced by the painful, free-floating fears we all have, and always will, that whisper endlessly in our ears: *trust no one.*

Fear has a wonderful memory, and it can enable people to stay frozen forever. Your fears live deep in your reptilian brain, within an almond-shaped haunted house called the amygdala. It's about as close to your spinal column as your brain can get—making it the perfect place to launch your body into action before your mind has a chance to think. The inhabitants of this haunted house include the ghosts of betrayals past—striving to keep you safe, as all fear does— but limiting your life in the process.

To trust others, and be trusted, you sometimes need to clean house, and face down the fearful memories that cloud your judgment, poison your mood chemistry, and trigger your temper.

It's hard to let go of the dark parts of the past, and it's a job that's different for everybody, and more difficult for some than others. That path is for your steps alone, but we all have a feeling in our heart about where it starts. If you look for yours, you'll find it.

Reconciling your most troubling thoughts is just the beginning, though. To reach the level of trust that leadership demands, you'll need to replace the once-protective fears from your worst days with new memories: positive, rewarding moments of ego subordination, nonjudgmental acceptance, validation, generosity, and rationality. These are the trusting—and trust-inspiring—memories that take us to a state of mind that is most simply described as love.

Since all relationships and encounters are influenced by the biology of thought and emotion, controlling the chemistry of interpersonal reaction is a vital part of rising beyond bitterness, to belief in others.

Although it's quite common for people to describe the quality of their personal encounters with the word *chemistry,* some people don't realize the literal presence of this chemistry.

How we act around others affects not just their thoughts, but their neurochemistry, as their bodies react to those thoughts.

The actions of other people tweak our own neurochemistry, creating a two-way street, in which "you" and "I" become "us"— for better or for worse: in connection or opposition. Chemistry can engrave memories so deeply that they're virtually indelible. These chemicals can live on long after the action that created them is gone.

That's why it's critically important to make this chemistry work for "us" instead of against us.

A single overt act of trust building, such as validating another person can, in key situations, create a chemical reaction that's equivalent to one ignited by sex. Sometimes I characterize this reaction to my FBI and private industry trainees as The Sex, Validation, and Rock 'n' Roll Response.

Validation and sex both trigger a flood of the excitatory neurotransmitter dopamine, as well as the contentment neurotransmitters serotonin and GABA. These three feel-good neurotransmitters—once activated by the precipitating acts of trustworthiness—are joined in the journey toward trust by the famous pleasure hormones known as endorphins, and by the bonding hormone oxytocin, most recognized for its peak production among women shortly after giving birth, and among all people shortly after orgasm.

These behavior chemicals combine to create a comforting neurochemical bubble bath for the brain that elicits a distinct, enduring psychological and physical feeling of pleasure. This stable sense of well-being is largely lodged in a dopamine-driven part of the brain called the caudate nucleus—known as the primary pleasure center of the brain, which is a major site for romantic attachment. When the caudate nucleus functions poorly, due to a bad biochemical or behavioral environment, it can contribute to disorders characterized by worry and agitation, including obsessive-compulsive disorder, anxiety disorders characterized by paranoia, and ADHD.

People who are lucky enough to have either good mood chemistry or happy environments—or best of all, both—tend to be blessed with brains and bodies that are *looking* for reasons to feel good, instead of bad.

This somatic expression of well-being powerfully reinforces its mental counterpart: the intellectual perception of being understood, and appreciated.

The line between building trust mentally and physically is blurred, and mutually reinforcing. When the verbal and nonverbal messages that inspire trust activate the pleasure centers in the brain, they reinforce not only the power of the message, but also the trustworthiness of the messenger.

This was demonstrated in 2012 by a group of neuroscientists at Harvard who discovered that—as I mentioned in the first chapter—an average of 40 percent of a person's daily communication is about their own opinions, actions, and feelings. In this experiment, when people were talking about themselves, their brains were in a condition of dopamine overdrive and neurochemical bliss. Even when they were offered money to change the subject, most continued to talk about themselves.

If you let other people do most of the talking, the pleasure centers of their brains will light up, and they'll tend to trust you. It's that simple.

Similarly, scientists have measured the bonding hormone oxytocin during various situations, and found that it increases when someone meets a friend, or even a pleasant stranger.

Bonding hormones can increase from just shaking a stranger's hand, or even from a casual touch. In one interesting experiment, a clerk at a convenience store lightly grazed the hand of every other customer when giving them change, and researchers asked the customers about the interaction when they walked out the door. Those who had experienced the subliminal touch rated the clerk much more favorably.

For that matter, oxytocin has even been proven to rise as a result of a loving look from people's pets. It's really that controllable and predictable.

However, an opposite psychophysical effect occurs during manipulative or coercive contact. Negative verbal and nonverbal messages create the evolutionary-psychology force colloquially known as brain hijacking.

This force is reflected physically as the stress response—first characterized in 1915 as the fight-flight response, by W. B. Cannon, and in the 1990s as the fight-flight-freeze response, by C. L. Stauth, in various books and articles. This common physical response bathes the brain in a veritable battery acid of the stress hormone cortisol, and activates the stimulative, sympathetic branch of the autonomic nervous system, resulting in excess production of hormones associated with agitation and anxiety.

It also results in interference with logical thinking—commonly called brain freeze—by depressing function of the primary neurotransmitter of thought and memory, acetylcholine. The sad result is that sometimes people who don't trust each other can't even think straight during an uncomfortable encounter.

This fight-flight-freeze response is mirrored in various physical characteristics that reveal and reinforce distrust.

Among these physical reactions is blood vessel constriction, which partly results in cold hands, as well as in the fear-euphemism of *cold feet*. The stress response also creates shortness of breath, which can contribute to a telltale reveal among people who commonly fail to inspire trust: fast talking, a synonym for distrustful behavior. The stress response also elicits muscular inhibition that causes some people to be, in effect, paralyzed by fear, resulting in mild interference with speech, or the feeling of being tongue tied. This inhibition can also reduce muscular coordination, presenting an appearance of being stiff, or awkward. Other physical manifestations include contraction of the pupils, creating the proverbial beady-eye appearance; impairment of digestive-system contraction, sometimes characterized as butterflies in the stomach; and limitation of peripheral sight, causing literal and figurative tunnel vision.

All of these physical responses provoke further mental distress, through feed-forward activity that's carried from the body to the brain. This perpetuates a downward spiral of distrust, limiting people's ability to grant trust, or inspire it.

This panoply of physical traits—with their obvious giveaways—make people who are exposed to fight-flight-freeze behavior feel oppositional, evasive, and unresponsive.

Once those feelings start, they're hard to stop, as the body develops a mind of its own.

Unfortunately, the Type-A people who often seek leadership positions tend to be born with high-adrenal physical characteristics, which makes them more vulnerable than calm, laid-back people to the brain-hijacking forces of stressful situations. Their adrenal abundance—typically regarded as a gift of the strong and energetic—can easily tilt them toward negative behavior, allowing a productive condition such as aggressiveness to slip into the destructive condition of aggression.

Therefore, the potent psychophysical force that's created by following the Code of Trust is simply *not* built-in second nature to many Type-A people. Sometimes, the harder they pursue leadership, the further it recedes.

If that sounds like you, don't feel bad, because that was me, too. It took me a long time to learn to get out of my own way, stop being my own worst enemy, and worry more about others than myself.

When that happened, a weight was lifted off my shoulders: the weight of my own ego—which I'd thought was holding me up, but was really holding me down.

These days, in an era of innovative health care, many people—especially hard-charging types—turn to quick medicinal fixes. New generations of mild medications do help some people with frank mood disorders to calm down, or to control their depression, and improve their relationships. But my work in this area has convinced me that the best approach to controlling the chemistry of trust is not through medication, but behavioral modification. This belief helped lead me to the creation of the Code of Trust.

I explored the biochemistry of trust for some time with a government group known as the IARPA, the Intelligence Advanced Research Projects Activity, but we made very little progress in finding dependable ways to promote trust by using only physical measures, such as the administration of oxytocin. It seemed to work for some people, but others experienced a paradoxical effect, and actually felt more alienated.

For most people, the best purely physical approach for optimizing the biochemistry of emotion is just to work hard at staying healthy and fit.

General health has a powerful impact on mood chemistry and cognition, so it's hard to be at your best if you regularly sacrifice your health on the alter of either unbridled ambition, or out-of-control indulgence. Your chemicals of contentment and your capacity for higher thought can be significantly depleted by exhaustion and worry, and even by a bad diet, or nutrient deficiencies.

For the same reasons that cautious use of caffeine, carbs, and alcohol often gives people a temporary boost in well-being, excessive use of them has the opposite effect—especially when they're used to self-medicate exhaustion and worry. It's easy to go off the deep end, and create a classic downward spiral that's common in our culture: bad habits triggering bad behavior, which leads to more bad habits.

Another important lesson I learned from Vern Schrader was: the best way not to *medicate* your stress is to not *have* it, and the best way to do that is to keep all of your expectations to a minimum. "When you manage your expectations," he said, "there's no deep end to go off."

Like many of the things Vern taught me, that's easier said than done, so sometimes it's necessary to rebalance your brain chemicals when they go awry.

To optimize the function of your neurotransmitters and hormones, the best strategies are the same ones that your mother recommended: eating a healthy diet (and that includes *vegetables,* and cleaning your plate before you even *mention* dessert!); getting enough sleep (including the deep sleep that helps rebuild brain cells); exercising regularly (with plenty of aerobics, to activate your body's own antidepressants and energizers); minimizing your exposure to toxins (including the ones you *like*); trying to relax every day; and spending time with the people you love (including *calling your mother* once in a while, Mr. Big-Shot!).

That's the end of Trust-Chem 101. Class over.

Here's your homework: Take a painfully honest inventory of your own chemistry of trust. Consider these issues:

- **Is your fuse too short?**
- **Do problems interfere with your sleep?**
- **Are you uncomfortable around new people?**
- **Do old betrayals still influence your actions?**
- **Do you have a thin-skin for perceived slights?**
- **Does failure hurt more than success feels good?**
- **Do you depend on external factors to normalize your mood?**
- **Do you take a certain pride in isolation?**
- **Do you get a guilty pleasure from seeing others fail?**

Here's reality: we all hold onto plenty of those traits, as the dark part of our hardwired brain says: don't let go.

Here's a greater reality: We all hold, at the very heart of our hearts, the better angels of our nature. Those angels, our beacons of choice, have one overriding message: what you hold onto stays, and what you let go of leaves—and what you do is up to you.

Like most of life's best lessons, it's so simple that it's almost too good to be true.

Him or Me
Parris Island

I went to the captain and told him about the theft. I owed that honesty to him, and to the Corps.

As I told him the story, his hands and jaw began to clench, and a red tinge rose up his neck so viscerally that it was like watching mercury rise up a thermometer.

"It's that damned *Howell*!" he said. "No *command* over his men!"

"Sir, the thief was in the *other* platoon."

"Which targeted *Howell's* man!" Nice leap of logic. He clearly held a grudge. The captain had never really learned to control his moods, and any kind of insult burned its way straight into his brain, and stayed there.

"Let me make one thing crystal clear. I do not want Sergeant Howell to take up a collection."

"Yes sir!"

But I'd given it enough thought to know that passing the hat was the only feasible solution. Howell's men wouldn't mind.

How did I know? I'd asked Joe College. It was a touchy, need-to-know subject, but I trusted him. Part of the trust was pure logic: He held his concern for Shane's success on the same level as his own, and wouldn't endorse a doomed option. And part of the trust was pure intuition, backed by elements as amorphous as the look in his eyes. There's a calmness and unblinking clarity in the eyes of people who say exactly what they think—free from the endless mind games of manipulation—and it falls indiscriminately on whomever they see.

In fact, Joe said the recruits wanted to give Howell, "the Old Man" (as in, thirty-five-years old) a going-away present as they left for parts unknown, and helping him with this project would be perfect.

Joe didn't request confidentiality regarding this conversation. Didn't need to. Trust is contagious.

Now, though, it was a hell of a mess, as I'd feared all along it would be—especially for me.

Three days later was the our last doughnut day of Recruit Training, which, even in the best of times, holds a bittersweet tinge, because the DIs invariably regard a few of their men as veritable sons. They see the recruits as images of themselves, and as emblems of the type of person who comes in as a kid, and leaves as a man who will sacrifice everything he has for the vision of fairness and freedom that became the country of America.

Not that the sergeants would ever *say* this, or even show it. God forbid! They were *DIs*! But I knew it was true, because that's how I felt, too.

Even on this dreamy day of brotherhood—or *especially* on this day—I was in turmoil. Somebody was going to suffer this day.

When I gave Sergeant Howell his doughnut, we were standing in the second story of the squad bay, watching the junior enlisted Marines outside march in close formation, moving as one, their dress blues bright against the green grass, and their brass gleaming.

"I never get tired of seeing this," Howell said.

"It's a sight."

"I'd hate like hell to ever lose it."

"Me, too. Once this stuff is in you, it stays, doesn't it?"

"Roger that." Howell tilted his head down and a little to the left. "That, um, problem, Lieutenant?" he said hesitantly.

"Yeah, right. That's all good now. We got Top Cover on it. So go ahead and take care of it."

"*Really?*"

I glanced over, but he was looking away, and all I saw were the names of his four kids tattooed on his arm. "Really."

"Good man, LT!"

I hoped others would see it that way. But I doubted it. I took a long look at my Marines, because I thought it was probably my last.

I'd decided to take the fall. How could I not?

It was him or me.

Saying Good-bye

When recruits graduate, they get a week off to go home, then they report to Marine Combat Training at Camp Lejeune, North Carolina (home of the body-armored mega-mosquitoes I mentioned in the first chapter, when I got my midnight ride to the bombing range).

By the time they're in Lejeune, we never see them again. We rarely even hear anything from them, or about them.

But that didn't happen this time. Unfortunately.

The captain approached me early one morning about a month after the last group had landed at Lejeune, with a smile that looked more ugly than friendly. "We *got* him!" he said.

"Got who?"

"*Howell! Nailed* him!" I felt sick. "That recruit you told me about—Fink, or Frink—when he got to Lejeune, he started bragging about how somebody stole his eighty dollars."

I interrupted. "It was eight hundred dollars, sir."

"His whatever-amount money—and Mr. Loudmouth is telling everybody how his DI took up a collection. So *now* Howell's ass is *mine!*"

He savored the moment and smirked. "Give me the rundown on your order to him about not taking up a collection."

I felt like I had a belt around my chest. I had to force my words out. "Sir, I did not discuss that issue with Sergeant Howell."

"Say *again?*"

"I did not order the sergeant, sir. The sergeant did not disobey a direct order, sir. The fault is mine, sir."

"I can *not. Believe!* I'm *hearing* this." His carotid artery bulged from his neck, and sweat began to slicken his face.

"It was *my* mistake, sir."

He was quiet for a moment. "I never took you for a lifer, Lieutenant Dreeke. I *did* think you could survive your tour at Parris Island. You *fooled* me. Tomorrow you will report to the Battalion Commander to initiate the disposition of your case. You will explain the breech of conduct and tell the Lieutenant Colonel exactly what the *hell* you were thinking."

"Yessir! Tomorrow, sir." I stood stiff, raised a salute, and he glared at me, motionlessly—waiting . . . waiting . . . —and returned the salute. I snapped mine back and walked away.

I wish I could say that I left with my head held high, but that would be a lie. I walked away like a sick, scared kid.

I took a last look at my group of brothers, marching in the sun, and longed to be one of them.

I wondered how I'd be able to tell my wife.

I was shaky with uncertainty. But I knew this: on this day, I had finally been a leader of men.

I hoped that in the years to come, this one day would somehow seem sufficient.

I'd done the right thing. No regrets.

Just dread.

Quantico
Twenty Years Later

A room crammed with CEOs and corporate officers began to empty after I finished my presentation on the importance of trust building in the politically sensitive area of classified work. This group was composed mostly of people in the defense industry who were fulfilling government contracts—with the usual preponderance of former servicemen—so it was fun for me to be among a tribe of guys who spoke the same language as me, and held the same values.

As generally happens, some of them came up to the stage afterward to chat. At the end of the line I saw a face that seemed familiar. As he gradually moved forward, I began to put his face in context: it was from a long time ago, had something to do with the Marines, and centered around some problem.

I'm good at remembering faces. It's just one of those quirky brain skills that you either have, or don't.

When he got to the front of the line I put up my palm and said, "Don't tell me. I know you're name. . . . You were at Parris Island."

"Right so far, Lieutenant."

His voice narrowed the search. "Joe! We called you Joe College."

He laughed. "Got me! And now I actually *have* a degree."

"Joe College," I mused. Memories flooded back.

"Joe CEO, now, Lieutenant," he said, with pleasantly casual pride.

"You don't have to call me Lieutenant now, sir."

Calling him sir was sort of a joke, but I always treat the men who run these companies with respect.

"I'm honored to call you Lieutenant, sir. You changed my life, Agent Dreeke."

"I *did*? You were buddies with the trainee who got ripped off, right?"

"Yes. Still am! Shane Frink! The Mayor of Falluja! Shane distinguished himself over there. And continues to do so. He's still in—over in Pendleton—and now he talks about you to his own men. Talks about Sergeant Howell, too."

"*Really*? Why?"

"Sir, me and Shane learned as much from you and Staff Sergeant Howell as we did from everybody else put together. About taking care of the men around you. About sticking your neck out."

Most of the details had come back to me. "We *all* learned from Sergeant Howell," I said.

"Sergeant *Major* Howell, you mean! Big man down in CENTCOM. *Still* a good guy to know."

I was impressed. That was the highest rank an enlisted man can reach, and CENTCOM—the U.S. Central Command, based in Florida—runs all military operations in the Middle East, North Africa, and Central Asia: the hot spots, where cooler heads prevail, and history now pivots.

"So it all worked out?" I asked Joe. "I'll be honest. I did what I could to take the fall, but I thought we were *all* screwed. I stayed in, but lost my Company."

"You got it the *worst*. The guys you top-covered did *great*. The Lieutenant Colonel was no fan of the Captain, and loved that kinda old-Corps thing. He kept an eye on us."

"So *that's* why I survived. I thought I was just lucky."

"No sir! You made your luck. I just wanted to say thank you, sir!"

As he held his hand out, I swallowed and felt a lump.

It's impossible not be touched by something like that. We all occasionally deserve it—because we've all helped people—but as a rule, fate and coincidence rarely conspire to create the serendipity of reward.

It's just as well, though, because taking care of people is not about the reward.

"Keep in touch, Joe."

"I will."

I knew he would.

He did. His company, a cryptography lab, is in the area, and sometimes we go flying together. He's one of the men I trust at the controls when my son is in the plane, and that alone is helping my son to learn the lessons of trust.

Trust is not only contagious, but travels through time—penetrating the illusory and ever-changing boundaries of status, power, money, and politics. Trust proven true in the real world is indelible, and starts anew with each day.

Know this: All leadership is a transfer of trust. It stays with no man or woman, but is in a constant state of forward movement, into the future, for the better.

It is this movement, and the willing surrender of leadership's burdens, that makes power possible, and makes it worth pursuing.

Leadership is not about you.

If you now can see that this simple fact is a gift, and not a bittersweet penalty, your lessons on the Code of Trust are complete.

And so we end—with the same lesson with which we began. Let it be the talisman of your travels. Let it be your friend.

PART II

INSPIRING TRUST: THE FOUR STEPS

— 5 —

STEP ONE: ALIGN YOUR GOALS!

The Real World
Quantico, Virginia

MY DAY HAD COME. My ship was in. I had it made. Or so I thought.

I sat in my spacious (by government standards) office, at my lavish (by government standards) desk, on an upper floor of the FBI Headquarters, staring at an outline of an article on a yellow legal pad, which had more cross-outs than words, even though I'd been honing the thoughts on it for months.

Numbered one through five, it summarized the five basic tenets of trust.

The ideas for the article, and the years of experience behind them, had put me where I was, and had always wanted to be: working as the head of an important program—which turned out to be the Counterintelligence Behavioral Analysis Program.

My job was to help agents throughout the country understand the motives and methods of the foreign spies that threaten America's safety, and make sure the agents were handling their cases ethically and effectively, in accord with the Code of Trust.

I had this leadership position mostly because people trusted me:

good people, bad people, the smart and less smart, people I knew well, and people I hardly knew at all.

"So," I asked myself, my eyes fixed on the list, "what do I *call* this?" It was more than a strategy, but less than a leadership system. It was a set of standards. An ethic. *A code of conduct!* At the top of the page, I wrote A Code of Trust. Then I Googled that, to make sure I wasn't stealing somebody else's concept. There was nothing remotely remotely close. There weren't even any ideas that closely resembled mine: in the public domain, or in the Bureau. So I crossed out "*A*," and changed it to "*The*."

The Code of Trust. I liked how it sounded.

I felt very good. For about ten seconds. The next question was: How does somebody actually *implement* this? In the real world?

Yes, I'd defined the essential qualities that made a person trustworthy. Now: How does that person *become* trusted? There is a difference.

I went back to work. About six weeks later, I had a system of implementation. I wrote my article, and it was accepted by the *FBI Bulletin*.

Turns out, I'd finished the work just in time to help an old friend.

Going Nuclear
Detroit, Michigan

Special Agent Lyla Khoury trudged out of the Detroit FBI Headquarters—a gargantuan tower with stunning waterfront views on its east side and neglected vacant lots on its west—got into her car, put her head on the steering wheel, and cried for approximately one minute, a stress technique she'd learned from a psycho-babbly leadership book for women. Her boss, an Assistant Special Agent in Charge, had just chewed her out, and told her to close her case.

Lyla didn't get him at all.

The way she saw it, her goal—to nail her target—would be messy and even morally complex, but her ASAC's goal was to wrap every case in a neat package, or get rid of it. She thought he was robotic—a statistic-obsessed technician, instead of a true investigator—and called him Inspector Gadget behind his back.

She'd lost her temper at the meeting—knowing it wouldn't help—but she just couldn't stay calm about a case that might create another nuclear nation in the Mideast. Her famous last words, before the shut-down order, were: "What part of *boom* don't you get?"

He didn't buy her dire assessment. He gave her three weeks to close it down, or—in her opinion—work a miracle.

(The issue here, I must add, may or may not have been nuclear. It may have been chemical, biological, or something else. The exact nature of the threat is not the moral of this story.)

She headed home. To an even more painful problem.

She opened the front door and called out, "Amira, I'm back!" Her daughter was now the home's only other occupant.

The reply, she later told me, was: "And?"

"And?" basically meant: "So *what*? You're going to ignore me at *home,* and that's supposed to be *better*?"

In the kitchen, her daughter had her phone in her face and didn't look up.

"Have you given some thought to what we talked about?" Lyla asked Amira, as she searched the refrigerator for something that looked at least *somewhat* like the makings of dinner.

"Hang on." Amira finished her text, seemingly as slowly as possible, and said, "A little."

"And?"

"And I don't want counseling. I'm not the problem. The problem is the *life* I'm living. So. Yeah. That's about it."

Lyla felt like throwing her hands up, but if she did, Amira was sure to go nuclear. So Lyla softly said, "Poor choice."

Her daughter rolled her eyes. "Oh my Lady *Gaga*! At least I'm *consistent*!" At sixteen, Amira had perfected the dark art of smart-ass comebacks, having harvested her repertoire from TV shows about dysfunctional families, chefs, models, wives, and naked people.

"How's your wrist?" Lyla asked.

"Gone!" Amira said, pulling her hand into the sleeve of her sweater. "Whole goddamn *hand* is!"

"Watch your language!"

That got the usual response: no language at all.

"Amira, you've got to understand that I just want you . . ."

Amira interrupted: "To be more like *you*. So! I've got one question. How's that *workin'* for you?" That nugget of sarcasm was courtesy of Dr. Phil.

Lyla's day, with no respite from conflict even in her own comfort zone, was turning into a nightmare within a nightmare. Fifteen years earlier, she'd held golden dreams in her heart: wrapping up her career as a public defender, having a baby, taking a year off, joining an elite investigative organization, rising to the top, and then: public office, with her loving husband and beautiful kids standing behind her at a podium. Even back then that dream was ten years old, made realistic by toil and sacrifice from an early age. Lyla's dreams had always started with "Once upon a time. . . ." Now they started with "Someday. . . ."

On this day: no husband, a house with a bigger mortgage than value, chronic insomnia, IBS, a pissed-off boss, stagnant career, and a distant daughter who expressed her anger by cutting herself, dating a loser, ignoring her homework, slapping her own mother, and settling for a career as a hairdresser. Lyla was mystified by her daughter's defeatism, and invariably found ways to blame herself.

On the positive side: Maybe she could prevent World War Three. Then she'd be a hero, her daughter would see her differently, and her dreams would rise from the ashes.

That's life, she thought: no matter how heroic you are, nobody calls you a hero until you win.

But Lyla didn't have an ounce of quit in her. That's what I'd liked best when we first met, five years earlier, at the CIA Training Center.

"I've got a problem at work," Lyla told Amira, "and I may be gone a couple of days, so you'll have to stay with your father."

Amira's shoulders sagged. "Gone *where*?"

"Quantico."

"Have a ball."

"And no seeing Spike while I'm gone." That was her daughter's boyfriend, who had a spike in his ear.

"Mah-ah-ah-ah-m!" A new record: five syllables.

"My house, my rules."

"Now you sound like *dad*!" The ultimate dagger.

Lyla retaliated. "And if you run *away* again, don't bother to come back!"

Amira looked stricken, and Lyla regretted it immediately. She longed to take the words back. But that's just an expression. Words don't come back.

Amira glared at her phone with glassy eyes.

Lyla went to her office and called me. I remember her saying that either her boss was out of his mind, or that she still had a lot to learn.

Your Own Lesson

This is the most important chapter in the book.

It's the chapter that will start the transformation of your trust-worthiness into leadership.

By this point in the book, you've seen the value of the Code of Trust, and may have integrated most of it into your life. If you did, you are now worthy of the trust of almost anyone—even though most people may not yet recognize it.

Those closest to you have probably noticed some changes. You might be having fewer disagreements with them. It's likely they think you're a better listener, and they probably listen more carefully to you. Your influence with them may be expanding.

This is not a contrived, short-lived effect, due simply to better people skills, or management orchestration. It's a predictable, replicable outcome of an evidence-based methodology, reflecting a fundamental shift in your outlook.

It is the living embodiment of the power of trust.

I've seen many people adopt the Code, and it almost never fails to make them trustworthy. When it doesn't, it's invariably because they fail to properly implement it. In flying, we call that pilot error, and it causes more than 80 percent of all serious problems. In personal relationships, the percentage of failure due to human error is far higher.

Nobody's perfect—but some codes of behavior come as close to perfection as you'll find in this life. One of those codes decrees that if you suspend your ego, don't judge, validate others, honor reason, and act generously, you will be worthy of trust. That's almost certain.

But even when you're worthy, half your work remains undone.

The other half is conveying it.

Your trustworthiness can become vastly more obvious, and when it does, the circle of those who trust you will expand beyond your dreams, and your tribe of trust will suddenly appear, as if it's always been there.

To be a great leader, trusted by many, you need to follow four basic steps. These steps are the endgame of trust: the last lessons I can teach you.

The Four Steps to Trust are so effective that they can change the way people see you almost overnight.

They will elevate and widen your influence, bring complete strangers to your side, and rocket you toward your goals.

As I mentioned in chapter one, the Four Steps to Trust are:

(1) *Align Your Goals!* You'll achieve the power that only combined forces can attain.
(2) *Apply the Power of Context!* People only trust those who *know* them: their beliefs, goals, and personalities.
(3) *Craft Your Encounters!* Creating the best possible environment for every interaction sets the stage for success.
(4) *Connect!* Speak the language that everyone wants to hear: the one that focuses on them, and their needs.

Those steps, as you see, aren't rocket science. The hard part of the whole equation is simply human error. We all have elements of vanity, carelessness, laziness, and insecurity in us, so we need to be absolutely determined to proceed properly in every personal engagement, no matter how minor.

Where does that determination come from? It comes from the gleaming vision of your ultimate goal.

With that vision dancing before your eyes, you'll be motivated to make the short-term sacrifices that being trusted demands.

Let's be logical: what I am asking of you—to consistently put others first, and control your baser instincts—is a major task, fraught with sacrifice, and can be made practical and achievable only when there is a lofty reward in the waiting.

Some of the sacrifices you'll make, though, will start to feel good, the same way a long jog or a hard week of work makes you tired in a *good* way. It's a reminder that you've done the right thing.

These sacrifices may feel like an intuitive action within your own family—because you've already established trust in that limited environment—but among a large group of people, this code of conduct can feel like walking the plank. Out in the cold, cruel world, it's common for us to raise our shields, look for enemies, and limit our trust. We do it out of fear—to control the risk of failure—and don't take the chances that trust demands.

These are fears you need to overcome, and chances you need to take.

Realistically, the only way you can inspire trust that's deep enough and wide enough to confer limitless leadership is to gather *all* of your relationships, associations, and networks into a single group that is so cohesive and congruent that it feels and functions like a family.

Lots of companies and organizations refer to themselves as families, but few really are. That's usually just a marketing ploy, and therefore an insult to genuine familial groups everywhere.

Sometimes, sadly, families aren't even families, but still pretend to be.

You don't need to posture. You can have the real thing.

But first you need to have a goal that glimmers before you so brightly that it promises the almost mythological prize of a happy ending: in your professional life, in your family, in your community, and in the mortal mission of your own personal journey through life.

That's why this chapter is so important. It shows you how to memorialize a goal so glorious that it empowers years of deference, acceptance, validation, rationality, and generosity.

Such goals do exist. They are so dazzling that they're often called dreams. All leaders have dreams, and all great leaders have great dreams.

Nelson Mandela's dream was to free 35 million South Africans from virtual slavery, and it gave him the strength—and the *patience:* the temporal version of humility—to vault past twenty-eight years of imprisonment to the presidency. FDR's goal of restoring peace and prosperity to America—to *literally* save the world—carried him beyond horrifying physical limitations. Imagine the magnitude of the dreams of people like Abraham Lincoln, Mohandas Gandhi, Susan B. Anthony, Martin Luther King, Cesar Chavez, Margaret Thatcher, and Winston Churchill—as well as that of latter-day leaders who may someday rank with or near the greats, such as Benazir Bhutto, the Dalai Lama, Nobel Peace Prize–recipient Aung San Suu Kyi, and Elon Musk. Their dreams are known by millions, and their dreams made their greatness possible, as much as their greatness made their dreams possible.

Dreams don't always come true, though. Sometimes they don't even come close. But falling short of your ultimate goal can be fine, if you come close enough to savor most of its rewards.

Perfection, in this world, isn't necessary, and perfectionism—a well-disguised form of fear—is typically the enemy of contentment. Even so, striving for perfection—while embracing its vast unlikelihood—can be richly rewarding.

As the English poet of spirituality Robert Browning said, "A man's reach should exceed his grasp, or what's a heaven for?"

America's own poet of practicality, Yogi Berra, phrased it like this: "You've got to be very careful if you don't know where you're going, because you might not get there."

At the very least, having a dream gives you hope. That's simple logic: You can't possibly have a dream without hoping to reach it—and hope is arguably the most precious of all human resources. It's very real, even when it's never fully realized. It always feels good, makes sacrifices bearable, and heals the wounds of regret. It is the heart and soul of motivation, and the wellspring of optimism.

Hope fires the drive that keeps us alive, and softens our long day's journey into night.

To paraphrase the Berra phrase, you'll never achieve your dream if you don't have one.

Bottom line: only great goals inspire personal greatness.

Because of this, the First Step to Trust is more than just the beginning of an action plan. The first step, along with the others, make the Code work every bit as much as the Code makes the Steps work.

Without the Steps, the Code is a lifeless philosophy. Even the finest philosophies, if not implemented—in the real world, among real people—are no more than legends: fictional accounts of a way life might be, if only someone had the courage to live it that way.

In *your* world, only your own life, and your own actions, can bring the Code to life, and turn it into leadership.

Loose Cannons Quantico

In the Behavioral Program's version of a war room, Detroit Agent Lyla Khoury led her team's presentation with self-deprecating charm and steely authority, and I was reminded why she'd caught my attention at a seminar sponsored by another three-letter government agency: she was a younger, female version of me—but much smarter.

My team—a psychologist and two case agents, or Field Assessors—were casually interspersed with Lyla's people, including her Assistant Case Agent and her undercover agent. The seating was a show of democratic equality—which didn't really exist. In actuality, my team was her team's last hope, and if we didn't come up with something, they'd all be scrounging for new assignments.

Lyla's previous case was reason enough to cherish this one: She'd been tasked with reviewing a bottomless pit of practically prehistoric cold cases in the basement of the Detroit HQ. She thought it was punishment, for losing her cool on another case. Detroit, I'd learned, considered her a loose cannon. Behind *her* back: "Whatever Lyla wants, Lyla gets."

But in typical Lyla fashion, she'd kept digging until this case caught her eye, and struck gold.

Now she was painting a picture of danger and intrigue that had my team riveted, using words and phrases—substantiated by hair-raising PowerPoint images and graphs—that included "faux Arab Spring," "rogue sects," "ticking time bomb," Mideast holocaust" and the one that makes even seasoned FBI agents go nuclear: "nuclear."

She'd dug up a spy ring that was sending nuclear secrets to an Arab nation.

Short version: An emeritus professor of physics at a major Detroit-area university, who'd emigrated as a child to Dearborn, Michigan—home of America's largest per-capita population of Arab Americans, most of whom had come there to work at Ford—was the nexus of a league of pro-Arab technologists who were stealing nuclear secrets. The professor, who we'll call the Professor, was a spotter: an assessor of local academics and professionals who worked in nuclear physics, and were willing to give or sell him information.

Like so many clandestine groups, its purpose was couched in altruism—in this case: using nuclear power to, in his words, "make the desert bloom."

Nuclear power is different from nuclear weaponry, but it can still lead to it.

Because the Professor was old, worked for a shaky but official U.S. ally, was focused on nuclear power instead of bombs, and ran a ring that had slowly aged into senility, he conjured a certain sympathy—even among Lyla's bosses.

But Lyla—the daughter of emigrants from the same country, and a lifelong resident of Dearborn—used her own identity in counterpoint.

The fact that the Professor was old, she said, just meant that he'd been a traitor for many years, guilty of crimes that could—worst-case scenario—lead to the future that now terrifies everybody: nuclear attack by some crazy sect that isn't even a country.

Everybody was concerned, but we stayed rational. My team approached each case in a Spock-like, logical methodology. In situations like this, it's the only way to keep from getting emotionally hijacked.

I put the Code to work: "I'd like to start at the end of this," I said, "and work backwards: What's your ultimate goal, Lyla?"

"To get my ASAC on board."

That was a goal, but hardly ultimate.

"Why isn't he on board?"

"To be honest, I don't know."

That was hard to believe. She was pitching, not strategizing. "And what if you get his buy-in?" I asked.

"Then my goal is to tag my target."

Closer, but no cigar.

"And arrest him?"

"Him and everyone he's recruited."

To me, it sounded more like a can of worms than a viable mission: a maelstrom that would freak out America, without achieving equal strategic value. Most of the damage had been done, and was already outdated, and I'm always more worried about damage to come. If we exposed the Ring of Codgers, the more dangerous current spies would hunker down. I saw why her ASAC was hinky.

To me, it looked like this was going nowhere.

If you were leading this, what would you do?

Some leaders would call her out on her inconsistencies and flaws, in front of everybody. That can feel good if you're frustrated, but kicking ass in a crowd just raises shields. To build a productive plan, I needed Shields Down, Information In!

Some leaders would just let her do it her way, and sink or swim—with the risk on her, and not on them. Cagey leaders would deftly disengage, and appoint a committee or consultant to ponder it. Others would play it even safer, and kill the op. The no-guts-no-glory guys, of course, would roll the dice and pay the price: see the hill, take the hill.

By this time in my career, I was finished with hills, and focused on mountains. I'd seen enough of winning battles and losing wars. It just created unnecessary conflict, and pushed problems up the chain of command, as egotistical flameouts tried to grab their moment of glory.

I had bigger piranha to fry—and it was always, so to speak, the *same fish* in the frying pan.

I had the *same basic goal* in practically every case: Achieving congruence and honest communication among everyone. Whenever I could get all of the agents, ASACs, and Supervising Special Agents on the same page, miracles came out of nowhere.

Every year, I worked about eighty cases like Lyla's, and I can tell you exactly what my goal for her case was: To get her to communicate with her ASAC and SSA in an open, honest way that would serve everybody, all at once. That decentralization of egotism is the central principle of the Code—so again we see how the Code makes the Steps work, as well as vice versa.

I'd found that any team that was running its operation in accord with the Code of Trust and the Four Steps invariably made the right moves.

I had the same ultimate goal of congruence and good communication with everyone in my life: my colleagues, my family, my friends, my business associates, and my casual acquaintances, up to and including my Junior G-Man buddy who rented kayaks in Miami Beach (whom I still envied from time to time).

If you can achieve this one simple but lofty goal with your own team, you can always come up with a good plan.

That doesn't mean that my specific goals need to be yours. Everybody's different, so everybody's goals are different. But when a leader sets a goal that serves a whole group, and stays true to the Code of Trust, teams are easy to lead, and plans are easy to make.

A Marine motto I mentioned earlier is: whenever two Marines are together, there's a leader—and the leader is always the one with the plan.

I had a plan, and I hoped to soon make it Lyla's plan.

I stood and addressed the room. "This is really interesting," I said. "Lyla, you're amazing—you've got my guys stoked. It's noon, so let's break. Lyla, do you have time for lunch?"

"Of course!"

One on One

"How do you think that went?" Lyla asked.

"You're a great presenter! How do *you* think it went?" Why be negative? There's always something positive to say that lowers shields, and paves the way for honest reflection.

Besides, I'd rather ask the questions that open the door to possibilities than to give the answers that whittle the available ideas down to just my own. Definitive answers are especially dangerous when you're the boss, because—right or wrong—everybody's tempted to jump on the bandwagon.

The right questions shoot people straight toward their unguarded, inner wisdom, and make cooperation and congruence their choice, instead of their burden.

"I probably could have done better," Lyla said.

"How?"

"I got ahead of myself, by putting all the emphasis on the operation instead of the office politics. If I can't light a fire under my ASAC, there *is* no operation."

"Good point. We should figure out why *he* should do what *you* want. Why do you think he should?"

"Because my way will work?"

"Yeah," I said, without much enthusiasm.

"Because my target's a *traitor*!"

"Right." I let that hang.

More in exasperation than inspiration, she said, "Because the only way my ASAC succeeds is if I succeed!"

Bingo. "Good *call*! Because I'm sitting here thinking: The only way I can succeed in this case is if *Lyla* succeeds. It's just human nature. I wrote about that in the *FBI Bulletin*—you might want to check it out."

I caught a couple of positive nonverbals from her: raised eyebrows and strong eye contact. With just that little flip in perspective, she was back in the tribe! This time it was the tribe of agents who sometimes had to trade their lives—literally or figuratively—to make America safer. That's a serious affiliation.

"How do the Detroit guys see you?" I asked. "What's your context?"

"Pushy. Over ambitious. Smart but a hothead. Second-generation Arab girl who wants to make good."

"What if they thought you were being pushy, smart, and over-ambitious for *their* agenda?"

"Good rhetorical question."

See, I told you she was smart. So I told her, too. "I love working with smart people."

If ever there was a power word, "*love*"—if used appropriately and accurately—is it. Even when you use it casually, it triggers dopamine and serotonin in the same subliminal way that sunshine lifts your mood.

"What do you think your ASAC would consider a success in this case?"

"Something bigger than what I'm doing, that would put him on the map."

"Like what?"

"Something like revitalizing the Professor's network, and getting some new, real-time intelligence."

"That's not possible. *Is* it?" I positioned that goal like the Holy Grail.

"I'll think about it. I've been focused on the bird in the hand."

"Talk to your team, and we'll reconvene in the morning."

I got a glimpse of the same spark in her eyes that I'd seen five years before.

"So how's the family?" I asked, expecting the usual answer: good, how's yours?—and thus ending the meeting.

"Don't let me start," she said. But she did, probably because she knew I actually cared.

I got the whole story.

"Any advice?" she asked at the end, with tears still in her dark brown eyes.

"Let me sleep on it."

The Woman with the Plan

Studies show that sleeping during a process of problem solving usually improves the end result, partly because even during sleep, your brain is still working on your problem—but in a different way.

When you're awake, your brain usually takes the shortest path of connected brain cells to a fact that it wants to find. Taking the shortest neuronal pathway is very efficient, but only to a point. If you're really struggling to remember, it can overload that path with bioelectrical activity, creating the traffic jam of thought that we all call brain freeze: the failure, typically under pressure, that comes from trying too hard.

Sometimes you just give up, and then the fact suddenly appears, as if by magic.

It's not magic but simple biology. Your brain is under the least amount of pressure when you're asleep, and it settles for taking longer, less direct routes to information. It rambles around, runs into all sorts of interesting things, sorts options, and sees the big picture. That's why you sometimes wake up with great ideas, strong gut feelings—or the elusive fact you'd been trying to find.

A similar phenomenon occurs emotionally. When you're too

focused on a goal—usually something that's very immediate—your fixation can become the enemy of the goal's achievement. That's why you need to step back from the daily grind while you're setting your ultimate goal, and summon visions of your own big picture: your view of your ideal, almost perfect life, and best possible self—not just in the here and now, but in a future that can be almost unfathomable, if you fail to look hard enough.

Your vision of that perfect life and ideal self—your dream—is always there, and maybe you've seen it in your nightly dreams, but felt it fade away in the hard light of day.

Maybe you *did* see it during the day, but thought it was so distant that holding it in your heart would be a torment.

Don't give up. Even just glimpsing your goal gives you a chance to grab it.

If you have the courage to hope, your ultimate goal sometimes appears as spontaneously as a fact you actually knew but couldn't find. It bursts from behind clouds of lesser goals, and obstacles that seemed insurmountable but weren't.

Your ultimate goal may initially seem too amorphous for action: an all-encompassing goal that's too obvious and remote to bother with. But being all encompassing is its value. It becomes the North Star of your journey, and your travels become not just a process but a mission.

Your mission, for example, may be to achieve enough financial independence to work at your dream-job. Or to not have a job at all. Or to work hard at a serious hobby, like painting, or writing. But if you don't designate one of those as your ultimate goal, you might get side-tracked into thinking that your mission is to make a big salary, or save every penny, or to invest with the skill of Warren Buffet.

Those are reasonable goals, but they are not your mission, and may not even be necessary in achieving it. You might achieve your mission of working at your dream job by just adjusting your expenses, or finding a more practical dream job that you like even better.

When you know your ultimate goal, the decisions you need to

make each day become so much easier, because you simply have to ask yourself: Is what I'm about to do or say going to *help* me reach my ultimate goal, or *hinder* me? You become virtually immune to the emotional hijacking that can occur when you face a petty insult, or need to need to swallow your pride.

Even just knowing your ultimate goal grants peace of mind, because you realize that each of your intermediate goals isn't make or break.

That happened to Lyla. When I saw her the next morning, she was practically a new person. That's not unusual. When valid philosophies are adopted by strong people with big brains, they can have breakthroughs that change their lives, in a metamorphosis that can happen in a moment.

The first thing she said was, "Robin, my *real* goal isn't to kickass on this case. It's to keep America safe. I grew up listening to my parents talk about the old country—stuff you don't wanna *hear*—and I *know* what we have here, better than most people."

"I wonder if protecting America is also the ultimate goal of some of your people in Detroit."

She nodded hard, and I knew she was picking things up fast.

She took over the meeting in the war room like a star athlete in a big game, and created a *new* plan—thinking on her feet, and listening to the ideas of everyone. The plan centered on luring the Professor into action long enough to link the Over the Hill Gang with the newer circles of nuclear espionage that his old ring had spawned.

Everybody loved it. Made sense to me, too.

After the meeting, she called Detroit, and I overheard a positive, pleasant conversation, with her doing a lot more asking than telling.

When the call was over she came to my office and abruptly asked, "What do I do about *Amira*?"

I meandered into a story about my buddy whose mother-in-law drove him crazy, because every time she visited all she could talk about was her *new* new diet, even though she was steadily gaining weight. I asked him why she made such an issue out of dieting, and he said maybe it was because even though she was only mildly over-weight, she felt judged.

Before I could get to the end, Lyla said, "So the moral of the story is that one way to stop *having* problems with people is to stop *causing* them—right, Obi-Wan?"

It felt good to finally be the guru instead of the acolyte. "Yes, Grasshopper."

"Huh?"

"Sorry—that's not your context. Old TV show about a Zen cow-boy. Anyway, what's Amira really good at?"

"Art. Painting. Drawing. Music. Anything that's creative. And," she added dourly, "doesn't *pay*."

"Is that where she's headed with the hairdresser goal?"

"I think it's more of a cute-girl phase. She's more melting pot than me, but she still looks like Jasmine in *Aladdin*. Tell me why I shouldn't want her to get a degree, have a real profession, and drop all this emo crap?"

"Is that what she wants?"

"No."

"Well, that's *one* reason why you shouldn't. People generally do what they want. Not just kids—everybody. All you can really do is find the part of their goal that fits into yours, build some bridges, and go from there."

"Robin, she's *cutting* herself."

"You've got to a find a way to stop that. But if you loosen the apron strings, would that make her more likely to hurt herself, or less? That's not a rhetorical question. Everybody's different."

"She's so stubborn she'd stop the whole rebel-without-a-cause thing just to *spite* me."

Her eyebrows pinched together and she looked profoundly boxed in: damned if she did, and damned if she didn't—the Classic Catch-22.

Then exhaled powerfully, relaxed visibly, and started to laugh. She was so smart!

She realized she'd seen a very pragmatic option, just by recognizing that she was trapped, and letting go.

She was in a good position for the hardest question of all. "What's your ultimate goal with Amira? Not *for* her—*with* her: the part *you* can control."

"*Ultimate?*" She sat quietly for almost a minute. This was not the time for me to lead the conversation. It was time for her to be the leader. "Not to sound like a one-note symphony, but I think it's basically the same thing I want to do with Inspector Gadget—just start having a clear relationship, like you said yesterday, and let the chips fall. Then I can at least get my own two cents in. Is that simplistic?"

"*I* don't think so. It's simple, but it's the simple things we trip on. Especially Type-A people, like you and me: we get all caught up in the brain surgery, and miss the little things that bring people down."

She drifted off for a second. "I've got an idea!" she said.

But her team converged on her, and I didn't see her or her team again for several weeks, when they all came limping back.

Find Your Allies
Quantico

"Good news and bad news," Lyla said on her return visit, as we headed for the war room. "The good news is, I got my ASAC on-board, and I'm getting along better with him. Even though he wants to *shut us down* again. But I can see *why,* this time. The bad news *really* sucks."

I didn't ask what it was, because I was still buoyed by the good news. The bad would come soon enough, and I thought we could handle it.

Whenever I see a smart team working in tandem, I know they'll make good decisions, and that's all you can really count on in this world. The best-laid plans don't always work, because fate has an agenda of its own. But a good plan, inspired by a great goal, is something we can all create on our own.

The best thing about monumental goals is that they attract the help of others, with a power far greater than your own. Lyla now held to her heart the goal of helping America, wasn't shy about showing it, and had aligned herself with her colleagues far more closely than before.

Helping her was no longer about helping Lyla get what Lyla wants—it was about helping *America* get what it wants.

Not one person in her office had failed to affiliate themselves with that goal, and her influence was expanding.

By now, if you're as smart as I know you are, you've probably tried to formulate your own ultimate goal. It's probably something you can say in five seconds—a handy rule for winnowing your goal to its core.

Your ultimate goal is undoubtedly worthy of being shared, and pursued by others, because it's almost shocking how similar all of our wants and needs are. The psychologist Abraham Maslow famously reduced the human hierarchy of needs to just six categories: physical well-being; safety; love and belonging; esteem, self-actualization; and self-transcendence.

Your own dream in life may well be one or even all of those ultimate goals, or something that fits snugly within one of them.

When you are certain of your ultimate goal, or mission, you can generally find many people who'll want to help you further that mission, as you further theirs. When you align your mission with those of other people, you all become stronger, and move closer as a group to being leaders.

To align your mission, you need to look at other people as honestly as you do yourself. That can be hard, because we're all tempted to preserve our prejudices against those we consider enemies, rivals, or obstacles, or simply irrelevant.

But even enemies are human beings, and deserve understanding. You undoubtedly share some common interests and beliefs with those who oppose you most. Trust can be found in that common ground, and lead to a new relationship.

Not everyone you approach, though, will want to align their mission with you, because many people still believe that for them to succeed, somebody else has to fail. That commonly occurs when more than one person is trying to achieve the same goal, such as being CEO of a company.

But even in competitive situations, you can still find unlikely partners, and build a powerful team of rivals. Everyone on your team can grow in skills and stature, even as you compete internally, and that will increase the odds that somebody on your team will reach the goal. Then that person can help the others, as your group's rising tide lifts all its ships.

Even if you don't rise, you'll probably be in a better position to reach your goal later, or to achieve something similar. At the very least, you can expect to be treated well by the person who does reach the goal, and you might become that person's successor, or chief aide.

Some people, though, are just too fearful to accept this code of conduct. To be a true leader, you need to understand these people's insecurities, and still find ways to like them, and help them achieve their own goals.

Occasionally, though, people have goals that you just don't approve of—morally, tactically, or personally—and when that happens, you should choose not to align with them. It's impossible to be partners with everybody, no matter how understanding you are.

Even when you break from someone, you should still make them feel that your relationship, from your perspective, is more about them than you. That might lead them to think that ending the partnership was their idea, and stop them from having hard feelings. If you're humble, nonjudgmental, validating, reasonable, and generous, that person might refer you to someone else whose goals are more like yours.

In business situations, your decision not to link missions with someone will often happen in a meeting. Show everyone there your strong, committed stance on the issue at hand, don't make the conflict personal, and behave kindly to the person whose goals you oppose.

That kind of behavior builds a leader's reputation as a person of principle, rationality, and consideration. Word gets around, and often brings you to the people that you *do* want to be with.

If the person you don't want to align with becomes belligerent, just keep your cool, and let them be the bad guy, since that's what they seem to want. Word gets around about that, too, and elevates your stature by comparison.

No matter what happens, always stay approachable, because opponents don't always remain oppositional. People change, and so do their goals. When that happens, be ready to realign your missions.

For example, by the time I'd become head of Behavioral Analysis, I'd changed my own ultimate goal. It had previously been to be a leader, but by this time it was *to have healthy, happy relationships with the people around me.* That was an even greater goal, because I'd realized that if I focused on that grand goal, all of my means goals would fall into the proper place, and the proper priority. When you find that you're no longer self-serving, majestic things often happen, seemingly spontaneously.

With this new ultimate goal, I was able to vastly widen my alignment of missions, and my tribe of trust grew beyond my dreams.

Once you align your missions with your allies, you'll have far less to worry about. You can keep a laser focus on your own ultimate goal, and not get bogged down in lesser priorities, ego wars, betrayal, selfishness, demographic differences, and other distractions.

The single best way to align yourself with others is, of course, to understand, validate, and adopt their goal as one of yours. Then they'll open the door to their trust to you as naturally as they would to an old friend.

Many people, though, don't want to even *think* about the goals of others, because they fear that this perspective will subjugate them, subvert their own goals, and undercut their authority. As I've mentioned, I often encounter trainees in my trust seminars who essentially say, "I'll get walked on like a *carpet*!"

That sounds like a reasonable fear—but it almost never comes to fruition. When you follow the Code of Trust, it puts you above pettiness, and allows you to remain the driver of your own dream. People don't think you're a punk—they think you're statesmanlike.

Being deferential to others is the *opposite* of being submissive: it identifies you as the bigger person in what could have been a debacle of mutually assured destruction.

Leaders who seem to cede power are often simply sharing it, in order to have greater control over an outcome—rather than over a person—as they move toward their own goal, as inexorably as a river to the sea.

The process of aligning your missions invariably starts with *listening* to people—and not just with your ears, but your heart and mind: hearing what they *don't* say, and reading between the lines. It's the only realistic way to inaugurate trust, and to find the elements of their goal that you admire, and that will help you achieve your own goal.

For those who love the sound of their own voices—which is, let's face it, most of us—this takes work.

Do you remember me mentioning a psychology experiment in which researchers offered money to people in exchange for engaging in conversations that shifted the focus from themselves to the person they were talking to?

Most of them, as you may remember, couldn't—or wouldn't. They were happy to trade the loss of money for the pleasure—biochemical and psychological—of talking about themselves.

That undoubtedly felt good—as long as it lasted. When it was over, they weren't the winners. They were the egotists who had sacrificed financial gain for a few moments of self-reflected glory.

Leaders are people who listen and learn, and when you finish talking with them—mostly about yourself—you feel better about them, better about yourself, and far less afraid of deferring your own goal to theirs. It's simply a matter of *we* becoming *us*.

Aligning your mission with those of others can be complicated, but the rewards are immense, and often exponential, as each person who becomes part of your ultimate goal recruits others, and those people enlist even more.

This path to leadership really isn't that complicated. You've undoubtedly set goals before. You just didn't supercharge them by incorporating them into the Code and Four Steps.

If you haven't set an ultimate goal for yourself, do it now. As the saying goes: it's not rocket surgery—or something like that.

It's really just Leadership 101, and Lyla had learned most of it, largely by trial and error, in less than a month.

As she walked into the war room, though, her shoulders were sagging, and I soon found out why.

The Woman with Plan B

"When we approached our target," Lyla told the room, as an image of the Professor came onscreen, "we thought this would be the highlight of his waning career."

Just looking at him—with white, frizzy hair, and eyes that seemed to be too deep in his head—you could see why she thought that. He was at an age when most professionals are relegated to total obscurity, and are pointedly ignored when they offer help.

"Ron, our undercover," Lyla said, "reinitiated contact with the Professor with an invitation, supposedly from his country's ruler *himself,* to reinvigorate the ring, which was virtually defunct. The bait was that his country was on the bubble of having a functional nuclear power station, and needed to fill a finite number of gaps.

"And the Professor was like, 'Sorry, not *interested*!'" She shook her head. "Can you *believe* it?

"So we ask him what he *was* interested in, and he said he wants to *meet* the ruler. In *person.* In *country.* And tell him what a true patriot he'd been for all those years. Plus, he wanted to visit their nuclear facilities. So. There's that."

It sounded like a target's demand for a "witch's broomstick"—an impossible prize to deliver. Sometimes that's a measure of the subject's grandiosity. In this case, though, I thought our subject just wanted validation for all his years of sacrifice.

It made sense to me, but others in the room thought the request was just nuts, and could be overridden by offering things like money and power.

People started throwing out ideas, and it was my duty—based on the ideas' relative merits—to throw most of them all the *way* out.

It seemed like the only decent option was go back to an original idea: To summarily arrest him, sweat him for the names of his associates, and bring as many of them to trial as we could. Otherwise known as: Square One.

Lyla killed that idea and drove a stake through it's heart—not just because her ASAC wouldn't sign off, but because, she now realized, he shouldn't. It would create a stir, but wouldn't serve America's greater interests.

One of my guys—call him Steve—got a sly smile on his face and held up his index finger.

Lyla pointed at him, and he stood up. "We go to the Professor, and here's what we say: "Guess what, given your reluctance to help your country, we've done some *research,* and we came up with evidence that ties you to negative incidents that happened here. You're a *mole,* Professor! Admit it—or prove you're not, by doing what we need!"

Brilliant! It would turn the tables in a way he'd never see coming. The confusion alone would flip him. I quickly signed off on it.

"Two things," Lyla said. "One. I want an ambulance within a block. He's already on oxygen supplementation, and if he so much as hyperventilates, we get him immediate attention. Two. *I'm* at that meeting. If it goes south, nobody goes down but me. Besides, we need another figure there who's flown in from the homeland with the bad news."

She paused. "*Three* things, actually. If HQ doesn't love it to death, it's out. All of us here"—she made eye contact all around the room—"are in this for the long haul. If this doesn't fly, something else will."

Lyla and I adjourned to my office and she called her ASAC.

"Hey, Gadget, we've got a new plan. At least I think we do. But I really need your take. Miss me?" He said something that made her laugh. "That's how I feel, too." I heard him laughing as she hung up.

"You call him Inspector Gadget now?"

"He takes it as a compliment. He calls us The Brains and the Brawn. Unfortunately, I'm The Brawn. I tried to amend it to The Brains and the Broad, but he said that could not only get him fired, but on TV."

She flew back that night.

Dearborn, Michigan

"*As-salaam alaikum*"—peace be upon you—Lyla said to the Professor, as she and her undercover agent entered his small home.

"*As-salaam alaikum,*" he said, holding the handle of his oxygen cart, which had a clear tube leading to his nasal cannula.

Lyla, wearing a purple silk hijab that covered all of her auburn hair, bowed slightly as she crossed his threshold.

Her people were listening in a van outside, and the ambulance was on the other opposite side of the block. But she was still scared, she told me. It was her first undercover assignment, and there were countless ways to blow it—or get hurt, even in a controlled encounter, which do occasionally go sideways. There are certainly safer lines of work than undercover espionage.

They sat on a hard, old sofa with a TV tray between them that held Meramieh tea, redolent with sage, in a fine porcelain teapot with small matching cups.

He was very calm, apparently flattered that someone from the homeland had come to hear his requests.

With solemn graciousness, Lyla shattered the geniality with a delicately phrased accusation that he was suspected of being a mole, and traitorous to the homeland, but could redeem his reputation by reviving his activity.

He remained calm, at least outwardly.

"I appreciate your dilemma," he said quietly, but sadly. "Misunderstanding is the currency of our mutual service to the home we love. Surely there are many ways to solve this. Perhaps I could take a polygraph test. But what I cannot do is what you ask." He gestured toward the oxygen cart, and a small table covered with medications. "You can see why, *sayidaty*"—ma'am.

Lyla, ready with Plan B, C, D, said, "I do see why, and I cannot ask you to do what you cannot do." She paused and sipped tea, as if contemplating the standoff. "Tell me, are you still able to write?"

"Yes."

"At some length?"

"Yes, *sayidaty*."

"Then our ruler"—she said his name, but I can't—"will be very happy, I believe, if you could write your memoirs. That will reveal your authenticity in various ways, and will do much more. It will serve as an inspiration to others, also in voluntary exile, who wish to make our desert bloom. And it may result in the visit you wish to make."

It was a shrewd, if convoluted, example of linking missions by giving people what they want.

"I would be very honored." His eyes glistened. "*Sayidaty*," he said, "do the people still hunger, as they once did? It's been so long, and I cannot base my beliefs on what I read, or see on Western television, or even hear from those I am supposed to trust."

Lyla told him the truth, almost reflexively. "It is *not* so bad now."

"The children?"

"The children come first, as always."

He was visibly relieved, and moved.

That was the first time she felt he might be a good man.

Later, she told me, the exchange made her hands begin to tremble, and she didn't know why. I think I do. I think she felt shame for tricking an elderly gentleman, and an absolutely equal measure of pride, for doing something for her country that she would never do for herself.

When she got home, yearning to decompress, she called out, "*Amira?*"

"We're in here."

Amira—whom I met later on, and who *did* look like Disney's Jasmine—was on the couch with her boyfriend.

Amira's dream now was to own a high-end salon, featuring special cuts she was designing herself. Her boyfriend's dream was to manage the business end.

The first thing Lyla noticed, she told me, was a tattoo on her Amira's forearm. "That's very pretty," Lyla said. "It really is, and I'm not judging. But you promised to *talk* about that—*first*, and I've gotta say, sweetheart, I think this is bullshit." For better or worse, her language around her daughter was less guarded, but oddly—or not—her daughter's language was notably tamer.

"Mom, it's so cool! *I* did this, with my own makeup, and then a layer of hairspray. It stays color-fast for weeks, but you can scrub it off. I *invented* it, mom. Google it!"

"She could start a franchise," her boyfriend said, "or get a use patent!"

"Wow," Lyla said.

The spike in Spike's ear was gone. "Jerry—what happened to your spike? It was growing on me."

"My dad asked me to take it out."

For a half second Lyla wanted to say, "Good." She said, "Parents!" The kids laughed.

Endgame
Ten Months Later
Quantico

"He died," Lyla said on the phone.

"The Professor?"

"Yeah. I watched the graveside service, but at a distance. Not many people there."

"The price of patriotism," I said, not really kidding.

"I didn't realize until almost the end how happy that writing the memoirs made him. As he relived it, he felt justified for doing things that were hard for an honorable man. When I helped him, we talked about everything from family to politics, and I know he was sincere about making the desert bloom. He wanted his country to be America's strongest Arabian ally, because he loved both places equally, and wished they *were* equal."

"Complicated."

"Two sides to every story."

"How's the operation going?"

"Through the roof. He told us everything about everybody, and we've got tabs on all the new guys. They think they're still working for the homeland, but now they're working for us. And I don't think all of them are interested in seeing the desert bloom. So we're working on those people, and it's under control. It's actually supporting our alliance. Maybe the Professor got what he wanted most, after all.

"How's the family?"

"Amira's an *inventor*!"

"I know. You mentioned it." About five times. Proud parents don't keep count.

She rhapsodized about Amira, and said, "I finally figured out my ultimate, *ultimate* goal. It's to be an overtime professional *and* an overtime mom. For decades, that was the American Dream, but these days it's more like a dream within a dream. Especially for a single parent."

"Are you getting there?"

"Gettin' closer. So . . . *thanks,* Robin. I really mean it."

I said what I almost always say when a close ally offers thanks.

"No, Lyla, thank you.

— 6 —

STEP TWO:
APPLY THE POWER OF
CONTEXT!

Wherever You Are,
Now

DO YOU REMEMBER THE STORY in chapter two about the math wizard who blew me off in the *Seinfeld* restaurant—and started working with *other* FBI people: anybody but me, quite pointedly?

It was because we weren't on the same wavelength. I wanted to tell him stories about the Yankees and the FBI, but he was a grad student in high tech who wanted me to stick to the facts, stay on task, and cut to the chase.

Most people like stories, but back then I thought *everybody* did, since they provide the nuance and human touch that's usually so important in communication. But the guy in the restaurant wasn't "most people," and I didn't have enough sense at that time to talk to him within the context of his own perceptions.

Do you recall my axiom: Never argue context? In my younger and dumber days, I didn't even know context existed. That's the main reason I blew it with the guy in the restaurant.

It's possible that you're not a story person, either. That's just how some people are, and it's fine. If so, this chapter is tailor made for you. The only story in this chapter is your story. It starts wherever you are, and it starts now.

Your own story—including how you like to be addressed, and how you can effectively address others—is going to help you take the critically important second Step of trust building: understanding how to communicate with people within *their* context, not yours, in order to inspire their trust, and make them happy to align their missions with yours.

Step Two animates the prime axiom in the Code of Trust: It's All About Them.

So once again we see that the Steps make the Code work, just like the Code makes the Steps work. Ideas without action are fine, but they're best in books of fiction.

However, when you're addressing more than one real-life person at a time—as I am in this nonfiction book—you can't be on everybody's wavelength at once, so you need to mix up your delivery, offer a little something for everybody, and convey ideas with layered styles of communication.

I'll show you how to do that in this chapter.

One thing you can count on: This chapter doesn't have a story, and is *not* All About Robin. That's a wavelength with just one listener, and even *I* get tired of hearing myself talk.

So now you're going to tell your *own* stories, to yourself—and it starts with the story of your life.

The Story of Your Life

I know the story of your life. Everybody does. To a point. I'll see if I can get it right.

I know, for example, that if you're reading this book, you're probably a bright person who's very ambitious. You're aware that you have shortcomings, but aren't afraid to tackle them. You know that trust is a two-way street, and you long to trust people, but you're not gullible—so sometimes you have to act as if you have more faith in people than you really do. That makes you dependent on the approval of others, but that's a price you're willing to pay to lead your team. Because of this, you'll probably succeed.

Why are you like this? Because most people are—or wish they were. That was just a fill-in-the-blanks description: one that shows you how fortune-tellers can sound so accurate.

Why did I say "if you're reading this book?" It created inclusion, and offered you a rationale for accepting positive comments.

All of these statements fulfill the first principle of trust: because I put others first, it's all about you, not me.

They reveal parts of you that are relatively common, and archetypal. But your whole story is unique, and you're the only one who knows it. You're an absolutely singular, ever-evolving product of nature, nurture—and even yourself, since there is a "you" in you that nobody put there. There will, quite literally, never be another you.

So—to make the upcoming information more meaningful—stop for a moment and think about your own one-of-a-kind singularity, and the special people who have been able to penetrate it: the people you love to talk to, who seem as if they can almost read your mind. Then think about the people you know who are so impenetrable that they seem like they're from another planet.

If you did stop and think about those people just now, I'm guessing that you had more thoughts about connection than disconnection, and that there were many similarities among the people with whom you connected well.

That's healthy, and realistic. I've worked with Russians, Iranians, Koreans, Californians, spies, criminals, and CEOs, and virtually every person had remarkably similar desires and emotions, at the very core of their personalities. I was almost always able to reach them, if I just delved deeply into that core.

Those who seemed utterly unreachable were walled off primarily by a poor ability to communicate. Initially, that was a surprise to me. I thought the big barriers would be ones of ideology, nationality, and life experiences.

I discovered, though, that as different as we all are—in the many obvious ways that show on the surface, and hide what lies beneath— almost all human beings, at heart, have the same fundamental drives, dreams of love, and fears of loss. Even in our haunting and primal loneliness as individuals—born alone, bounded by one body and one life, and destined to die alone—we're all confined mostly by barriers we built ourselves.

If you leap beyond those barriers, you'll get a glimpse of our vast similarities.

The science of finding human similarities—which are the *defining characteristics of context*—is archaic, but emerged as a technology in the 1920s, through the work of Dr. William Moulton Marston, the psychologist who discovered the presence of systolic blood pressure, which he later applied to his invention of the modern polygraph. In his 1928 book *Emotions of Normal People*, Marston introduced the concept of personality typing, breaking it into two basic character types—active and passive—categories that people usually refer to now as Type A and Type B.

You're probably a Type A, like most people who study the subject of leadership.

If you're not a Type A, you're even more unique than most. Maybe what makes you different is that life has thrown you a lot of curve balls. Life happens, and fate doesn't always play well with others.

Because of this, after Marston characterized the two most basic personality types, he then categorized the two most fundamental situations in life: favorable, and antagonistic.

Using that added context, Marston created four subsets of human behavior, which he arranged in a quadrant. They are:

(1) *Dominance,* resulting in activity in an antagonistic situation.
(2) *Inducement,* resulting in activity in a favorable situation.
(3) *Submission,* resulting in passivity in a favorable situation.
(4) *Compliance,* resulting in passivity in an antagonistic situation.

This behavior-typing system, which he named DISC, was so simple and sensible that most of the subsequent behavioral typing systems are based on it.

Marston was wise enough not to judge, and saw each of these types of behavior as valid and equal, representing reasonable ways to solve problems in a world that none of us can fully control.

For example, he thought that there is often power, wisdom, and creativity in being passive, and even submissive. He considered passivity, as a general rule, to be relatively more applicable to women than men—in an era when that wasn't considered insulting. At that time, society tended to place somewhat more value on the relatively more passive qualities of empathy, cooperation, and nurturance— which women, more often than not, tend to excel at.

In fact, with the help of his wife, Marston created a fictional character who is still part of the American culture, evincing femininity paired with super powers: Wonder Woman—who, in Marston's estimation, has "all the strength of Superman, plus the allure of a good and beautiful woman."

Marston's work emerged at about the same time as that of history's second-most famous psychiatrist, Freud's colleague Carl Jung, who created the concept of archetypes, as well as analytical psychology: the study of integrating opposing traits into a functional personality. Jung called the two most common personality traits extroversion and introversion, which are similar to the DISC categories of active and passive.

Later iterations of the same essential DISC system were created by Inscape Publishing (which assigned DISC categories of: Dominance, Influence, Steadiness, and Conscientiousness), and Triaxia Partners, which calls its system the Personal DISCernment Inventory.

The FBI, as part of its continuing efforts to understand human behavior, has used these and other personality typing systems since the 1970s. When I began teaching these systems, as the head of the Counterintelligence Behavioral Analysis Program, I sensed the need for further refinement of them, and created one of my own.

Mine, as you'll see, adds a layer that gives it broader applicability, and it has since been taught at not only the FBI's National Academy for Law Enforcement Executives, but also at many business, military, university, and government seminars. The breadth of its value speaks volumes about the importance of figuring out where other people are coming from, and how best to reach out to them.

Mine added an element that was strongly influenced by the work of another DISC disciple, Dr. Tony Alessandra, author of *The Platinum Rule*. Alessandra created an extension of the classic "do unto others" Golden Rule, the biblical admonition that advocates treating other people the way *you* want to be treated.

Alessandra's Platinum Rule is different, and profound. It says: treat others the way *they* want to be treated, even if it's not the way *you* like.

My system, the Communication Style Inventory, combines certain elements of Alessandra's with derivatives of the classic DISC categories.

It starts with what I consider to be the most important aspect of communication: Addressing people in the way that *they* prefer. Their communication style is a vital element of their context, and ignoring it is tantamount to arguing context.

Figuring out how to address them is easy, because it's generally the way that they address you.

I think there are four basic types of communicators: starting with people who are very *direct* (and speak *while* they think), and people who are *indirect* (and speak *after* they think). These two categories are naturally coupled with the two classic traits of being *people oriented,* or *task oriented.* They combine to create four general types:

- Direct, Task-Oriented Communicators.
- Direct, People-Oriented Communicators.
- Indirect, Task-Oriented Communicators.
- Indirect, People-Oriented Communicators.

I'm convinced that these four communication types strongly influence—and are influenced by—the four most common DISC styles of behavior, which I categorize as Dominance, Influence, Steady, and Conscientious.

My system therefore consists of two quadrants, overlaid upon one another: my version of the four-trait DISC, and my four-type Communications Style Inventory.

I called it the Communications Style Inventory because I wanted it to have a cool, unusual acronym: CSI. Then, after I fell in love with the acronym, somebody mentioned the TV show—so my natural, ego-free reaction was, "Too bad. They'll have to live in my shadow." So far, that hasn't happened. But this book will change that! Maybe.

(A brief diversion on humor: if the joke is on you, you've placed yourself within the universal communications context of humor, which is arguably the most uniting of all human perceptions.)

Because I consider the CSI to be even more salient than the DISC categories, let's look at it first. Then we'll overlay the DISC types on it, to make it even more accurate.

After that, we'll add one more layer: demographics, such as age, sex, and locale.

Many people focus primarily on demographics when they try to define somebody's context, but I think demographics are less important than they once were, because we're now a more inclusive and diverse society, with more cross-cultural sharing through the Internet.

My communication system is easy and fun, consisting mostly of things you already sensed, but hadn't systematized. When you learn the simple system, you'll have a huge head start on talking to people in their own context, inspiring their trust, and aligning their missions with yours.

The drill right now is for you to figure out your own communications style. You've had an intuitive feel for your style almost all your life, so now the goal is just to bring it to the cognitive forefront.

When you can categorize it—as a start to this process—you'll be better able to figure out the communications style of other people.

While you're categorizing your style, you'll probably recall times when a reasonable message to you was sabotaged by the way it was delivered. That's so common that it created the saying: Don't Shoot the Messenger—which wouldn't happen so often if people were better messengers.

As your insight into communication styles increases, you'll probably rise above the need for people to always address you in your own preferred style. You'll feel comfortable speaking their language. When that happens, you'll get that pleasure jolt that comes when people truly connect, and their dopamine, serotonin, and oxytocin systems start firing on all cylinders.

That's a golden moment in the inspiration of trust, and is often the preamble to their mutual linkage of ultimate goals.

It's when you start to make a friend for life, and form an alliance that lasts forever.

Step Two is huge. It's all downhill from here.

The CSI: Communication Made Simple

One subset of communication that's familiar to all teachers is the breakdown of people who excel as (1) visual learners, (2) auditory learners, and (3) kinesthetic learners. If you're a visual learner, you'll love the graphs and lists in this chapter. I get that—I'm a visual learner, myself. For me, a picture, acronym, or short verbal cue is always worth a thousand words—so you're getting about 10,000 extra words here.

Of course, I also like the other two forms of learning, based mostly on what it is I'm trying to learn. When I learned to fly, nothing beat the kinesthetic memory of having the instruments right in my hands.

So this generalization—like *all* of the generalizations presented in this chapter—contains crossover, nuance, and gray area.

Here's what the CSI looks like, presented in a quadrant graph:

THE COMMUNICATIONS STYLE INVENTORY

DIRECT COMMUNICATORS	
(People who think *while* they speak)	
Task-Oriented People	People-Oriented People
INDIRECT COMMUNICATORS	
(People who think *before* they speak)	

As the graph indicates, there are two fundamental styles of communication: Direct and Indirect.

Direct Communicators

The Direct style is preferred by people who tend to speak freely, say whatever is on their mind, and think things through later. Sometimes they say that they're "thinking out loud," and want everyone to know that whatever comes out of their mouth isn't written in stone.

Direct speakers like the give-and-take of verbal exchange, tend to be open to the ideas of others, and feel that they truly benefit if someone changes their mind about something.

For them, conversation is an art, and even when it morphs into a *rambling* art for art's sake, they take pleasure in your company, and usually feel that you're someone they can learn from.

They think this unfettered, unstructured style of communication is conducive to honesty, transparency, and creativity.

They don't feel threatened by opposing perspectives, and welcome the opportunity to incorporate some of your opposing ideas, in the tried-and-true, *compromising* style of horse trading.

Like almost everyone, they want *you* to talk to them this way, and when you do, you can often have very productive, pleasant conversations, as your discussion follows the classic Socratic dialectic structure of: thesis, antithesis, synthesis.

Indirect Communicators

The other primary communications method—the Indirect style—is preferred by people who like to think about things before they speak. They expect you to take most of what they say very seriously, and can get impatient—believing that you're arguing context—if you coax them to change their statements to fit your own point of view.

They sincerely believe that they are being respectful of you when they consider their words carefully, without wasting your time in the needless give-and-take that often ends exactly where it started.

They're proud of being precise, highly rational communicators who don't go off on tangents, or say things they don't really mean. They're lovers of logic, with reverence for one of the five rules of the Code of Trust: Honor Reason.

When you adopt their style, they appreciate it, and your talks can be short, exact, and productive.

Just because you prefer one communication style, it doesn't mean yours is better, and that you can't vary from it. Everybody's different, and if you can't validate that simple truth, you'll never inspire widespread trust.

Adopting another person's preferred communication style—known as behavioral mirroring—is a simple practice that yields such valuable and replicable results that Joe Navarro and I wrote about it in the *FBI Bulletin*.

The fancy word for the technique is isopraxis, and responding to it is so deeply ingrained in the human psyche that it's common for infants to smile when their mothers smile, and to arch their eyes when their mothers do. You probably practice isopraxis yourself from time to time, without really being aware of it.

Isopraxis works because we all crave similarity—and even sameness—as much as we do individuality. That's contradictory, of course, but the blessing lies in the balance.

Take a moment to do this simple inventory of your own style.

THE CODE OF TRUST

Count the number of Direct and Indirect communication–style qualities that apply to you, as well as those that apply *equally,* on the CSI Checklist.

Your score will give you a reasonable idea of where you fall on the scale of communications styles.

The scale may *describe* you quite accurately, but it will never define you. You can change, if you want to: a little or a lot.

Maybe you should nudge yourself, if you're so attached to your style that it limits your communications.

CSI CHECKLIST

DIRECT VS. INDIRECT THE TYPE OF COMMUNICATOR YOU ARE	
A DIRECT PERSON	**AN INDIRECT PERSON**
❏ Takes risks with relish.	❏ Avoids risks whenever possible.
❏ Makes swift decisions.	❏ Makes decisions thoughtfully.
❏ Is confrontive and expressive.	❏ Is nonconfrontive and ameliorative.
❏ Is impatient and relentless	❏ Is patient and easy going.
❏ Talks and tells.	❏ Listens carefully and asks questions.
❏ Is outgoing and entertaining.	❏ Is reserved and appreciative.
❏ Offers opinions freely.	❏ Guards opinions carefully.

Number of direct descriptors: _____

Number of indirect descriptors: _____

Number of completely equal descriptors: _____

That doesn't mean you have to. If you're a *diehard* Direct Communicator—or the opposite—and insist on communicating in your own preferred style, you'll always have certain people on your wavelength, and you may well be able to form unshakable alliances with them.

Realistically, though, sticking straight to one style will decrease your ability to inspire widespread trust.

Play with this concept in real life, and note your results. When you try to talk in a style that's not naturally your own, you'll probably find that it's not so hard—partly because you have traits that favor both styles.

If you are heavily weighted toward one style, and struggle to adapt, your payoff will be an expansion of your intellectual capacity for understanding. It's common, for example, for multilingual people to alter their thought processes when they speak in different languages—and altering your communication style is a form of that. It's the verbal equivalent of walking in someone else's shoes.

Word of warning: Speak your own mind, even in someone else's style. Also, don't corrupt this connecting device by using it for manipulation. If you do, you'll sound phony.

The ultimate takeaway: Be aware of how you sound—and how other people sound to you. To communicate most fluently, speak their language.

Pick 'em: People vs. Tasks

Now let's look at the left/right aspects of the CSI quadrant: Task-Oriented people vs. People-Oriented people. These are the rock-bottom, ultra-fundamental personality types that play a huge role in how you like to communicate.

You'll note that they are in the same general vein as Marston's categories of Active vs. Passive, and Dominant vs. Compliant, as well as Jung's categories of Introversion vs. Extroversion.

The Task-Oriented and People-Oriented types are also shaded by the biochemical aspects that we talked about previously. Task-Oriented people are more prone to have a biochemical makeup that's rich with dopamine, adrenaline, thyroxine, and the other stimulating, adrenergic neurotransmitters and hormones.

These people can be crack-of-dawn go-getters, but sometimes their flame dies fast. The faster they move, the faster they can fall. But if they know when to say when, they're often extraordinarily productive, fun, and inspiring.

On the other hand, the People-Oriented types are more likely to be dominated by the calm-and-content branch of the nervous system, which is mediated more by serotonin, endorphins, oxytocin, and GABA. They're the tortoise that can beat the hare, but sometimes they start the race too late to win. They're often satisfied with what they have, which can make them very pleasant company—but also complacent. When they use their extraordinary endurance and personal charm carefully, they can become the proverbial last man standing who is loved as much as admired.

Each pole is of equal value, if utilized wisely. Common sense says: be yourself—and better yet, be your best self.

Uncommon sense says: yes: Let you be you—but try to go with the flow of the crowd, or you'll get trampled, or find yourself walking the point with no backup.

It's also smart to adapt to the situation at hand: if it's crunch-time, save calm and content for later—but when the job is done, *act* like it's done.

Task-Oriented Types
In addition to the biochemically driven traits of Task-Oriented people, they also have largely behavioral characteristics. They use a disproportionate amount of their get-up-and-go on the *functional* details of the job at hand, and are far more interested in the *product* they are creating than the *people* with whom they are creating it.

When these people are game-planning a project, they tend to break it down into tasks, phases, and deadlines—then, almost as an afterthought, they staff-out the assignments of others.

They're interested in the achievement of the goal as a whole, and are relatively indifferent to who makes that happen.

Task-Oriented types are often very practical, and do tend to get things done on time, and on budget. They're great at planning, follow-through, details, staying calm in a crisis, and emanating resolve and confidence.

All these things make them look great on paper, and they often rise to the top in large, impersonal corporations.

When watching movies or TV, Task-Oriented types focus more on plot than characters, and when they talk, they communicate more about facts, figures, and minutiae.

One way to help spot a Task-Oriented person is by observing their body language, a subject we'll delve into in chapter eight. There are two basic styles of body language—open vs. closed, and dominant vs. submissive—and Task-Oriented types tend to often reflect the closed, dominant style, which includes: arms folded, facial features compressed, and palms held toward the body.

A challenge for Task-Oriented people is developing good people skills. They are often prone to asserting themselves by creating fear, instead of inspiring love. This hampers their ability to evoke genuine enthusiasm, loyalty, and selfless teamwork.

Because they do subordinate people to projects, it's typically more difficult for them to inspire trust. That doesn't mean they can't. They just have to work harder at it, and not be afraid to stray from their natural inclinations, from time to time.

As you may have assumed, they are generally Direct Communicators, although the most thoughtful of them can be Indirect.

They occasionally find that they have no allies when they really need them. They tend to be successful as long as their projects succeed, but when things go south, so do they, and they're soon forgotten—unless they successfully soften their hard edge of full-focus on projects over people.

Of course, everybody loves a winner, so sometimes all of their deficits are immediately forgiven when they succeed.

Even when they fail, they still tend to look good on paper, so when they search for another job, they often end up with solid lateral moves, or even spectacular ascensions.

Of course, like all of these traits, it's important to not see them as exclusive packages, because when it comes to these quadrants, we are all a majestic blend of each.

People-Oriented Types

The polar opposite of Task-Oriented people—the People-Oriented types—tend to be most concerned about assembling great teams, as they make one brilliant pick at a time. They think the most important element in accomplishing a task is *who* gets it done, instead of how it gets done.

Their strengths tend to be coordination, delegation, motivation, remaining popular during difficult situations, and creating camaraderie. They're often adept at Indirect Communication, and can be the center of lively, give-and-take conversations.

They don't hog the spotlight, curry credit, or lust for power, so sometimes they're overlooked—but not if their organization is relatively small, or is driven by a culture of soft power.

One of the "tells" of People-Oriented individuals is that in their writing and speaking style, they use more pronouns, more personal incidents, and more stories.

Their body language is usually open, characterized by uncrossed legs and arms, good eye contact, and expressiveness.

They're typically averse to bluntness, criticism, and pushing weak people out of the way, but that can actually heighten their power within an organization.

They often stay safe from punishment or downsizing when the company needs to find a scapegoat, or cut costs, and they tend to keep their positions no matter how tough times get. That's one of the perks of not having enemies.

It's therefore not uncommon for a People-Oriented person to spend his or her entire career in just one company, sometimes ending up in an ever-enviable C-Suite.

Even though we're now framing this conversation primarily in terms of business, the same basic rules apply in every type of group, including families and friends. Social and familial relationships function differently, but people are still unique, and still want to be treated that way.

Here's a checklist to see where you are. Note which descriptor applies to you, and then add them.

Who, Who, Who, Who—Who Are You?
(Sorry, I was channeling the *CSI* theme song. Natural mistake in this chapter.)

To see who you are in terms of my CSI quadrant graph, apply

CSI CHECKLIST

TASK-ORIENTED VS. PEOPLE-ORIENTED THE TYPE OF COMMUNICATOR YOU ARE	
A TASK-ORIENTED PERSON	**A PEOPLE-ORIENTED PERSON**
❏ Is formal and proper.	❏ Is relaxed and warm.
❏ Favors facts and statistics.	❏ Likes opinions and nuance.
❏ Focuses on projects.	❏ Focuses on performances.
❏ Keeps feelings private.	❏ Readily shares highs and lows.
❏ Focuses on time and deadline.	❏ Values flextime and workarounds.
❏ Loves logic and linear thinking.	❏ Factors-in feelings and intuition.
❏ Lives by plans and goals.	❏ Is spontaneous and freewheeling.

Task-Oriented descriptors: _____

People-Oriented descriptors: _____

Completely equal descriptors: _____

your Checklist Score from the Direct/Indirect quadrant to your Checklist Score from the Task-Oriented/People-Oriented quadrant.

You'll land somewhere in one of these four categories:

(1) A Direct, Task-Oriented Communicator.
(2) A Direct, People-Oriented Communicator.
(3) An Indirect, Task-Oriented Communicator.
(4) An Indirect, People-Oriented Communicator.

When you're trying to determine who fits into what category, try to first determine if the person you're with is Task Oriented or People Oriented, because that's usually the easiest thing to tell, and is the most important.

Then try to figure out if they're Direct or Indirect, primarily by just listening to them talk, and secondarily by observing their body language. If someone is speaking in well-orchestrated paragraphs and staring at you straight on, with their arms clenched over their chest, they're Direct. Maybe, to you, they're *too* Direct— unless you're very Direct, too, in which case they might be your soul mate: or, if you're both *inappropriately* too Direct, your cellmate.

By this point in the book, you know something about me, so test your communication-typing skills with this quiz. I'll give you the answers in the next paragraph. Am I: (1) expressive? (2) a risk taker? (3) somebody who'd rather listen than talk? (4) free with my opinions? (5) patient? (6) reserved?

Here are the answers, in the same order as the questions: yes; yes; no; yes; no; yes. If you got at least three out of five, you're already tuned in enough to effectively read other people.

The combination of those attributes reveal that I am, as I mentioned, a Direct Communicator.

Now rate me on these qualities. Am I (1) logical and linear? (2) intuitive and emotional? (3) focused on people more than projects? (4) a statistic aficianado? (5) deadline oriented and punctual?

Here are the answers: not really; yes; absolutely yes; no; and: not according to my wife, which means, *definitely* not (*obviously*—no question about it!).

That adds up to me being People Oriented.

Therefore, I'm a Direct, People-Oriented person.

That describes who I *am,* but not always how I *act.* I've learned to feel very comfortable tailoring my communication style to the person I'm with. After all: *it's all about them.*

Which leads us quite naturally to the key question: who are *you?*

Take a moment, add the numbers, find the gray area, and you'll know something about yourself that just might, if applied astutely, change your professional and personal life.

At the very least, what you just learned about your communication style will tell you a great deal about where you land in the DISC personality inventory.

My version of the DISC personality inventory—characterized by the behaviors of: Dominance, Influence, Steadiness, and Conscientiousness—is similar to Marston's, and to the other DISC categorizations.

Following is a graph of my DISC system—superimposed on the CSI, which I consider the most important tool for excellence in communication. You'll see that the two typing systems are very congruent, and influence one another.

I call the two combined systems the Communication Style Guide.

Take a look at the graph, and then I'll give you practical advice about how to implement it.

It's self-explanatory. As I promised, no stories: just graphs and lists, for several pages.

All of you Ultra-Direct people can digest this whole thing in less time than it takes to toss back an energy drink. Then you can occasionally glance at it before meetings with various types of people, and soon it'll be second nature.

THE COMMUNICATION STYLE GUIDE

DIRECT COMMUNICATORS	
Task-Oriented Communicators	People-Oriented Communicators
Indirect Communicators	

How to Implement the Communication Style Guide

Here's how to put this knowledge to work, starting today.

By now, you know your own CSI type and your own DISC type, and you probably recognize the types that apply to the people you're closest to.

The following eight lists break down these four categories two ways: (1) How to motivate each of the four types of people, which is of special importance if they report to you; and (2) How to deal with each of the four types, if you report to them.

Of course, this knowledge is equally important to team members who are of equal status.

The same system also applies to families and friends, and can be especially helpful in encounters with strangers.

The lists about motivation show you what people from the various types want for themselves, and what they need to master in order to achieve success.

The lists about dealing with people show you how to effectively work and socialize with each of the various types on a daily basis, based upon which type you are.

Because the lists are broken down like this, you can *focus mostly on the ones that most apply to you, and to the people you're around most often.*

The others are not required reading, but will certainly inform any student of human behavior.

1
Motivating Someone Whose Primary Style Is the Dominance Style

WHAT A "D" DESIRES	WHAT A "D" NEEDS FOR SUCCESS
Power and authority.	Identification with the organization.
Prestige and position.	Individualized commitment to others.
Material remuneration.	An emphasis on internal values.
Challenge.	The ability to pace tasks, and relax.
Accomplishments and results.	Difficult assignments.
To know "why," on all issues.	Clear understanding of expectations.
A wide scope of operation.	Understanding people through logic.
Direct answers.	Empathy.
Freedom from control.	Methodology that's based on prior experience.
Efficiency of operation.	Awareness that penalties exist.
New and varied activities.	An occasional reprimand.

How to Deal with People if Your Primary Style Is the Dominance Style

If your style is primarily Dominance,

   *To **deal with another Dominant:***

   • Just be yourself.

   • Be direct and straightforward.

   • Allow the other Dominant person to take on difficult assignments that will challenge their logic and analytical ability.

- Delegate, and allow the Dominant person to speak his or her mind.
- Offer options, whenever possible.
- Allow the Dominant person to take control of certain projects.
- Help the Dominant person to be aware of the effect that his or her abruptness has on others.

To *deal with an Influencer:*
- Relax and lighten up a little.
- Be friendly, democratic, and willing to discuss situations freely.
- Make sure that you give this individual recognition for accomplishments.
- Allow this person to interact with a variety of people, and provide them a reasonable degree of independence.
- Show interest in the Influencer as a person.
- Help the Influencer to prioritize, manage time, and meet deadlines.

To *deal with a Steady person:*
- Provide abundant recognition of the person throughout the company.
- Take an interest in a Steady people: as people, and in their work.
- Offer sincere appreciation on a personal level.
- Give Steady people plenty of warning about changes.
- Control your urge to be blunt with them.
- Allow the Steady person to work at an established and self-regulated pace.

To *deal with a Conscientious person:*
- Evaluate the Conscientious person on performance of long-term goals, rather than short term.
- Communicate exactly what you expect.
- Provide projects that require precision, organization, and planning.

- Don't apply too much pressure.
- Be available to discuss key strategies in stressful situations.
- Help the Conscientious person to keep projects moving by eliminating excessive checking and rechecking.

2
Motivating Someone Whose Primary Style Is the Influence Style

WHAT AN "I" DESIRES	WHAT AN "I" NEEDS FOR SUCCESS
Popularity and social recognition.	Control over his or her own time.
Monetary rewards that allow expensive living.	An emphasis on objectivity.
Public recognition of ability.	An emphasis on business.
Freedom to speak candidly.	A check on being overly ideological.
Rewarding working conditions.	A fair, democratic supervisor.
Group activities, outside work.	Introduction to influential people.
Demographic relationships.	Control over his or her emotions.
Freedom from control and attention to detail.	An elevated sense of urgency.
Expressive validation.	Carefully analyzed data.
Identification with the company.	Close supervision.
Camaraderie and conversation.	An emphasis on precise presentation.

How to Deal with People If Your Primary Style Is the Influence Style

If your style is primarily one of Influence,

To *deal with another Influencer:*
- Allow him or her sufficient time in the spotlight.
- Concentrate more on details, facts, risks, and probabilities than you normally do.
- Give the other Influencer a chance to be heard.
- Keep their assignments varied and interesting.

To *deal with a Dominant:*
- Respect the Dominant's time.
- Don't overgeneralize or exaggerate.
- Back up your statements with facts and logic.
- Stress results and details.
- Assign difficult assignments that challenge the Dominant's natural skills of logic and analysis.

To *deal with a Steady person:*
- Pay attention to deadlines.
- Allow the Steady person to work at an established and regulated pace.
- Don't assign last-minute projects to a Steady person.
- Create competitions in which everyone can win.
- Provide a stable environment that establishes permanence, security, and consistency.
- Encourage his or her participation in the decision-making process, even if they're recalcitrant.
- Encourage feedback on various issues, even if not needed.
- Approach matters in a systematic, low-key manner.

To *deal with a Conscientious person:*
- Be supportive and responsive.
- Deflect pressure on them whenever possible.
- Help the Conscientious person see the big picture.

- Establish realistic parameters of your expectations of them.
- Answer all their questions carefully, even if they seem obvious.
- Offer them detailed instructions, and monitor their progress.

3
Motivating Someone Whose Primary Style Is the Steady Style

WHAT AN "S" DESIRES	WHAT AN "S" NEEDS FOR SUCCESS
Maintaining the status quo.	Special preparation for upcoming changes.
The security of their situation.	Remuneration that results in visceral rewards, such as a better house or car.
Positive references and reviews.	Generous fringe benefits.
A happy home life.	Help with introduction to new groups.
Procedures with established precedents.	A spouse who is sympathetic to his or her career.
Sincerity.	Help with finding short cuts and work arounds.
Secure limits on their territories of operation.	Being understood on a deep level, devoid of superficiality.
An extended time to adjust to any changes.	An orderly, well-packaged presentation.
Frequent and effusive appreciation.	Reassurance.
A powerful sense of identification with the organization.	The feeling that their accomplishments were meaningful.

(continued)

WHAT AN "S" DESIRES	WHAT AN "S" NEEDS FOR SUCCESS
Increasing recognition as their seniority increases.	Quality products that reflect well on themselves.
Special, unique products.	Able associates.

How to Deal with People if Your Primary Style Is the Steady Style

If your style is primarily the Steady style,

To *Deal with Another Steady person:*

- Encourage and support their organizing efforts.
- Point out problems in a nonthreatening way.
- Encourage the Steady person to make independent decisions.
- Appeal to their sense of loyalty and team spirit.
- Explain the reasons for various needs and demands.

To *deal with a Dominant:*

- Communicate in a concise and straightforward way.
- Be confident.
- Be professional and businesslike.
- Provide options for their review and decision.
- Don't take their criticism personally, because it's probably not.
- Offer them options and projects that challenge them.
- Help provide the delegating that they may not be adept at.
- Keep discussions of personal matters to a minimum.

To *deal with an Influencer:*

- Help the Influencer prioritize and organize.
- Help the Influencer meet deadlines.
- Give recognition to the Influencer for their accomplishments.
- Provide freedom to them, but with clearly defined limits.
- Give them assignments that require motivating people.
- Allow free discussion, and be open to their ideas, even when they're not pushing hard for them.

To deal with a Conscientious person:
- Demonstrate procedures in an efficient, logical manner.
- Don't mix personal and professional comments unless you know the person well.
- Keep praise simple and concise.
- Give the Conscientious person time to plan for change.
- Establish agreeable time constraints, and don't push them unless absolutely necessary.
- Grant the Conscientious person dignity, even when they fail.

4
Motivating Someone Whose Primary Style Is the Conscientious Style

WHAT A "C" DESIRES	WHAT A "C" NEEDS FOR SUCCESS
Adherence to standard operating procedures.	Work in which precision has great value.
Limited exposure to blame or risk.	Clear plans, parameters, and deadlines.
Security and protection.	Help with feeling more confident.
Positive references.	Help with seeing the seeing a larger perspective.
No sudden changes.	Help with preparing rebuttal arguments in a disagreement.
To be part of a group.	Emotional and professional support during difficult times.
Personal attention.	An abundance of explanations, and introductions to new tasks.

(continued)

WHAT A "C" DESIRES	WHAT A "C" NEEDS FOR SUCCESS
Strict limits on responsibility.	Exact job descriptions.
People who will help with changes and challenges.	Help with focusing too much on details.

How to Deal with People if Your Primary Style Is the Conscientious Style

If your style is primarily the Conscientious style,

To deal with another Conscientious person:
- Praise the Conscientious person, but keep it simple and concise.
- When you want behavior changed, specify exactly what you want to change, and outline how you want this to happen.
- Keep the Conscientious person informed about impending change.
- Provide support and guidance in difficult situations.
- Emphasize deadlines and parameters.
- Help the Conscientious person avoid obsession with perfection.
- Encourage the Conscientious person to be less hard on himself or herself.

To deal with a Dominant:
- Encourage the Dominant person to take charge of certain projects, but choose the project carefully.
- Make sure that the Dominant person understands time lines and deadlines.
- Give the Dominant person options, whenever possible.
- If the Dominant person clashes with you or criticizes you, don't take it personally.
- Compliment the Dominant person more on professional achievements than personal attributes.

- Voice your expectations clearly to the Dominant person.
- Listen to the Dominant person's suggestions, even if just as a courtesy.

To *deal with an Influencer:*
- Give the Influencer only the details that are necessary.
- Recognize that Influencers like practicality more than theory.
- Help the Influencer establish his or her priorities.
- Join the Influencer in enthusiasm and optimism.
- Occasionally pay the Influencer a personal compliment.
- Because Influencers are often right-brained, visual people, help them learn with visual aids.
- Reinforce and reward the Influencer's positive behaviors.
- Show Influencers how to implement ideas.

To *deal with a Steady person:*
- Give the Steady person adequate time to train or adjust to new situations and methods.
- Be patient.
- Show the Steady person how their actions benefit others.
- Compliment a Steady person's teamwork and dependability, and let him or her know that other people are also appreciative.
- When you must correct a Steady person, don't be blaming and judgmental, and don't personalize the critique.
- Tell a Steady person exactly why he or she needs to meet certain requirements and deadlines.
- Allow the Steady person to work at a consistent and self-regulated pace.

These guidelines for communication are consistently effective, but an inescapable truth of life is that things change, and it's important to change *with* them. So here's another quick compilation with tips on how to deal with someone in different situations.

Your Situational Game Plan
Fine-Tuning Your Communication Technique
for Different Times—and Different People

Regardless of *your own* communication style, here are the best ways to communicate with others in *their* communication style, *depending upon various situations, and stages of an encounter.*

The Planning Stage
When you're with a Dominant person:

Focus on goals and challenges, and stress the degree of dominance and control that the D has over the task or project at hand. Be respectful, but don't shed your dignity or downplay your self-esteem. If a D thinks you don't respect yourself, it will be harder for him or her to respect you, and your plan. Keep it short. No digressions. Save your jokes for other people.

When you're with an Influencer:

Focus on the high degree of input that the Influencer enjoys in the task or project you're approaching, and offer your approval of and need for their management and operational style. Make them feel that they're being welcomed to an efficient, friendly environment. Practice your best people skills, but remember that you're still dealing with a Direct person.

When you're with an Steady person:

Game-plan the project or task in logical increments, and use some anecdotes, if appropriate. Stress the importance of maintaining stability while improving results, and express appreciation that the S excels at this. Tell the S exactly what you need from them, and why it will be so important to you.

When you're with a Conscientious person:

Emphasize your own professionalism, and the need for someone with their high level of professionalism to to contribute to the job.

That will reassure the C that they're entering a secure situation that they can thrive in, without needing to play the games of office politics that they dislike. Explain everything in a logical, accurate, and specific manner.

During the Opening Dialogue
When you're with a Dominant person:
Limit the socializing, and don't act as if you're trying to make a new friend, or that if you are friendly, you get special breaks. Get to the point, emphasize reason and responsibility, and focus on the final outcome: goals and results. Don't be intimidated by the D's expansive, controlling demeanor, and don't try to top it, or even match it. Always let a D be a D.

When you're with an Influencer:
Be casual and friendly, but stay on topic. Offer them some personal information that relates to the job at hand, and try to get a sense of their own feelings and aspirations. Find out how they've achieved results in prior experiences, and try to relate those to the current task. If a team is being assembled, tell them specifics about the members.

When you're with an Steady person:
Be informal and low pressure, but stick to business. Be patient with the S, and don't expect them to immediately feel comfortable with new ideas or procedures. Even if you are the boss, don't act like it. Let the S know that you realize that work is the great equalizer: It exalts the humble, and humbles the exalted. That philosophy lies at the heart of their dependability, and if you acknowledge it, their trust in you will expand exponentially.

When you're with a Conscientious person:
Get down to business quickly, but tactfully. Don't encroach upon their area of expertise, or even their physical space. Let them be the expert, and show that you respect expertise greatly. Feel free to mention details and processes, because that's what they're best at.

Make friends. You can never have too many friends, and Cs can be friends for life.

During the Course of the Project
When you're with a Dominant person:
Remain results oriented every step of the way, and have clear reasons for your expectations of their actions and approval, whether the D is above you in the organizational hierarchy, below you, or at the same level. Focus disproportionately on questions that relate to the desired results, especially if they are procedural, "what" questions. Try to anticipate what those questions will be, and give straight, short answers. Always make sense. Never embroider.

When you're with an Influencer:
Be enthusiastic about the progress of the project as it unfolds, without worrying that it might make them complacent. Ask open-ended questions that may reveal the I's motivations and ultimate goals, and validate them. Anticipate answering many staff-based, "who" questions. Show interest in their team.

When you're with a Steady person:
Always be as sincere as you possibly can, because these people have a hot-button radar system for phony praise or "motivational" criticism. Focus on questions that show your concern about and knowledge of the ever-changing puzzle of tasks and relationships. Have good answers for technical, logistical, "how" questions.

When you're with a Conscientious person:
Be businesslike, without being cold. Ask questions that allow the C to express his or her knowledge, strategies, and concerns. Expect them to ask very specific "why" questions about the projects, processes, and the team's motivation. If they seem frustrated, you can alleviate it better with empathy than a rah-rah pep talk.

When You're Pitching Proposals and Ideas
When you're with a Dominant person:

Emphasize efficiency, as well as the specific, personal rewards that they will receive from the proposal or idea. Avoid anything that seems to challenge their established territory or point of view. Be strong, but not confrontational. If the D has objections, you don't have to accept them, but don't dismiss them peremptorily, because a self-satisfied D can be very impatient with people who argue context. Dealing successfully with a D takes tact, but it can be worth it, because Ds are often people of power and influence, and their efficiency and protection can make your life much better.

When you're with an Influencer:

Emphasize how the new idea will not only save them time and aggravation, but will offer them added excitement and pleasure. Assure them that they will receive as much recognition as those who seek it more actively than they do, as well as those who are hands-on contributors to the project. Assume that their level of morale will generally tend to indicate the mood of their entire group.

When you're with a Steady person:

Assure them that continuity and the reigning culture will still exist if a new idea is implemented, and tell them explicitly that they will enjoy a continuation of harmony and predictability in their environments. Try not to spring change on them suddenly, and consider taking them aside before your pitch, to help them feel that they are driving the process. When they offer their perceptions of the project's pace and practicality, assume that they're accurate.

When you're with a Conscientious person:

Emphasize the logic and careful consideration that went into the concept you're pitching to them, and let the C feel that their cooperation will be an important element in the concept's success. Give them even more time than the other three types to accept a new idea or method, and to adjust to it's novel demands. Explain as many details as you can, while still making the change sound sensible.

When Negativity Occurs
When you're with a Dominant person:

Don't be shocked if they overreact, because they are accustomed to being proactive and in control, rather than reactive to a situation that's out of their control. Also, to them, success and achievement are integral elements of their self-worth, so setbacks hit them hard. Resist the urge to confront their overreaction, or to join it, and accept the likelihood that they will be blunt, and possibly blaming: of not just the project, but the people involved. Don't fall into the trap of being overly defensive, but be ready to offer objective, logical strategies to turn things around. Emanate calmness, but make it clear that you're as concerned as they are.

When you're with an Influencer:

Be aware that problems will create a natural dissonance with their generally positive outlook, and don't be surprised if they shift toward the Dominant approach, as a way of dealing with the problem. Because an I is a Direct People Person, they're at their best when a project is going well, so if they suddenly show some of the negative traits of a D, don't take offense. Stay empathetic, and try to see the problem from the diverse elements that compose their typically holistic, global perspective: financial, social, hierarchical, personal, etc. Have some anecdotes ready about others who faced similar problems and succeeded.

When you're with a Steady person:

Don't mistake their low-key reaction for indifference. They may be more upset than they act, but they believe that things will turn out best if they keep calm and carry on. Acknowledge their pain, even when they don't display it, and offer gratitude for showing an attitude that will help stem panic. offer ongoing support. if necessary, probe them to find out what they really need, and offer ongoing support. An S can be an invaluable ally in a crisis. It's historically common for an S to rise to power during times of cataclysm: Consider the ascension of Presidents Eisenhower and Obama: politically different Steady people who calmed the county in eras when that was of paramount importance.

When you're with a Conscientious person:

Focus mostly on reassurance. Let the C know that the crisis is in the hands of people who don't mind confrontation or problem solving, and who are already smoothing the rough edges of the issue. Tell them that their best contribution is to continue working as well as they always have. If they are high-functioning Cs, that will be a cue for them to work even harder, which will ultimately be of great value in solving certain elements of the problem. When the problem is over, let them be among the first to know.

When Presenting a Panel of Options
When you're with a Dominant person:

Provide as many variables as you reasonably can, with each backed by solid research and logic. If the D is with a team, direct the decision specifically toward them, as if their opinion is by far the most important. Be aware that pushing for a particular option may trigger reflexive opposition. Because of the Dominant person's strong personality, it can be effective to ask for a decision almost immediately, in a classic direct close. If they're a superb D, their first instinct will be the best.

When you're with an Influencer:

Employ an upbeat approach, with the inference that at least two of the options are excellent, and don't require intense scrutiny. Feel free to offer specific ideas for implementation or action, because that aspect might be a weak component in the I's arsenal of skills. Because the Influencer does not subscribe as much to absolutism and control as a Dominant, it can be appropriate to end the meeting without a vociferous, powerful assent, along the lines of an assumed close.

When you're with a Steady person:
Offer the options in an objective, inclusive manner, giving the Steady person plenty of room to sort methodically through the ramifications of each. Bring as much information to the meeting as possible, but don't feel the need to display more than is necessary, because that can overwhelm an S. Keep some of the details to yourself, unless a certain point needs to be resolved. A direct close may not be necessary, but it's wise to get a very firm commitment to action, because Steady people, if left to their own devices, can overthink things to the point of paralysis.

When you're with a Conscientious person:
Be ultra-reasonable, in both senses of the word: rational, as well as understanding. Patience pays, but don't prolong the session unnecessarily, because the detail-obsessed C's resolve may waver if certain details become too conflicting. Ask very respectfully for a firm decision before you leave, or you may have a hard time ever getting one.

At the Point of Delivery
When you're with a Dominant Person:
Focus on the event of the delivery with the same vigor as you did the creation of the product or service itself. Keep the delivery message short and sweet. Meet your deadline. Keep your budget. Fix the glitches before delivery, with your own sacrifice of time and money—and *expect* glitches. Even if there are no glitches, the D might find some, so have some Plan B's at hand. Act as if you expected everything to turn out great, and it did—but don't do it boastfully. Give the D the credit for success, and let them know you'll be spreading the word of their achievement.

When you're with an Influencer:
Make a sleek, smart presentation, but keep it low-key and personal. If there have been complications and work-arounds, keep them to yourself, and focus on the end result. Spread the praise, and start

with the Influencer. Be responsive to suggestions for tweeks, and don't take offense. Realize that the Influencer is a people person, but is still a Direct communicator. Be generous with follow-up help, partly for your own sake. Extended contact will build your relationship with the Influencer, and a solid relationship with an I can survive multiple rocky roads and failed projects.

When you're with a Steady person:
Focus on the reliability of the product or service that you're delivering, and make it clear that you've just made the S's life easier and more pleasurable. Show appreciation for their patience, since an S takes pride in their abundance of that virtue. Stress the personal attention that they will continue to receive, as a natural aspect of your own ability to provide stability.

When you're with a Conscientious person:
Don't expect a grand gesture of grateful acceptance—just be thankful that your task was to please a personality type that is noted for being pleased, and pleasing others. As always, show appreciation that singles out the value of the person's particular style, and remember that it's almost impossible to praise someone too much. Make the C a sincere promise, on a personal as well as professional level, that you will stay in close touch, because the end of your job may be the beginning of the C's job. Stay in their loop with periodic reviews, and assurances of continued support: verbally, and in writing. Technically, a verbal contract is binding, but there's also a widespread, gut-feeling belief that a verbal contract is, in a sad irony, worth it's weight in gold.

That's All, Folks

A quick chapter. No frills. All about you.

No pep talk at the end. You know what you've learned, and you know what to do with it.

One solemn warning: Don't try to use this powerful information for manipulation. If you do, you'll get burned so badly by people's BS-radar that you'll wish you'd never learned it.

Power that's misused is worse than none at all.

Two Steps to go.

Let's move on, and move out!

— 7 —

STEP THREE: CRAFT THE ENCOUNTER!

Prepare to Engage

THE THIRD STEP TO TRUST is to apply a reliable system to your preparations for meeting people.

If you're as motivated as I know you are—since you've read this far—when you get together with someone of significance, you typically want to create or retain a connection of genuine trust, and hurdle untrammeled over the usual barriers of context, chemistry, and conflicting agendas.

The importance of your preparation for these meetings is too critical for you to leave to chance, charm, talking points, or good intentions. To be a successful leader of a company, an organization, or a family, you will need to prepare for each meaningful encounter as thoughtfully as a military leader would plan for battle.

You will, in short, need to Craft the Encounter.

In the FBI, we call a phrase such as Craft the Encounter a "*term of art,*" implying that many simple, common acts that people often take for granted—including preparing to meet with others—can be systematized and personalized until this act emerges as a virtual work of art.

After you master the craftsmanship of preparing to meet people, others around you will adopt your techniques—either by imitation, osmosis, or training—and help you to further expand your circle of trusted associates.

This meticulous process isn't simply for your sake, but for that of the people you meet. Their time is valuable, and they have problems and opportunities of their own. It's all about them, and you need to honor that fact of life to successfully link your mission with theirs.

I developed my system for crafting encounters shortly after I became director of the Behavioral Analysis Program, and it quickly became one of the most valuable lessons I ever learned, and later taught.

Part of my job was to help agents prepare for meetings with foreign spies, most of whom were not only suspicious and guarded, but also equipped with unmatched expertise at uncovering subterfuge. Overcoming these obstacles required the high level of competence that this system provides.

My agents used the same system to recruit their own American spies, a job that's even harder than dealing with foreign operatives. The agents had to ask these citizens to dedicate themselves to an abstract ideal—the security of America—with no compensation, the possibility of risk, and the added burden of absolute confidentiality and total anonymity.

In both of these spy-ops scenarios, the only preparation system strong enough to function flawlessly was one centered around five cardinal rules of connection that you already know: the Code of Trust. Once again, we see that this set of character-building principles has the power to offer multiple applications.

This will not be the last time that the Code will inform a different system. In the next chapter—in which you'll learn a system for finalizing a connection of trust—the Code is repurposed once more, as a Code of Communication.

The Code really is that ubiquitous. In your pursuit of honorable, lifelong leadership, the Code will serve you equally well as a guide to each of the following three phases of connection:

1. Achieving a realistic perspective of yourself, others, and general human behavior.
2. Planning for your means goals and ultimate goal, and finding others who need your help, and want to help *you*.
3. Executing each trust-inspiring system properly, culminating in the effective deployment of the Four Steps to Trust.

It is the Code alone that empowers all four of the Steps, just as the Steps give life to the principles of the Code.

Although my preparation system is unique, it rests on the foundation of a classic military procedure that has governed the planning of countless combat and support missions, known by the acronym SMEAC. Let's break down SMEAC, and you'll see how I moved it from the terrain of conflict to that of connection.

SMEAC
The Military Planning System

S = Situation. In the military, preparation starts by reviewing the big picture and the main players. You need to know your target, know yourself, and know the territory on which you'll meet. This preparatory phase is analogous to my own Step Two to Trust: Apply the Power of Context.

M = Mission. The second phase of SMEAC is to establish your primary goal, which is usually a means goal that serves an end goal. This military phase is analogous to my Step One to Trust: Align your Goals.

You probably just noticed that in my system of trust, I placed goal setting ahead of the situation (or context), because I believe that a goal, if chosen wisely, can be even grander than those who pursue it—and that it is this grandness that inspires everyone involved.

Prioritizing the goal over the self honors the first principle of the Code: Suspend Your Ego. And it fulfills the theme of this book: leadership is all about them.

E=Execution. The third phase of SMEAC is to establish an initial plan of action, based on the first two phases: learning the context of those involved and identifying their missions, and then preparing to engage. This phase is analogous to my Step Three to Trust, which we're studying now: Craft Your Encounter. In a battle, opposing forces initially focus on their plans for the first shot that goes downrange. In an operation of connection, people focus first on their plans for an opening remark.

A=Administration and Logistics. After your first shot—or your first remark—an encounter unfolds, and you need to be prepared for as many variables as possible. Preparing for variables is the other element of Craft Your Encounters, and its activation begins immediately after the opening remark.

Unfortunately, few things ever unfold exactly as planned, because—guess what?—whoever you're dealing with probably predicted your most likely actions, and if they're wary or distrustful, they may have devised a plan to oppose them.

In the Marines, we reduced this follow-through phase to its fundamentals: Beans, Bullets, and Band-Aids—or food, weaponry, and first aid. In the heat of engagement, though, even preparations as simple as those can blow up in your face. So plan creatively, be nimble, and be quick. Semper Gumby!

C=Coordination. At some point, you'll probably need help to Craft the Encounter, and to link missions with other people. Even though the power of one is legendary, I'll take the power of two any day. Three is even better, and a team is best. The FBI has become a global leader in the initiation and development of teamwork, particularly under its current Director, and operates from another fact of life: we're all in this together.

Lack of coordination among disparate forces has tanked countless missions throughout history, but as a student of trust, you've got a huge advantage. At this point in your studies, coordinating your actions with others is probably something you can do in your sleep.

I learned SMEAC decades ago, and it's still employed by every branch of the military, and beyond. Last week at my Civil Air Patrol squadron meeting, a Cadet Colonel scrawled the acronym across a blackboard as the basis for a CAP mission.

SMEAC is deadly efficient, and many lives have been entrusted to its efficacy. However, for a *nonmilitary meeting of the minds*, my relatively similar system of Craft Your Encounters is even more efficient.

The set of techniques for Craft Your Encounters is probably the simplest system in this book—so simple, in fact, that I already revealed the whole thing:

(A). *Prepare for your opening remark.* I'll soon show you how, with a seven-point system.
(B). *Plan for the various responses to that remark.* My system for that is organized around the classic five-W model of inquiry: who, what, when, where, and why.

The Power of Crafting Trust

The techniques for the first element—preparing your opening remark—will help you to, in effect, turn a cold call into a warm call.

Know this, though: *Every* call—on the phone or in person—is a cold call, for a simple reason. People change, and so do situations. Trust is born anew in each passing encounter.

Trust is arguably the strongest force in all of human interaction—often even more actionable than love—but its very indispensability renders it vulnerable. A slight breach of trust—or even a perceived breach—can shatter years of devotion. Think of trust as a glass hammer: a powerful tool, when applied properly, but less than use-less if it's used wrongly. If you take advantage of trust, or even take it for granted, it can be gone in a flash.

The delicacy of trust is one more reason to craft your first re-mark into a veritable poem of connection, and be ready for every likely variable. This will be easier for you than you'd think, since your first remark and your responses to the variables all reflect the Code of Trust: 1. Suspend your ego. 2. Be nonjudgmental. 3. Vali-date others. 4. Honor reason. 5. Be generous.

You should try to work all five into your first remark. With these five principles infusing your proverbial first shot, you'll be far less vulnerable to the fog of war that inevitably follows the first volley in a battle—primarily because the Code *will help you avoid a battle,* or any kind of contentious, overly dramatic, ego-driven meeting.

If you put the Code at the center of an encounter, you'll inspire a meeting that's driven by logic, reason, and generosity. It will be devoid of the battle of wills that many people still think is inevitable.

You might be the only person at that meeting who's acting with humility, respect, and restraint, but that's okay: it makes you the leader.

These five principles have the power, in and of themselves, to keep you from trying to force your agenda, or to manipulate people into helping you. Making that mistake might seem like a shrewd maneu-ver, but it usually backfires. If that's the kind of meeting that you're preparing for, you're preparing to fail. Even if you "win," your vic-tory will be brief.

The most effective way to create a partnership is to put your faith in the Code, and let the rest of the process take care of itself. With the right foundation, your dreams won't necessarily come true, but they will never collapse, and they'll never tempt you to do some-thing that you'll later regret, or that others will never forget.

Advising you to let go may sound contradictory in a chapter about influencing the course of an encounter—but as I've often men-tioned, there's an element of Zen in all human connection that virtually mandates letting go. Simple reason: in every connection, *another human being is involved*—and nobody likes to be pushed, or held back.

The equation of coercion is self-limiting: Pushing = Pushing Back, and Holding Back = Pulling Away. After great effort, the sum of your exchange typically reverts to zero.

When you let go, you often need to be patient, but patience has majestic qualities, including the creation of a safe harbor that pulls people in when their fear-based instincts are telling them to pull out.

Fortunately, your patience will be bolstered by the trust systems that you're learning. They transform a fluid, interchangeable art form into a linear process, building a tight structure that allows hard-charging, Type-A people to let trust unfold at its proper pace, without causing undue stress.

Stress clouds the brain—creating, in effect, a neurological fog of war, as neuronal pathways—the linked brain cells that lead to thoughts—clog with excess activity: Plan A, Plan B, C, D, E, F, & G. It creates the same brain freeze that comes from saying tongue-twisters—which have nothing to do with the tongue, but simply the brain's impaired ability to correctly pronounce words that sound quite similar, and therefore occupy similar or adjacent neuronal pathways.

The same cognitive phenomenon is so dangerous in a military battle that troops are taught and trained one lesson that stands above all: *don't panic.*

In military and in civilian life, the protective structure of a dependable system gives people the confidence to stay calm, which naturally clears the congestion of thoughts that clog the pathways. When you eliminate the stress that comes from trying to force things, your frontal lobes rejoice, reason reigns, and you get an immediate turbo-charge to not only your IQ, but also your emotional intelligence quotient, or EQ.

So let's take this stress-busting, deal-making system for a test-drive.

(A)
Prepare Your Opening Remark:
The Seven Point System

1. Establish a time limit. Time is such a precious commodity that even life itself is often measured by its length. At the outset of a meeting, show your respect for someone's time—their *life*—by promising them that you won't waste it.

Start the conversation with something along the lines of:

- "I know you're very busy, so . . ."
- "I appreciate your time, so I'll be brief."
- "I won't be long. . . ."

This may also imply that *you're* busy, and that offering them your time is a recognition of their worth.

Even if neither party is busy, it's still wise and courteous to establish a time constraint. It keeps the meeting moving, and heightens its importance—while still relieving the stress that comes from not knowing when something will end. Predictability is a powerful force against stress—that's why many freeways now have digital signs telling you how long a traffic jam will slow you down. It keeps you from stressing out and doing something dumb.

If you see that the other person is becoming impatient and wants to end the meeting, you can deliver a message of urgency not only verbally but with body language, such as checking your watch, or picking up your briefcase or coat.

Establishing a time constraint is extremely valuable when you approach people unexpectedly, especially if they're strangers.

I've taught this technique to the many FBI agents who need to make a cold approach to people, and it has invariably led to more relaxed, shields-down encounters.

If someone thinks that you're going to tie up their time, they'll pull away, but the more freedom you give them, the longer they'll stay.

2. *Ask for assistance.* We're all biologically programmed to love helping others—even strangers. It's in our DNA, a carryover from humankind's earliest days—recognized by evolutionary psychology as a factor that's now embedded in our neurons. This urge is a key component of our emotional-intelligence quotient. It separates us from most of the animal kingdom, and it's intimately related to our heartfelt appreciation of trustworthiness.

Some people are hesitant to ask for help, because they think that they'll owe the other person a favor, or that they'll be seen as needy or annoying. Oddly, though, if you ask someone for something that's reasonably easy to provide—such as information, or a moment of their time—it automatically prompts them to warm up to you.

In my development of trust techniques, I named this mechanism for bonding—during a cold approach—"the *assistance theme*," and taught agents to craft it into their opening remarks.

As I mentioned previously, this phenomenon is referred to by evolutionary psychologists as the Ben Franklin effect, for the Founding Father who famously ended a feud by asking an enemy for a favor. Franklin realized that, "He that has once done you a kindness will be more ready to do you another, than he whom, you, yourself, have obliged."

Recent studies showed Franklin was right: People were even more prone to help somebody they'd already helped than they were to help someone who'd helped them. As I explained in chapter one, researchers say that it if you help somebody, even if you don't like them, or barely know them—but continue your dislike or indifference—it just doesn't make sense to you, and creates an annoying static in your brain that's known as cognitive dissonance.

Most people would rather just accept someone as a friend than to deal with the confusion of this mental conflict.

It's important, though, to make it easy for people to oblige. All Ben Franklin asked for was the loan of a book.

To give someone an easy way to do you a favor, ask them if they know today's weather forecast, or if there's a coffee shop in the neighborhood, or if they would mind waiting a few seconds while you finish something.

When they accommodate you, and you thank them, you've created the beginning of a bond.

3. *Offer something.* The opposite action of the Ben Franklin effect—offering instead of asking—can create the same connection.

That might sound momentarily paradoxical, but it's easy to understand why people like to receive gifts as much as to give them. You've experienced this many times.

The urge to give and the urge to get—intertwined since the era of our hunter-gatherer ancestors, when one person willingly shared his or her success—causes your brain to register a sense of safety and tribal connection, and rewards its receptors with dopamine and the other neurochemicals of contentment. After all these millennia, we're biologically and psychologically conditioned to think—even if subconsciously—that gifts that are given will result in gifts received, and vice versa.

When the brains of both people are bathing in this warm broth of contentment, connection comes naturally, and trust is on the way. In my seminars, I refer to this method of building trust as reciprocal gift giving.

The gift you give can be material, or something as ethereal as a compliment.

Material gifts can hold abundant meaning even when they are of little commercial value. I like to give people FBI memorabilia, because even though it has no monetary value, it gives them an association with a famous American institution. Other thought-that-counts gifts that I give include sprays of hand sanitizer, and breath mints. When I proffer these tiny tokens of consideration, even to total strangers, it almost always elicits at least the reciprocal gift of some friendly conversation.

The key to reciprocal gift giving, though—and, once again, the Zen—is to neither seek nor expect reciprocity. If you're just giving in order to get, it's not really giving.

If you give freely, though, expecting no reward other than your own brief dopamine release, people are still likely to reciprocate, and it can inaugurate a cycle of exchange that sometimes lasts a lifetime.

However, to heap Zen upon Zen, another truth is that there is such a thing as giving too much. The most obvious example is offering something with so much material value that it could be considered a manipulation, or even an outright bribe. A more common mistake, among those of us who adhere to the Code of Trust, is to focus so intently upon other people—as a well-meaning gift of attention—that we stay relatively hidden, or make them feel overexposed.

People can feel uncomfortable when you leave them in the dark about who you are and what you want, or when they think you're prying. Therefore, it's wise to inject a modest element of quid pro quo in most exchanges: When people reveal something about themselves, return the favor. Then they'll feel like they know you better, and have a sense of your own expectations. Even then, though, keep the balance of attention in their favor.

4. Stick to the subject: them. Most people can't start a conversation without using the word "*I*." But you're not most people: You're a leader (natural born or not) so the first words out of your mouth are about *their* goals, *their* expectations, and *their* lives. When you open with "*you,*" the conversation has a different tone, and it usually heads toward a more productive outcome.

Go straight to the most important subject: their thoughts and opinions, which will guide your relationship with them more than any other element of their context.

Skip past any recitation of theirs that's intended to demonstrate how they *should* feel, and find out how they *really* feel. When people veil their underlying beliefs, keep searching for them, and you'll find them: Because people *want* you to find them. They're only concealing them because they don't want to look pushy or inappropriate.

If you know they're people oriented, ask how they're doing. If they're task oriented, ask *what* they've been doing.

Don't use a display of your own strengths and achievements to convince them to be your ally. The less you try to impress them, the more you will. Your ability to connect will impress them far more than anything on your résumé.

When you do make them feel safe enough to open up—mostly by just listening without judging—you'll soon know exactly what you can do for one another.

You'll walk away from the meeting believing that you're closer to your ultimate goal.

They'll walk away with a biochemically gratified brain, thinking that you're a great conversationalist, and looking forward to the time when they can see you again.

5. *Empower and validate them.* Many people try, subtly or bluntly, to inaugurate relationships by trying to gain a competitive edge. They scan for faults, and focus on your vulnerabilities, believing that the Big Brother or big-bully approach will intimidate people into allegiance.

Sometimes it works—until the other person can escape—and sometimes it just heightens opposition. It never results in a lifelong relationship of trust.

Trust, by its absolute nature, is not characterized by hierarchy, but the equality of mutual benefit.

For you, empowering and validating others will be a natural instinct—and one more reminder that simply honoring the Code of Trust will carry you through countless uncertain moments.

By this stage of crafting an encounter, you're already prepared to validate and empower people in least one significant way: by recognizing the importance of their time.

So take the next big step, and discover what their priorities are, and how *you* can align your resources with them to facilitate what they're seeking. Be as generous as you reasonably can, and make the offer relatively open ended.

That may sound like an offer to let them steamroller you, but if you make a generic blank offer, people will tend to ask for *no more than they really need.* People aren't stupid, and they know you won't give them the moon just because they ask for it.

They're also smart enough to know that the best way to get nothing at all is to ask for too much.

If you hold back on your willingness to help, though, it will be hard to truly connect.

A corollary to the principle of offering to help as much as possible is knowing the correct answer to the question, "Will you do me a favor?"

The *wrong* answer is: "What do you need?" The right answer is, "Of course."

Either way, the next thing they'll say is, "Here's what I need." If it's too much, or something you can't do, it's perfectly natural to back away, or to just offer what you can.

People will understand. They knew they were asking for something you might not be willing or able to do—that's why they called it a favor. No matter what you do for them, though, they'll always remember that when they asked you for a favor, the first thing you said was Yes.

When you're trying to find out what people want, look at their desires from their perspective, not yours. That's a derivative of the Platinum Rule, and it's usually the only validation that reasonable people need. If they're unreasonable, you probably don't want to link missions with them, anyway.

Don't put your own goals or ideas above or below those of others, nor in opposition, or even juxtaposition. If you turn a meeting into a race, you'll lose—because leaders put other people first.

As I've mentioned many times now, you don't need to blindly *agree* with people, but to just *understand* them.

If you agree with everything they say, they'll think you're a phony. If you see things from their point of view, they'll see you as a friend.

6. *Manage your expectations.* As my Jedi Master Vern Schrader taught me, the best possible attitude is to have no expectations of people whatsoever. That's always my goal. However, it's sometimes impractical to go into a meeting with no idea at all about what the outcome might be. Therefore, manage your expectations

very carefully. When you tell someone how they can help *you* reach *your* goal, don't ask for more than they can give. If you do, they'll pull away.

Don't even *think* about wanting more than you can get. Inflated expectations are such a hot button that even when you don't voice them, people sometimes sense them, and back off.

We've all seen movies in which the curmudgeonly mentor makes impossible demands that somehow push the protagonist to victory. But the whole process unfolds in a montage. With the theme song. In real life, success doesn't come from pretense or pep talks, but from proven processes, such as the Four Steps (which doesn't even *have* theme song. Yet.).

It's quite reasonable to presume that people are capable of meeting certain standards—and that they share some of your dreams—but capability and aspiration are a far cry from attainment, so don't expect miracles.

Set your sights as high as you like, and feel free to challenge people, but if you think that you can control someone's actions with just the height of your hopes, they're bound to fall, and you'll both fail.

When your hopes are met, you can raise the bar higher, but inflated expectations will crush more dreams than they inspire.

It's often most effective to just back off, and let the *other* person decide what they want to give. Why? Because that's what they'll do, anyway.

If you meet someone whose goal is plainly antagonistic to yours, apologize for wasting their time, wish them well, and move on. As long as you stick to the principles of the Code, they'll probably still consider you an opponent—but not an enemy.

That's important. It takes ten friends to control the damage caused by one enemy.

Destruction is easy. Creation is hard.

7. *Explain yourself skillfully.* It's not enough for your heart to be in the right place. Your mouth needs to be there, too. Vast numbers of noble intentions have been sabotaged by poor delivery.

Your vocabulary, tone, pace, and nonverbal language need to

match the high level of your intentions—assuming, of course, that your intentions *are* at a high level. If they're not, don't even try to inspire trust, because people can spot the good delivery of bad intentions from a mile away.

That's especially true in the digital era. In our ongoing revolution of sophisticated presentation, the delivery of messages has outstripped the evolution of personal development. Therefore, pitchmen, and even genuine presenters, are now considered guilty until proven innocent. In an age of skepticism, the gold standard is sincerity.

I'll give you more detail on how to properly present yourself in the next chapter, in which the Code of Trust morphs into a Code of Communication, but even planning your first remark requires attention to delivery.

Here are the fundamentals:

- Don't rush it. You'll risk sounding like a scam artist who has something to hide.
- Forget every manipulative trick you ever learned. If you need tricks to sell your idea, you need a new idea.
- Present your positive intentions with positive language, and don't build up your idea by tearing down others.
- If you don't have much information about the person you're with, don't offer what *you* would want, if you were them. You're not them. First, find out what they want.
- Expect people to be wary, and try to overcome it with logic. Even fear responds to reason.
- If someone replies to your opening remark with sarcasm, insults, or condescension, respond with sincerity, compliments, and respect. It's the only way to prove their misgivings were unwarranted.
- Make people smile. If you can do that, they'll want to be around you. Once they cross that bridge, they'll be on your side.
- Be friendly, even in the most serious situations. It's never just business. It's always personal.

That's the end of Part "A"—and it's all you need to know to hurdle past the opening moments of an engagement, or a reengagement.

Construct and rehearse your opening remark—on your own time, in your own place—until it shines like a beacon of welcome.

Preparing for Part "B" is harder. It involves the most complex entity on earth: another human being. At that point, the process shifts to real time, and the real world, where Gumby Powers reign.

As always, the best way to be flexible is to be prepared.

(B)
Prepare for the Variables: With Beans, Bullets, and Band-Aids

Making your first remark in a meeting, like launching your first shot in a battle, inevitably invites the fog of war. As the terrain clouds, variables sprout with seeming spontaneity. But nothing surprises the well prepared.

To avoid the surprises that make your stomach roil, you need to be ready with information that can address every variable that may reasonably occur. This data is your nonmilitary equivalent of Beans, Bullets, and Band-Aids.

A well-crafted opening remark can set a positive tone, but other people will almost never be completely on your wavelength during that first meeting—because *they're not you*. That's the whole point of getting together with them.

They have their *own* methods, context, and goals—so variables are inevitable.

It takes finesse—grace in action—to achieve a meeting of the minds. The nuance and fluidity of this finesse invariably rests upon the efforts you put into preparation and practice.

In the reasonably peaceful realm of nonmilitary missions, most of your practice consists of simply gaming the variables that may occur, and knowing what to say when the time is right.

Therein lies the heart of preparing for variables: amassing knowledge.

That's harder than it sounds, because knowledge is more than just a pile of unfiltered facts. Knowledge is, in its most fundamental sense, *the truth.* You can't, for example, have knowledge that the earth is flat—despite the fact that it sometimes looks that way—because it's just not true. Knowledge, by definition, is not what you think—it's what you *know.*

As you know by now, truth lies at the heart of all trust, and it must be conveyed to others with unblinking, unselfish honesty.

At the heart of most instances of distrust, though, is a lie—generally delivered with cold calculation, or bald-faced manipulation.

Because knowledge is truth—and truth creates trust—your search for it must be scrupulous. It can't be self-serving, or deceptive. Those are qualities that are meant to construct a fortress of power, but they usually just build a house of cards.

When you uncover the knowledge of who people really *are* and what they really *want,* you'll probably know everything necessary to make them an ally.

The best simple system for finding this knowledge is the central mechanism of unbiased, objective journalism: the classic 5 Ws—who, what, when, where, and why. That fact-finding model dates back to the first century, B.C., in Greece, where it was expressed with exactly the same words, in a different language: *quis, quid, quando, ubi, cur.*

When applied conscientiously—without regard to its impact on your *own* goals—it's the best day-to-day way to amass enough knowledge to determine reality.

When you know the who, what, when, where, and why of others—and yourself—you'll be prepared for most variables.

At that point, the meeting—and all of the Beans, Bullets, and Band-Aids within it—will be yours to command.

Let's break down this ancient system for finding the truth.

The 5 Ws

Variable #1: Who?

If you're proceeding in a linear manner, in accord with the Four Steps, your research on knowing who you are, and who the other person is—within the framework of a meeting—has already started.

In Step One: Align Your Goals!—you identified your own mission, ultimate goal, and means goals, and those goals were almost certainly a factor in your upcoming meeting.

Unless the meeting is a total coincidence, which is unlikely, you already know the general context of the other person, as part of your implementation of Step Two: Apply the Power of Context!

If more research on people is necessary, the best venue for discovering details on their identities and goals these days is through social and professional media. Nothing fancy: just sites you already know, like Facebook, LinkedIn, and Twitter, along with White Pages and and other online directories.

If it's an important meeting, follow up this research by talking to the person's friends, associates, or supervisors—especially if they're mutual acquaintances. By now, I'm sure you know that the theme of those conversations should be, "I'm meeting with so-and-so— and I'm trying to discover their priorities and challenges." That lowers shields, and invites information. If your inquiry sounds like an interrogation—along the lines of, "Can I trust this person, or not?"—people will clam up, and your contact will come in feeling suspicious and invaded.

Unless I have a good reason, I generally avoid things like criminal background checks, or any kind of highly personal, private-eye investigation. What are you going to do with it? Confront somebody until they break into a tearful, movie-style confession, which leads to True Love, or Brotherhood?

Instead, look for things to *like*. I counseled an FBI agent once who was trying to set up a meeting with an important academic figure who had already turned down every other three-letter agency in the federal government. I told the agent to take a week and read every book and article the professor had ever written. He did, and in his request for a meeting, he mentioned a few key elements from them. He got the meeting, and they eventually became close friends.

All elements of context are significant, but I now believe that the most important aspect is whether they are a Task-Oriented person or a People-Oriented person. That tells you *how* to talk to them—which is typically even more important than what you talk about. If they're People Oriented, you need to tap that aspect of your own personality, and personalize the conversation as much as possible, using a storytelling style. If they're Task Oriented, focus far more on their goals, activities, and achievements than their opinions or personal interests, get straight to the point, and keep the conversation linear and logical.

Another factor that's important in recognizing who people are, in a general sense, is understanding them as members of their generation. The four primary generations of this era—Traditionalists, Boomers, Xers, and Millennials—have somewhat different thought processes, values, and standards, so look for ways to to appreciate them for what they are.

If you show respect for someone's generation—even if it's the same as yours—they'll feel more free to step beyond the boundaries of age, and relate to you on an equal, human-to-human basis.

Here's a quick rule of thumb on various generational topics of interest, and attitudes:

The *Traditionalists,* also known as the Greatest Generation, are all about formality, honor, manners, and historical perspective. They appreciate a thoughtful pace of conversation, the elevation of reason over emotion, good manners, and the views of people who realize that modernity is not necessarily synonymous with advancement.

They have a long-range vision of the changes that have altered America and the world, and can be impatient with people who have little appreciation for this big-picture view.

Their most significant events were the Depression, World War

Two, the Cold War, the postwar economic and industrial boom, the labor movement, the grand era of American trust that preceded the 1970s, and the rise and fall of the American middle class.

Their personal context is now dominated by their experiences as retirees, parents, grandparents, and people dealing with the challenges of aging, including the loss of loved ones, and the other trials imposed by physical frailty and mortality.

The best possible way to engage with them is to explicitly acknowledge the wisdom that aging naturally and inevitably confers, seek some of that wisdom, and express your gratitude.

The *Baby Boomers* honor and value experience in work and life, and respond to people who seek their thoughts and opinions, and value their broad perspectives—which aren't as broad as those of the Traditionalists, but are often more immediately relevant to today's specific issues.

Their seminal events were the Vietnam War, the Civil Rights movement, the political assassinations of the 1960s, the 1960s–1970s cultural shift, the Women's Rights movement, and the rise of the new economy, which is increasingly squeezing them out.

Their personal milieu includes their unique role as the transitional generation that understands older people as well as younger ones, the difficulties of enduring the Great Recession without having time to recover from it, and the necessity of adopting new technologies without having the intuitive understanding of tech that's shared by later generations.

Generation X members value creative ideas, tend to dislike micromanagement, are more wary than Boomers, and guard their own time carefully.

Their major events include their leading role in the integration of digital technology into daily life, Watergate, the Reagan years, the globalization of countries and economies, and the advent of tech-based entrepreneurship.

Their personal lives are strongly influenced by the shift from being the younger generation to a generation of parents. They are acutely aware of the pressures they face as the first generation to work in a fully globalized economy, and the hardships imposed by being the first generation in which being a two-wage-earner family is usually a demand, rather than a choice.

They are deservedly proud of their unique role as the generation that is equally comfortable with both high-tech and traditional industry, and the generation that straddles the industrial era and the digital era.

The *Millennials* are, to their enormous credit, the most nonjudgmental generation in American history, known for accepting almost everyone: except judgmental people (can't stand them!).

They are, also ironically, the least trusting generation, but the most idealistic.

They enjoy the unbounded energy of youth, but are also relatively more passive than the other generations.

Although they are in touch with far more people than most of the older generations, their relationships are often bordered by technological limitations, and constrained by some of the punitive aspects of political correctness.

These sensibilities have made them remarkably aware of nuances and contradictions that are lost on other generations, but their insights leave them occasionally overwhelmed by our current society's ocean of dichotomy.

One sensible way to see them is: the way young people have always been. The same essential qualities have been ascribed to young people from the days of the Flappers, to the Hippies, to the Slackers.

The events that interest them most are the growth of social media, the ubiquity of mobile devices, the threat of climate change, 9/11 and the war on terror, the Gender Rights movement, the burden of student loans and lack of affordable housing, and the lingering lack of opportunity that resulted from the Great Recession.

Bottom line: The key to finding common ground among the various generations is simply to listen. If you do that, you'll do more than just learn. You'll make a friend. You'll inspire trust.

Variable #2: What?

What you are is similar to who you are, but it's not part of the central, immutable elements of your context, such as your core personality, or ultimate goal.

The elements of your identity that are more temporary and mutable include your job position, locale, appearance, and topics of interest.

Because we all seek inclusion in a tribe—and feel most comfortable when someone approaches us as a tribal member—it helps to match what *you* are with what the *other* person is. I'm not recommending that you be phony, or untrue to yourself, because altering *what* you are doesn't change who you are. It just establishes you as somebody who is multidimensional, and has goals and missions that are even greater than yourself.

A person's employment position is one of the primary aspects of what they are, and it's wise to position yourself in synchrony with the other person's job. That doesn't mean pretending to be something you're not, but just relating to others on their own level. If you're a CEO and they're a sales rep, channel back to the days when you were in sales, and relate to them from that perspective. If you're the salesperson and they're the CEO, make an effort to think and act like a prospective CEO.

When you're both using that same technique, you'll tend to meet in the middle. If you're the only one who's using it, you'll meet on their turf, and that's even better.

If you're traveling, try to blend in with the local culture, customs, styles, phrases, and current events. Look at the local paper, check on their sports teams, see if the recent weather has been notable, and listen to the hometown radio. If your hotel has a concierge, ask what people are talking about, and what's special about the locale. In the Bureau, we call this looking for the ground truth.

The last piece of groundwork is deciding what you should wear. Dressing for success could mean wearing a thousand-dollar suit, or ripped jeans, depending on how you want to be perceived. If you want to be seen as nonthreatening, dress down, even if the other person is dressed more formally. If you want to look like a highly credible member of the establishment, dress up. If you want to create commonality, wear what you think they will (*without* looking like you dressed for a costume party).

I'll say this about my own personal experience, with no guarantees that it will work for you: I do best when I wear whatever feels most like me, which is generally something very casual, like jeans and a sweater. Why no guarantee? Because I'm at a stage in my life and career in which I've already established my identity, so anything that doesn't reflect that can look contrived. If you're still closer to the blank-slate stage of your life and career, it's probably smarter to dress the part of what you *aspire* to be.

You can also establish what you are by bringing a prop to the meeting. If you have good background info on the person you're meeting, it can be something in plain sight, such as a tie—but if you aren't sure how it will be received, it can be something that's concealed, such as a watch or device, that's revealed only when it feels right.

If you want to look nonthreatening, wear a plastic watch, but if you want to look like an authority figure, bring something that reflects success or power, such as a diamond watch. If you're looking for tribal affiliation, wear a Celtics watch in Boston, or a smartwatch at SXSW.

Although it's fine to look casual with your wardrobe and props, don't look unsightly. A psychology experiment showed that people assumed that a total stranger had many great traits, including intelligence, kindness, and trustworthiness, based strictly upon certain physical characteristics—a phenomenon called the "halo effect." The number-one characteristic that activated the halo effect was attractiveness.

So buff your halo. Look your best, no matter what style you wear. Grunge is dead. Dirty was never even alive. And when I mentioned ripped jeans, I meant designer jeans with hundred-dollar rips, of course.

Last and most important of all, remember something your

mother said: "It doesn't matter what you're wearing, as long as you're wearing a smile."

She was right. Experiments proved that, too. It's the Top-Secret Trust-Inspiring Method of the Federal Bureau of Motherhood.

Variable #3: When?

If someone asks a trust-based leader when they want to meet, the leader almost always cites the same time frame: "Whenever is best for *you*."

That doesn't mean you're required to be available at any time—it just means you put their feelings first.

Even if you need to say no to their first three or four suggestions, people will still remember that you offered to let them control the scheduling.

If they ask you to set the time, it's often wise to say that you're generally flexible, and will be happy to schedule around their needs. Then, even if you can't accommodate their first few suggestions, you still retain the mantle of leadership with your gracious, accommodating behavior.

When you do agree upon a time, be punctual. It's not just a matter of logistics, but validation and respect. If you are clearly the subordinate person at the meeting, it's even more important to be on time. Showing abundant respect makes all the other variables easier to manage.

The best way to be on time is to arrive early—especially since unexpected impediments often erode the extra time. Bring something to do while you wait, so you won't waste your own time, and start to resent the other person, which is especially possible if you're not only early, but they're late. Even if you try to conceal your resentment, an observant person will sense it, through things as subtle as your accelerated speech, or your desire to get straight to the point.

If they're late, don't take it personally. Consider their context: Was it their goal to be late, so that you'd be angry? Not likely. It is what it is. What it *isn't* is: about you. Just tell yourself that you're lucky to be meeting with someone so busy—or anything else that keeps you from taking it as a slight. Leaders know that sometimes people are just late.

If you arrive early for a meeting that's at someone's office or home, find a place nearby to wait, to keep them from feeling pressured by your early arrival. Pressuring people, even by just being early, can make them more resistant to you.

When you sense resistance, you'll inevitably start worrying: Do they like my ideas? Why do they seem distant? Am I asking for too much?

The more worried you get, the more pressure they feel, and the more they resist.

If the meeting is at a public place, such as a restaurant, it's fine to get there early, and find the best spot to meet.

Many meetings are spontaneous, and when that happens, don't plow straight into the heart of your message. Ask them if this is a good time to talk. If it's a bad time, and you don't read their cues, it won't go as well.

In the spur-of-the-moment meetings, be especially respectful of the other person's context—particularly if they seem to be Task-Oriented types.

Last week, for example, I was at my flight school, and ran into the owner, a West Point grad and excellent engineer, who is a very linear, Task-Oriented, Direct Communicator. He now bases his life around the exacting task of helping aspiring pilots to get up in the air and back on the ground in one piece.

If you've ever worked any kind of job in which a single mistake can kill people, you know how much I trust and admire this guy— who is also teaching my own son how to fly.

I've had many inspiring conversations with him, even though I'm on the opposite end of the Communications Style Inventory. One reason we communicate well is because I don't need to, as the phrase goes, "be myself," in every situation, with every person. Like most people, I have a variety of qualities, and I've learned to present different dimensions to different people. That usually pleases them, of course, but it's good for me, too, because I like pleasing people—and when I please them, they generally want to please me.

When I saw him, I tiptoed into a conversation about one of his favorite topics. But I could immediately see that he was distracted, so: "Is this a good time?"

"No," he said flatly. "Focused on something."

Twenty years ago, I would have thought, "Yeah, focused on *blowing me off*!"

Now I know that, as a rule, when someone blows off a person with an excuse, it's actually a *reason*—disguised as an excuse by that person's own insecurity.

So I wandered into another room where some guys were hanging around, and one of them pointedly asked me what was wrong with the owner.

"Nothing. He's focused. That's *good*," I said, as if I had the inside scoop.

And I did. The inside story is usually on the outside, and is shockingly apparent to people who are looking for reality, instead of trouble.

Besides, because the owner is a quintessential Indirect, Task-Oriented type, it's usually harder for him to switch gears—probably because people with that personality type are more compartmentalized and regimented, with a greater attachment to linear time. That's part of the reason they're so good at getting things done on schedule.

It's easier to accommodate spontaneous meetings if you're People Oriented, like I am. My time bends, weaves, and sometimes practically disappears—but is usually open to the inclusion of others, at a moment's notice. Deadlines? That's why I keep lists. *Long* lists.

Moral of story: Time is relative. It's one thing to you, and another to me.

But for both of us, when we're with other people, we're on *their* time.

Variable #4: Where?

Easy answer to that: You'll choose to meet them wherever they *want*. It will invariably be their own, individualized comfort zone, and they'll assume you chose that location in accord with their best interests.

It *will* be in their best interests, because their best interests are your best interests. The more comfortable they are, the easier it will be for you to get to know them, learn about their goals, connect, and align missions.

As always: Shields Down, Information In!

The Supersecret Spy Method (S.S.S.M.) for determining the ideal location of someone's comfort zone is to *ask them*.

It's common for people to draw a blank, though, especially if they don't know much about you and are trying to be equally accommodating. When that happens, use the S.S.S.M. Secondary Option, and ask them what *type* of place they like. Then do a little research, and find two or three places like that, and empower them with the choice.

If they don't respond to the S.S.S.M./S.O., drop the subject, get to know them a little better, and use that information to present new options.

(Sorry about all the acronyms, but without them, the government wouldn't even be able to deliver your junk mail, or collect your taxes, according to the Federal Committee on Redundancy Committee.)

About a year ago one, of my agents was trying to wrangle a meeting with an important Mideast source of HUMINT, but the target wouldn't commit to any particular meeting place—a sign that he didn't want to meet with us at all.

But my guy found out that what the source missed most about his homeland was the rich, aromatic coffee and tea, and fishing with his dad.

The agent called him back and offered three choices for the meetup: a Starbucks on a pier, a high-end teahouse at a local ocean resort, or a sunset cruise on a sport-fishing boat.

The contact—wealthy enough to charter his own plane

home—was genuinely touched by the consideration. He chose the
Starbucks, because he had a boat of his own. He later became an
invaluable source of help during the Syrian civil war. That cup of coffee, in one crisis alone, saved more than a thousand civilians from
being bombed.

Sometimes the place where people feel the least defensive
is—part Zen, part Sun Tzu—the place where they're defended best:
their own territory. That will generally be either their office, or their
home.

Task-Oriented people tend to feel strongest in their own office, and
People-Oriented types often feel most powerful in their homes, even
when (or especially when) their families are around.

This enhanced sense of power is not a problem, but an opportunity. When people feel safe, they say more, show more, and are more
prone to being fair than when they feel backed against a wall.

One of my West Coast contacts told me that the best lesson he
ever learned about negotiation came from a person who, at that time,
was considered the most powerful man in Hollywood. This veritable
kingmaker told my contact that when he met with serious people to
make serious deals, "The first thing I do is show them my jugular."

That may sound counterintuitive, but it's easy to imagine the
kind of executives that he dealt with: People every bit as smart and
tough as him. He knew they'd find his vulnerabilities, no matter
what. So he put his weaknesses out on the table, and negotiated from
there—unfettered by the machinations of anybody who thought
they could launch a sneak attack on his flank.

Where did *he* prefer to meet people? In his own office. Why there?
It wasn't because that was the locus of his power. It's because that's
where he could make them the most comfortable.

Variable #5: Why?

The primary Why in the Craft-the-Encounter formula is: why should
they even *talk* to me?

Inherent in that question is: why should they *trust* me enough
to talk?

You know by now that the correct answer has nothing to do with how you perceive yourself, your reputation, or your intentions. It's all about them.

You need to give them a logical reason to talk to you, and it should be clear and simple enough for you to convey in about thirty seconds. Your reason, to be as effective as possible, should be aligned with their priorities. If you don't know what their priorities are, craft your discovery of them into your opening statement.

If you don't feel like making the effort to approach them with anything better than an ice-cold cold call, it's probably best not to call them at all. If you do, there's still a chance they'll meet with you—probably out of courtesy—but it's more likely that they'll politely decline.

When they do back away, their explanation will generally not be: "Because there's nothing in this for me." In an age of political correctness that often emerges as velvet daggers of dismissal, we've all learned to veil the lesser angels of our nature, and let people down the easy way. Here are the top-five Greatest Hits:

- "It's not you, it's me."
- "We're just not a good fit."
- "We've decided to go in a different direction."
- "I'm looking for something a little different."
- "I'd love to, but just don't have time."

All those phrases mean the same thing: You failed to present your proposition as an opportunity. The most common reason for that is: it's an opportunity for *you*, not them.

If you don't know what's in it for them, keep looking until you find it. If you can't find anything, create something—even if it's just offering them good coffee on a pier.

But you can do better. Do enough research to know at least one thing that they want, and figure out a way to help them get it. If you're both in the same industry, or even the same town, you can probably give them some sort of boost in their career or personal life. It can be quite modest, and still be enough to entice them into a brief get-together.

The most obvious thing you have to offer—and generally the most valuable—is to link your mission with theirs. Even then, it's not enough to just say, "I've seen and heard good things about you, and I think we might be able to help each other." That will probably sound like a generic manipulation line. Be *specific*. Leave no doubt that you're being as honest, transparent, and straightforward as possible. Many people, and most leaders, have read numerous books about manipulating people, so you need to make it clear that you've moved beyond that.

If it's someone who has trusted you in the past, you can be even more direct, and say, "I think I may have found a resource for that challenge you're having," with no mention of your own needs, or any reciprocity. The only reason *not* to be that direct with a stranger is because most people are unaccustomed to the behaviors of the Code, and will think you're concealing a catch.

Sadly, that attitude often dominates our current environment of widespread distrust. People always feel very shrewd and savvy when they say, "If something sounds too good to be true, it is"—but think about how self-defeating that attitude is. Every great thing that's ever happened initially seems too good to be true: that's the very nature of progress—in technology, and in human evolution.

When you tell someone that you can probably help them, it's not a commitment—it's too early for that. It's an honest statement of intent.

If the other person doesn't want what you have, or wants something you can't give, that's fine. You still did the right thing by offering to help. That's what they'll remember about you, long after the details of your intentions are forgotten.

It's a truism that the first thing that excellent salespeople sell is themselves—and the self that they sell is almost always that of a person who believes that solving the buyer's problems is the best way to get customers, and keep them.

This attitude creates an atmosphere of cooperation, because the seller and the buyer are focused on the same problem. That takes most of the pressure off of the seller to sell, and the buyer to buy. It makes selling—typically one of the hardest jobs—into one of the most pleasant.

The success of great salespeople, therefore, doesn't come so much from *what* they sell, but *why* they sell: to solve customer's problems.

This paradigm also reinforces a major reason to apply the Code of Trust to all of the relationships in your life: *it feels good.*

That's as powerful as any Why that ever existed.

In the next chapter—"Connect!"—I'll tell you another spy story—one that shows you how I applied this system.

It will seem a little different from the orderly process I just described. Things always do, in the real world—populated by 7 billion people, representing 7 billion variables.

Some of it might seem so different that you'll think, "This isn't Robin's system." You'll be right. As soon as I teach a system, it belongs to the person who learned.

Now the system to Craft an Encounter is yours.

— 8 —

STEP FOUR: CONNECT!

T HE STAGE IS SET.
You've established your ultimate goal, found people who can assist you, and are ready—without reservation—to align your mission with theirs.

You've identified their context, and found reasons to respect and understand it. You've crafted your encounter with them.

It's time to connect, and forge the alignment of your goals into a mission that will change your life, and theirs.

You've never been more ready. For one main reason: At this stage of your study of trust, you've almost certainly integrated some or all of the Code of Trust into your life, because the Code is one of those things that you just can't understand without adopting. The powers of its principles are almost unfathomable until you've tried them.

To the uninitiated, they're paradoxical. *Leading by putting yourself last? Maximizing your authority by minimizing your ego? Validating the perspectives of people who oppose you?*

These counterintuitive lessons are understood only by those who've learned to artfully navigate the loftiest atmospheres of trust-based leadership—whether they lead a multinational corporation, a small business, a city, or a family.

If you've started *living* these lessons, you've personalized the power of not letting your vanity defeat you, and you've gained confidence from your burgeoning circle of associates. You've learned to keep manipulation and selfishness from slowing you down, and enjoyed the fast, smooth ride to leadership that's shared by those who glide down the swift river of fairness, reason, and goodwill.

If nothing else, you've already made one connection that will serve your life. With me. You've listened to my ideas and stories, and I've already imagined your reactions. So: Thank you for letting me tell you the story of my life, and welcoming me into yours. If we ever meet, we'll share a solid connection: yours, as a reader of a book I've written—and mine, as a writer of a book you've read.

Connecting, as you know by now, doesn't mean just getting together with someone, seeing what they're like, and hoping it leads to something. That kind of connection is nothing more than hooking up: it's for the careless people who aren't serious about leadership, long-lasting alliances, or reaching their ultimate goals.

Connecting consists of nothing less than forging a steel-strong bond of trust: seeing into the soul of someone, realizing they can bring you closer to your goals, and—most important—realizing that you can be of value to them.

Sadly, this process often hits a wall of fear, and either disintegrates, or takes a lifetime to unfold. It doesn't need to—and it shouldn't, because life's too short to suffer the waste that intimidation leaves in its wake. You can—with the right intentions, an attitude of confidence, and a mastery of the art of connection—begin to approach a high level of trust in the first moments you meet someone.

That doesn't mean it's easy. But the most potent powers never are. Right?

As you've seen, I'm a systems guy who goes by the numbers, whether I'm flying an airplane, planning a military operation, or recruiting a spy. So how does Step #4 start? It starts the same way it ends—by *communicating as effectively as humanly possible.*

I'll show you the five primary principles of the kind of communication that creates connections—and they're going to ring a bell.

Then I'll teach you the three main techniques that put these principles on their feet, and make them work in real life.

The Nowhere Man from North Korea
Quantico

As I've mentioned, in the FBI, when circumstances dictate extreme caution about revealing the identity of a certain country, we usually call it Erehwon—backward for *Nowhere*. So I'm going to tell you about a man from Nowhere whose country was one of the most dictatorial nations on earth. For our purposes here, think of him as a former citizen of North Korea.

I *can* tell you that he had become a resident of Southern California, and you can let your imagination work from there.

Torrance, California—at the south end of the L.A. Basin, America's sunny, beachy center of aerospace—has attracted one of the largest and most erudite Korean populations in the country. Among them are a small number of people who escaped the oppression of North Korea, if not the residual trauma embedded by living under a totalitarian regime, and the lingering dissociation from defecting. Many of them keep low profiles, and avoid any attention that might provoke retribution. But not all.

The émigré community of North Koreans in Torrance, along with that of nearby Fullerton, sometimes seems to constitute a country within a country: an enclave of isolated, fractured cultures—with traditionalism skewed by politicism—that's so different that it's almost impenetrable.

So it was not unusual for one of our newbie Counterintelligence agents—a bright and dedicated U.C. Berkeley grad who was rising like a rocket in the Bureau (let's call him Agent Youngblood) to consult with me, when I was director of the Behavioral Analysis Program, about a possible North Korean source of human intelligence.

"Mr. Dreeke," Agent Youngblood said, when he entered my office at Quantico, looking sharp in a navy-blue suit, "I've been trying to cultivate a man who might be a great source of HUMINT on North Korean missile technology. He's an engineer for a private aerospace company in Torrance that I read about in a local paper. Scary smart—PhDs in engineering and mathematics. I doubt he's a fan of the Kims, because he left North Korea for an international conference and never came back, but he's complicated. Didn't have a bad word to say about the North Korean government. I've reached out, but he won't talk to me."

"Why should he?"

"Why should he . . . what?" Agent Youngblood looked blank—as I so often did in the early days.

"Want to talk to you."

Agent Youngblood gave me what he thought were good reasons. He told me how he treated people well, how he was fluent in Korean and Mandarin, and about the wide range of Access Agents and other sources he'd cultivated. He said that the engineer—"Dr. Rhee," let's say—could become the lynchpin in his excellent dossier on North Korean missile capability.

I'd seen Youngblood's résumé and knew he was just stating facts, but it came off as vanity. Because it was. Key fact in connection: No matter how well deserved, don't offer even a *whiff* of egotism. Deal breaker!

It's not even logical. Nobody's perfect, or even close, so *humility is reality*. It's not a social grace. It's a fact of life.

To help Youngblood feel comfortable enough to back away from the self-absorption that was slowing him down, I smiled and nodded. HQ can be intimidating, and the safer people feel, the less they extol their own virtues.

"That was a great presentation about your thoughts," I said, "but to help you, I need to know more about what *he* thinks."

"I don't *know*. That's the problem."

"I'm sure Dr. Rhee is a complicated guy in a complex environment, but after you peel the layers off people, they're even more similar than different."

"I'd like to *think* that's true."

"You'll get there."

"But he doesn't even take my calls."

"Leave a message."

"I have. Twice. I phrased things in accord with his culture, and used a nonthreatening vocabulary. I was very direct: name, title, phone, email. All I asked for was a callback."

"That's smart. Good work. But it looks like we need to leave him a message that would inspire him even more."

"I think you're right." When you give someone critical feedback in the right way, it rarely registers as critical.

The first thing I told him was to focus less on the words he used, and more on the meaning of his message. If your heart is in the right place, it's almost impossible to say the wrong thing.

"Everybody worries about shoot the messenger," I said, "but that all depends on the message."

"But what would my message *be*? I need him, he doesn't need me, and this might be risky. So . . . ?"

As a reader of this book, I think you already know—especially from the prior chapter on crafting your encounter—what that message would be. It would be one that's congruent with the Code of Trust. Once you know the Code, the specifics of almost any message are little more than just filling in the blanks.

Thus, the Code of Trust is also the Code of Communication.

Here's a summary of what I told him, as a blueprint for his phone message—and almost any other message, ever.

By the numbers:

The Code of Communication

1. **Suspend Your Ego.** The first thing I told Agent Youngblood was: It's all about the engineer. Give Dr. Rhee a reason to talk to you that's in *his* best interests, not yours, or those of any other person or entity.

The reason should *not* be that you're a reliable Agent. There's only one subject at hand, and it's not you, Korea, aerospace, or America. It's *him*.

2. **Be Nonjudgmental.** Forget about right or wrong, good or bad. Don't judge him for not wanting to talk to you: If he doesn't, good for him. Don't even judge North Korea—that's his call. Don't wave the American flag. Realize that he probably won't say anything at all until he sees that he can't say anything wrong. Then you'll have the only *valuable* kind of conversation that exists: an honest one.

3. **Validate Others.** Elevate your nonjudgmentalism to the next level: understanding. No matter what Dr. Rhee says, look at it from his point of view. He doesn't need your approval—he just needs you to know *why* he thinks that way. That need is a human constant. Let's say that Rhee announces that he loves Kim Jong-un. Tell him that's interesting, and you'd love to hear his ideas. When he tells you, listen carefully to the details and find some that make sense, within *his* context—not yours. Tell him specifically why those ideas make sense, and thank him for the new perspective. His shields will drop, and a great conversation can begin.

4. **Honor reason.** Stick to the facts, and avoid any kind of manipulation. Don't exaggerate, hide negatives, or say anything that might sound like a debating tactic. Give him logical, verifiable *reasons* to trust you. Those reasons include offering an easy way for him to back out. From the time of Sun Tsu, great leaders have known that it's not smart to put somebody's back against a wall, or to back an army against a river.

5. **Be Generous.** Don't ask without offering—and offer *first*. Offer him the gift of choice, to heighten his sense of

empowerment. Empowerment creates freedom, freedom creates honesty, honesty creates understanding, and understanding creates trust. Give him the pleasure of doing most of the talking. Find out what you like about him, and tell him. If you meet over a meal or coffee, grab the check as if it's an honor.

I told Youngblood that he couldn't go wrong if he said something as simple as, "I really want to talk to you, and it'll be all about you, not me. I want to understand you, not judge you, and I'll be honest, reasonable, and appreciative."

Sometimes it's easiest to just flat out vocalize the Code to people: preach what you practice.

But all this was new to the young agent, and he seemed dazed.

We game-planned an answering-machine message, and I suggested that he deliver it in Korean. By now, you know why. Here's the English version of it, as well as I can reconstruct it from my notes:

"Hi Dr. Rhee, this is Agent Youngblood—I'm the local FBI guy here, working in counterintelligence, and I saw an article about you in the Fullerton Korean-language newspaper. I wanted to tell you how interested I was by the intelligent things you said, and it would be a real pleasure for me to buy you lunch, if you can squeeze it in. We can talk about a few things that might be interesting to you. I've met a number of people in aerospace here and in the Bay Area, and if I could introduce you to somebody that you'd like to meet, it would be my privilege. Also, I could fill you in on what I've been hearing about North Korea, if you're interested. Third, I work with a lot of analysts that would be interested in your insights on North Korea, so maybe it's of value to you to express them to people who have influence. If nothing else, we could just have a nice lunch at some place you like, or maybe some place you've been wanting to go, and talk about Korean culture, which I think is fascinating. If any of that sounds interesting, give me a call. If it doesn't, I'm embarrassed I even asked, and I'm sorry I wasted your time—especially with my poor fluency in Korean—and I won't bother you again. Thanks, though, no matter what, and I wish you the very best."

Agent Youngbood jotted all this down word for word, and translated it. Smart guy. It's easy to forget things in the heat of connecting. But he looked uneasy.

"Aren't we leaving too much to chance?" he asked. "This gives him such an easy way *out*—and I'm kind of a control freak."

"Me, too. But when I first started, a veteran agent took me under his wing and taught me what you might call the Zen of Spycraft." I told him about the great Jesse Thorne, whom you may remember from chapter one. "Jedi-Jess told me that *'control freak'* is an oxymoron, because *freak* means somebody who's *out* of control. He liked to say, 'Pull, don't push, because nobody ever got pulled into something they didn't want to, or stayed in something they were pushed into.' Another mantra was, "The only thing you can control in life is your *expectations*."

He was dubious. "What if it doesn't work?"

"It will—one way or another. If Dr. Rhee wants to talk to you, he will, and if he won't, you'll get a fast start on finding someone who will. The problem with meeting people who don't want to talk to you is that they never *say* anything. It's a waste of time to focus on the means goal of setting up meetings, when the only goal that matters is getting HUMINT that helps the country."

"Okay, but doesn't this make me sound kind of wishy-washy? Vulnerable?"

"Exactly!"

"And that's okay?"

"Do *you* like to deal with invulnerable people?"

He looked dispirited. He probably wanted to fly home to his wife with some hot spy stories, feeling like James Bond, and have her say, "Oh, James, your daring stories are so *exciting*!" (Remind you of anybody?)

Youngblood, though, clearly saw that this mission wasn't going to give him the dopamine rush he craved—and that it might lead to more drudgery than he thought existed in the spy business. To use (one final—I promise) Bond reference: he was shaken, and not stirred.

I was expecting that. As you know, most people get their biggest dopamine release from being the center of attention, and doing all the talking about their favorite subject: their thoughts, opinions, and lives. In short—themselves.

But you apparently have a higher calling. You know that leaders get their brain rush from aligning their missions with others, and reaping the rewards of the cardinal chemistry lesson of biochemical bonding: *the chemistry of trust is all about us.*

In fairness, though, it's hard for a great many people to forgo the instant gratification of basking in the spotlight—especially if they're insecure—but that's part of the reason they *remain* insecure: they don't rise to the leadership positions that offer them the greater pleasure of a promising future, as their bedrock goals beckon.

"Let's give it a shot," I said.

"Right now?"

"Before you sound too rehearsed."

He picked up the phone. "Practice it once, though," I said. "It'll keep you from sounding rehearsed." He gave me a look.

"Sorry, Grasshopper, I'm channeling my inner Jesse."

He went through it once. "Perfect!" I said. "Don't change a thing! But a little slower." The look again. "People don't trust fast-talkers."

He made the call. No answer. He left the message.

"Now what?" he said softly. "I'm clueless."

I'm sure he had ideas of his own, but he was smart to play dumb. It made him seem humble, and that's always something to be proud of. (Yes—ever more paradox—but that's the secret sauce of human connection).

"What we do now is stay flexible. In the Marines, we call that ethic Semper Gumby."

"Booyah!" He was getting it!

But *you* already had it. That's why you got the short version of the five principles of connection, candy coated in international intrigue. By now you know that the Code of Trust, repeatedly echoed by the Steps, has multiple layers of power.

Next: the three primary techniques that activate the five principles.

Once you learn these techniques, your lessons on the art of connection will be over.

The Three Techniques

With three dirt-simple, universal tools, you'll be able to connect with almost any person, in any context. They're three things you've probably been doing all your life—just not systematically.

I've taught these techniques to FBI agents, sales teams, C-Suite management groups, Marines, law enforcement officers, social engineers, and my own friends and family members.

Last week, I taught them to a cadre of Navy SEALs in California who were in a grueling, multi-month program of intensive people-skills training. I promised to teach them in two days how to create the type of interaction that each person prefers.

I told them that it would be easier than they thought—because the whole lesson revolved around a single fact of life (that you already know): connection, the ultimate emblem of trust, is governed by the universal desire to be nonjudgmentally validated.

When you provide that, you can learn people's goals, discern their character, and make an informed decision about linking your mission with theirs.

How do you provide that to them?

By using these three profoundly powerful techniques.

Communication Technique #1:
Direct the Course of a Conversation with Questions.
When you're discussing something serious with someone—such as linking missions—suspend your usual style of declarative communication and focus on asking, instead of telling. *Wield the power of the question.*

That power is illustrated by a corollary to the axiom, "Whenever two Marines are together, one is the leader—and the leader is the one with the plan." The corollary is: "Whenever two people are talking, one is leading the conversation, and the leader is the one with the questions."

Leaders ask questions fluidly and conversationally, with no fear of the answers, because all they want is the truth.

Truth—or reality—is the one firm foundation this life offers: in human relations, science, philosophy, art, and spirituality.

No matter what the truth is, it will lead you to the best way to reach the outcome you desire.

Communication Technique #2:
Influence the Outcome of a Conversation with *Active Listening*.

Listening can be as simple as keeping your mouth shut, but *active listening* is using a set of methods that systematically demonstrates your trustworthiness, elicits the information you need to know, reveals your own thoughts, and leads to the desired outcome.

The actions that comprise active listening evoke a wealth of true, unguarded information from someone, and make them happy to offer it.

At the end of the conversation, you know them, and they trust you.

That puts you in in the best possible position to make the right decision about goal alignment, and how to achieve it.

The next step will be yours, and you'll be operating with the power of knowledge, and the even greater power of trust.

Communication Technique #3:
Decode Nonverbal Communication.

Body language, facial expression, and the physical elements of speech, including tone and tempo, can make or break a connection.

Communicating is always a mind/body enterprise, and even the best message can be sabotaged by engaging in negative nonverbal communication, or by failing to correctly decipher the other person's nonverbal communication.

The first part of this three-part equation of connection—the power of asking—solved the next problem that Agent Youngblood had. His North Korean source, he soon told me—with unmistakable excitement (and, unfortunately, a degree of egotism)—had returned his call, and agreed to meet him.

The following day, though, Youngblood reported that Dr. Rhee had failed to show up for lunch. He was disappointed, somewhat insulted, and was ready to move on.

I gave him a better idea: Don't take it personally, call Dr. Rhee back, and keep your message—even if it's on a machine—all about him. Specifically, *ask if he's okay*. Did he have a problem? Not feeling well? Overworked? Ambivalent? Frame it as sincere concern—and better yet, *be* sincere.

Believe it or not, when people let you down, there's no reason to automatically take it personally, because it usually is—in actuality—rarely about you. It's about them (of all things!).

A day later, Rhee called Youngblood back, citing only a faulty memory for missing the meeting. That was probably true, and the rest had just been a reflection of Youngblood's insecurity. Or maybe Dr. Rhee really had been leery, and was just making an excuse, to be polite. If so, there's nothing wrong with that. There's a reason minor prevarications are called *white* lies, and they typically reveal a greater truth: that the person who tells them really *does* care about your feelings.

The first thing Rhee said to Youngblood on the callback was, "What is it you wish to talk about with me?" He sounded suspicious, as people often do when they're contacted by the FBI.

I knew exactly what Youngblood wanted to talk about: The recent launch of a Korean satellite—and whether it meant that North Korea was poised to launch a warhead. Dr. Rhee probably also knew that. But Youngblood was ready with the perfect response: "What would *you* like to talk about, Dr. Rhee?"

In a delicate exchange between two intelligent people, the blunt, bald-faced truth is typically not the first item on the menu. In fact, a hard truth that's delivered too quickly can create more misunderstanding than a white lie. (Thus, almost all good spies—and spy handlers—have good manners. Bond, as you may recall, was well mannered even on what was intended to be his deathbed, with a laser between his legs, when he asked Goldfinger, "Do you expect me to talk?" When Goldfinger responded, "No, Mr. Bond, I expect you to die," Bond didn't try to one-up the excellent reply—even to have famous last words. Now *that's* manners!)

Youngblood's good manners got him the meeting he wanted. The power of the question is hard to resist.

I was growing more interested in the exchange myself, because I'd run a search on Rhee through some government engines that most people don't have access to, and found that his specialty was rocket reentry systems. That made him valuable to private-sector space companies, because—lacking NASA's deep pockets—they were all trying to build satellite-deployment rockets that they could reuse.

My problem: noncombustible reentry into the atmosphere is also the most difficult challenge in delivering nuclear warheads.

Communication Technique #1
Direct the Course of a Conversation with Questions

The only thing that's more important than what you say is what you ask. An excellent measure of your mastery of the language of trust is your ratio of questions to statements. The person who asks the most questions is the one people want to talk to again: it's the person they trust.

People invariably respond warmly when you ask them questions that are specific to their lives, without being callously intrusive.

The person asking the questions is also the person who is driving the conversation. Win/win.

I've studied the power of questions for many years, and have compiled the essential actions that comprise a pragmatic, in-the-field Art of Asking: one that lies at the heart of the effective communication that creates fast, solid connections.

Here are eight simple tips for directing a conversation with questions, in approximate order of their importance:

1. *Use questions to create clarity.* Reality and honesty—revealed by clarity—are essential in the methodical movement toward ultimate goals.

If a plan isn't realistic, it's even worse than a distraction. It's a disappointment waiting to happen.

If even one partner isn't completely honest, it's not a partnership, but an exploitation.

Reality can be hard to find, but nothing reveals it better than absolute clarity of communication, and nothing creates clear communication better than questioning.

The simpler the question, the better. Rely on the same 5-W questions that you mobilized during your process of crafting your encounter. They will help you find the truth.

The *whole* truth, which is more elusive and more valuable, usually requires follow-up questions.

Even then, never assume that you fully understand the whole truth, especially in the early stage of an inquiry. Here's a Navy SEAL adage about assuming: "A-S-S-U-M-E makes an ass out of you and me."

Many people hide much of what they think and feel, mostly with good intentions and reasonable concerns, but despite that, they're rarely offended when you ask them what they really think—because we all yearn to be understood.

Also, most people aren't exactly sure how they feel about various issues, and asking them helps them figure it out. Asking a series of questions is such a brilliant tool for understanding yourself and others that it's been revered by scholars for 2,400 years as the Socratic Method, in honor of one of history's first great thinkers.

Another reason that asking questions cuts through confusion and creates clarity is that it's usually nonthreatening—because questions are, by their basic construction, nonjudgmental, and reflect a desire to validate the perspective of the person you're questioning. To make sure your questions follow those criteria, just stick to the Code. When people see that you want to understand them, they become eminently more receptive to your ideas, and more accepting of compromise.

A primary reason people won't compromise is because they think you don't see their side of the issue, and that if you did, you'd be offering them more. When you leave no doubt that you do understand, their resistance—which may be very reasonable, within their context—fades.

The search for clarity also pays homage to the fourth principle of the Code: Honor reason. Intelligent, honest questions signal the search for rationality, and take discussions to a higher level. They prevent you and the person you're talking to from getting emotionally hijacked by misunderstandings.

When a hijacking occurs, both parties can become defensive, manipulative, and confrontational. Objective questioning gets everybody off the emotional rollercoaster that a conversation can become when it sinks to the simplistic, declarative level of speech making and posturing.

Exchanges that are rich in clarifying questions also *simplify* any discussion, and make reality easier to identify. So often, anger and hate don't come from actual differences but simple miscommunication, so simplicity can be almost as beautiful as truth itself.

Simplicity reveals, and complexity conceals. People usually complicate things when they're afraid that their ideas are not intelligent enough or valid enough to withstand the tough-minded scrutiny that clarity enables.

When people cast off fear, take the leap of trust, and keep it simple, the reality that's revealed becomes a fertile field where collaboration can flower.

Concepts, of course, can be complicated, but that's no excuse for clouding their transparency with convolution.

For example, this chapter is, according to a word-counting site, written at the relatively easy reading-level of a nineth to tenth grader. Are its ideas easy? No, not at all—but the most powerful of all ideas are usually those that can be stated simply.

When you ask enough questions to know with crystalline clarity what someone really wants, you can almost always find some avenue for fulfilling their desires—or being able to tell them why you can't. Even if you can't help them, they'll still feel such a strong degree of understanding that they still consider you a person they can trust.

2. Influence actions by what you ask. Socrates loved this technique. He wasn't just your average, curious guy: He had *an agenda.* He wanted the people he was questioning to realize not only his own point of view, but the fundamental truths of humankind.

When people see enough of these fundamental truths to recognize reality, they usually act in *accord* with reality, which is invariably the most positive and productive course of action.

If you can help someone reach a moment of clarity—stripped of fear-borne and ego-driven illusion—you're not only doing them a favor, but also enabling them to make a wise, positive choice about linking their mission with yours. As a rule, they will see that it's in their best interests to create a mutually beneficial relationship— or you wouldn't have been exploring that option in the first place.

You can often use this technique to achieve the tried-and-true goal of assuring someone that the idea you're endorsing was theirs in the first place, even if it's undergone a few permutations since they first mentioned it. That's effective when you need to deal with insecure people who love the feeling of control. Your validation and empowerment help them lower their shields, and loosen the reins.

The American judicial system, particularly in a trial setting, is largely composed of the communications style of leading people to the truth by asking them questions. You've seen it happen in a hundred movies. Question builds upon question until reality—or at least the lawyer's sense of reality—is revealed.

You can achieve an even more elevated goal, though, than that of attorneys trying to win cases—which they sometimes do with spurious reasoning and dubious motivations. Your questions can help lead people to understanding, whether their answers *suit your own needs or not.*

If they don't, then you're the one who learned something new. Learning is good, because knowledge is power.

When someone teaches you something new, you can be flexible, adjust, and head to your ultimate goal on a somewhat different route. Semper Gumby!

3. Ask in accord with the Platinum Rule. You remember it: It lies one step beyond the Golden Rule of treating people the way *you* want to be treated—to treating them the way *they* want to be treated, even if that's not your style. Same goes for asking: empower people with the questions that lead them where *they* want to go.

This technique is similar to trying to influence actions with questions. The difference is: in this situation, you change your course of questioning when their answers reveal that they don't want to go where you're headed.

I taught this technique recently to a sales force that did door-to-door sales. They had some good policies aimed at making customers feel comfortable, including: park on the street, and take off your shoes before you enter someone's home. I suggested they go one step further, and ask the customer, "Our policy is to park on the street, but if you'd rather I didn't—because of a neighborhood-association rules, or anything else—where would you prefer I park?" And: "Our policy is to take off our shoes, but what would you prefer?"

Also, the sales team had similar products with varying degrees of quality and cost, so I recommended that they ask, "How long and how often will you use this?" That led to the question: "Which works better for you: to pay a little more—or to get a little less?" I acknowledged that this question might cut into their sales margins, but it would give them happier customers who'd be more likely to become regulars.

The Platinum Rule is pure essence of: it's all about them—and that concept is *especially* powerful in the realm of sales.

4. Ask instead of argue. When was the last time that a difference of opinion turned into an argument, and you won?

Before you say, "Yesterday," let's define winning as more than just getting your way on that particular day. That's usually easy, and can be achieved with a direct order, a raised voice, a passive-aggressive pout, a cold refusal, a threat, or various other means of domination and manipulation. *Winning* is when everyone walks away happy, trusting, and free from the desire for retribution, or disengagement.

Winning is maintaining the full, positive power of your alliance, and moving ever closer to your ultimate goal.

You can't achieve that by arguing—so the moment you start arguing, you've lost.

When you get your way in an argument, you usually don't even *know* you've lost. Smart people are "good losers," who hide their grudges and live to fight another day, and they're the ones to fear most. They have enough self-control to forfeit a battle in order to win a war—and if you've chosen to battle them, you've probably created a war, and may well have lost it before you even know it exists.

Disagreements, of course, are a given. The question is: what next?

Leaders, faced with conflict, start asking questions. They uncover the rational, real points of disagreement, with nonjudgmental validation of the other person's right to his or her own opinion. They put down their shields, and let the information in.

The best leaders parse that information carefully, looking for win/win. What's the end goal of the other person? What are their means goals? Their deal breakers? Does the other person fully understand the leader's goals and ideas? Does the other person have their own win/win ideas?

Let's just say the other person can't respond rationally and becomes angry and unreasonable. How do leaders react?

They certainly don't *match* the behavior, because that's like trying to put out a fire with gasoline. They let the less-controlled people vent—unless other people are there, who don't want to be around it—and nudge them gently back to reality. Fun? No. Rewarding? You bet!

The only focus of a leader is his or her ultimate goal: the rest is just window dressing—all in a day's pay.

Will the other person eventually settle down and see reason? Maybe, maybe not—and to a large degree, it doesn't matter. You achieve little by linking your fate to a loose cannon, and if you occasionally endure a temper tantrum in order to weed out those who aren't worth your time, so be it. You've made more room for the reasonable people.

If somebody does simmer down, and realizes they went too far, you haven't poisoned the relationship with your own reaction.

When it's clear that someone has a really hard time with overreacting to things, or becoming too emotional, it may be best for both of you to *not* have a close relationship. You don't need to become collateral damage in their insecurities, and they might be very uncomfortable with advice about how to deal with things more positively, no matter how humbly and sincerely you offer it.

Your reward is going home at the end of the day feeling good about yourself, and closer to your goals—even if you all you did was take a detour around a roadblock.

You asked every question you could. You didn't argue.

You kept your goals and self-respect intact. If you lost a potential ally, don't worry about it—you'll find another.

You will in almost all cases find another ally much sooner than the person you parted ways with will.

5. *Ask people about their micro-context*. Understanding someone's general context is pivotal, but nothing trumps asking somebody about their own, exact, personal needs and experiences.

If, for example, you're an FBI agent, you ask: "Have you ever talked to someone from the FBI before, and if you did, what was that experience like for you?" Same goes for selling cars: "Have you ever owned a Chrysler, and if you did, what did you think of it?"

Sure, you might not get a positive answer, but you'll get the most valuable information that exists: the truth. The truth is the ultimate fulcrum of connection: it's the best possible tell for when to go all-in, and when to pull out.

The only thing that's more valuable than the truth—generally defined as an absolute reality of what exists, combined with our own best abilities to perceive it—is the aspect of truth, mentioned previously, that the FBI refers to as the ground truth.

The ground truth, like the most standard version of truth, also recognizes absolute reality, but it adds the crucial ingredient of perceiving what is true within the context of others—instead of just ourselves.

Sometimes the ground truth about *ourselves* is a bitter truth to swallow, because people often have insights into our failings and challenges that even we don't see. Even so, that ground truth can be the most illuminating truth of all, and lead us not only toward connecting with others, but even connecting with the best possible version of ourselves.

Every lasting relationship starts with the truth.

Once you know exactly what people want, you'll know exactly what to say. It may not be what you *want* to say, and it may not be what they want to hear. But it will solve problems: now, later, and—with any luck—forever.

6. *Ask instead of accuse.* There are countless times when you need to confront someone directly and tell them they did something that's not acceptable. If ever there's a time to focus on your ultimate goal instead of your means goals, this is it, because confronting someone the wrong way can derail your ultimate goal.

The temptation is to confront someone by means of a direct accusation. You might be angry, hurt, or anxious, and will feel relieved by venting, via accusation.

Venting is a good way to get rid of negative feelings, and this form of catharsis can be emotionally healthy—but there's a time for it (later) and a place (alone, or with an empathetic third party).

Leaders don't vent—at least not in public, and never during a direct confrontation. They know it just doesn't work. It puts up shields, makes people conceal, creates enemies, and kills trust.

Leaders don't even *politely* confront people politely unless they're positive that they're guilty—and usually, not even then, unless it's necessary to protect others. Accusations often hinder leaders in the pursuit of their goals, and a false accusation is a recipe for embarrassment, or something far worse. Keep in mind that it's often easy to suspect the wrong person, because the guilty person may have contrived that situation.

When problems do arise, leaders forgo the often ritualistic practice of blame, and just try to find out what happened. More often than not, no one is to blame, and even when someone did trigger an unfortunate incident—but don't see it that way, from their own context—it's pointless and even destructive to confront them. Remember a cardinal rule of trust: never argue context.

The most fruitful avenue is to ask neutral, non-blaming discovery questions that help bring clarity to all of those involved—including the leader. Focus on just finding out what happened, and how to fix it.

Good questions, aimed at solutions instead of culpability, include: What are some of the factors that played into this? How likely is it to happen again? How do we prevent it? Does it have any silver linings? What are some things that all of us have learned?

Positive questions make everybody feel like they're part of the team, and part of the solution. People stop reacting with behaviors that are driven by fear of reprisal, and drop their defenses.

When shields come down and information comes in, solutions usually follow.

Some people are just too insecure to operate effectively within this positive, productive system, and on occasion it's in everyone's best interests to take them off a project, or team. As always, it's all about them, and if they don't feel comfortable with a trust-based style—and wish to discontinue their connection with it—they're still determining their own fate.

Wish them well, and help them find something that's better for them.

7. *Ask open-ended questions.* The best interviewers in the FBI,

as well as life in general, typically don't ask yes-or-no questions, or any question that can be answered with a single word or a phrase, because they want their targets to answer as expansively as possible. That shifts the content of the conversation to the person being asked, which not only pleases most people, but also prompts them to offer extra information.

Therefore, it's an effective tool to use for people who want to be the center of attention, as do most of us.

Questions that aren't specific are also less apt to provoke competitive, Type-A people from trying to one-up your question with an answer that's better than the question, or with an answer that makes the question sound ill-founded or naïve. A friend of mine who's a sports journalist told me that the most common way sportswriters question coaches and athletes—many of whom are hypercompetitive, and seem to enjoy making sportswriters look foolish—is to forgo the inquisitive format entirely, and just say, "Talk about . . . ," as in: "Talk about your team's defense tonight."

That creates such a blank slate that it's almost impossible to respond rudely or condescendingly—and if somebody does, guess who looks foolish?

8. Make statements with questions. There comes a time for you to talk about yourself. If you keep the conversation completely one-sided, people may become wary. They'll wonder who you really are, and what you really want.

If you've used all the tools of connection I've mentioned so far, you will have enabled people to lower their shields. The conversation will be about them, and—paradoxically, once again—the more you make it about them, the more they'll be happy to talk about you.

If they're emotionally intelligent people, they'll soon be pumping you for your own desires, needs, and goals. People who do this are the richest source of good relationships. When you find someone like that, you've usually found an ally with whom you can link goals.

Even when that happens, though, it's wise—and kind—to keep

most of the focus on them, even if it's asking them about your own actions or opinions.

For example, you might say, "I'm going to get an online MBA—do you know some good schools?" That reveals something about you, but it's still framed around them. It's a little more gracious, and when you make someone feel good, you both benefit.

Also, talking about your own actions by asking others about them makes it easier for people to give you honest evaluations—and if their replies aren't honest, they're more likely to harm you than help you.

Honest answers to questions about what you're doing can be supremely valuable, because they come from a context *outside* your own. People may know about problems, opportunities, or options you never even considered.

It's especially smart to introduce your *opinions* with questions—especially about controversial subjects that might trigger emotions. For example: "I'm starting to favor a flat-rate income tax. What are your feelings about that?" An even better version might be: "What do you think about a flat-rate income tax?" That gives people even more room to speak their minds, and it's far less likely to provoke defensiveness or divisiveness. When you get their opinion first, they're usually more accepting of a different opinion.

Another form of telling by asking is to ask a series of questions that gradually and indirectly reveal your own position, as did Socrates. It still communicates how you feel, but indicates your awareness of the pros and cons of the issue, as well as your respect for other ideas, and your intellectual integrity as a someone who's simply seeking the truth.

I knew a legendary FBI agent who rarely stated his opinion bluntly, and never contradicted or criticized people who disagreed with him, but was known as a man of firm beliefs. Everybody shared their ideas with him, and everybody learned from him. Here's how he started almost *every* serious discussion: "Help me understand why . . . ?"

The interrogatory style of making statements is a total reversal of the traditional manner, but it will quickly feel natural to you. Why? You've seen others do it. Think back, and even if you can't identify exactly who that was, I know who it was in a general sense: It was someone with keen intelligence, confidence, and gravitas—a professor, a president, or a successful executive. Or it was someone special in your own life—a parent, spouse, or friend, with no credential at all—other than the most revered that exists: a wise, respectful person.

It was, in short, someone you trusted.

The North Korean Question

Dr. Rhee met with Agent Youngblood at a place that the aerospace engineer suggested, which Youngblood told me was the worst Korean restaurant he had ever been to. Rhee—a privileged man, even by the demanding standards of beach-side So-Cal, where even the stray dogs have business managers—said it reminded him of North Korea.

"And that's good?" I asked Youngblood.

"Apparently. Because here's the kicker. He met with me because he wants my help."

"Good! Reciprocal gift giving!"

"He wants my help in getting him *back to North Korea*."

I'm an optimist. I can find something good in everything. Usually.

"*Why?*"

"He told me it's inevitable that North Korea will follow the lead of China, and gradually overcome oppression through the rise of the middle class. He said something like, 'I can help them see that money, not weaponry, is power.' He made a case that he and other scientists could help the North Korean government rethink its role."

Reasonable, yes—in a reasonable society. Naïve, absolutely. "Annnd . . . ?" I said.

"And he says his own skills in satellite delivery systems aren't related to weaponization, but just the peaceful development of a 'peaceful earth satellite.' But guess who used the exact same phrase when their last rocket blew up? Hyong Gwang Du," he said, with the Korean pronunciation—and little too much pride. "The Director of Scientific R&D in the North Korean space agency."

I was at a loss. If ever there was a time to manage expectations, this was it. "Well. Wow."

"I know. I just don't get it."

"Do *not* lose touch with him."

That was the day he hit bottom. For most people, that's good. But not everybody bounces.

Semper Gumby.

Communication Technique #2:
Influence the Outcome of a Conversation with
Active Listening

Asking questions is Part One of effective communication, and Part Two is listening so actively to what people say that you not only *get it,* but control the course of the conversation. Done well, you can influence a conversation so effectively that the endgame becomes predictable.

Almost anybody can listen to someone talk, and thereby make at least a casual friend, but somebody who masters the methodology of active listening has the power to create relationships of abiding trust—sometimes almost instantaneously.

When that happens often enough, you become a leader—whether that was your ultimate goal, or not. It actually is that organic.

I had an epiphany about the power of active listening a few years ago, when I was speaking at a conference for owners of large family businesses. At the traditional Sunday night meet and greet before the kickoff, I found myself standing next to a woman who was very wealthy, very beautiful, and so hollow behind her eyes that I knew without asking that she was suffering.

I tiptoed into her sphere of darkness. "It's not always easy being at these things, is it?" She forced a sad smile. "I'd rather be home," I said, "watching *Homeland* with my wife."

She gave me a measured look that quickly melted into one of relief. People trapped by suffering know immediately when someone can sense it. It's almost like a seventh sense, and sometimes it keeps people from going crazy from the kind of loneliness that only suffering can confer. "I'm afraid I'm not good company," she said.

"Problems?"

She sighed, tears welled, and I waited.

"I'm only here because my husband died. Last year. He knew what to do at these things. I don't. He knew these people. I don't."

After a painful moment of searching for something to say, I blurted, "That must really suck." (Yes, I know, that wasn't the politically correct "I'm-so-sorry-for-your-loss," but it came from my heart).

There are no wrong words, as I mentioned, that come from the heart—and people who are suffering *know* the voice of the heart when they hear it.

For those who can't speak from their hearts, that's the scary side of the seventh sense.

All she said was, "Yeah, it sucks," but the look on her face told me that my remark penetrated her protective shield.

Then she took a long pull on whatever was in her glass and started telling me her story. It was the saddest: life's sweetest fairy tale, matched without warning by life's most bitter lesson—that nothing in mortal life is certain, nor ever fully safe.

To offer more details would be an invasion of what little privacy she now has, given her current stature in the American business community.

I listened carefully, and instinctively relied on many of the methods that I'll tell you about next—long before I realized they could be formulated into a system.

After about ten minutes, I said something along the lines of, "So you knew there were problems that your *father* might have fixed, but if he had, it would have alienated your *husband,* and that's the conflict you just can't reconcile?"

Her eyes grew wide, and seemed to dry. "You're a good *listener. Thank you,* Robin. I thought you were just letting me talk."

She looked like she felt less alone—and in the solitude of loss, that can feel like new life.

She took a gulp of her neglected drink. "Do you know some of these people?"

"Some."

"Will you introduce me?"

"Of course."

In the process of those introductions, she was considerate enough to open far more doors for me than I was for her, due to her late husband's stature. I wasn't surprised by her kindness, since the saddest thing about kindness is that it comes far more commonly from suffering than it does from comfort.

That sad meet and greet, she later told me, marked the day she hit bottom, and began to bounce back to a better life than she thought possible, given the height of her fall from happiness.

It also created a solid connection that both of us remember well. I rarely hear from her now—although I read about her in business journals from time to time—but I know that if I need a friend, I've got one. She knows that, too.

My epiphany: All it takes to connect is an open heart, an active mind, and the desire to be less alone in a life that's already bordered too much by separations that *need not be.* If you have those qualities, you're a natural for active listening, and a great candidate to elevate that trait to an art—or at least a system.

As you've probably guessed, I've systematized it.

The Twelve Commandments of Active Listening

1. *Listen for what matters most.* You already know what matters most, in virtually all situations, to all people: *Them.* As always, *it's all about them.*

Even when someone is talking to you about abstract subjects, keep your focus on how those abstractions apply specifically to them.

Part of this focus is to continually ask yourself: Why *should* they talk to me? Furthermore, don't ask yourself why *you* think they should, but why *they* think they should.

What's in it for them? What can I offer? What are their end goals? Their means goals?

How do you find these things out? Ask them.

2. *Keep your opinions to yourself.* Code Principle #2: Be non-judgmental. It applies to listening just as much as it applies to telling, and asking.

If someone *wants* to know your opinion, they'll ask. If they don't, your opinion is irrelevant to the conversation.

If *you* know your opinion, that's good enough, because that's all you need to know to keep heading straight toward your ultimate goal.

If you're not sure of your opinion, probe them for a smart opinion. People love to be asked: about almost *anything.*

For example, when was the last time you asked someone for directions, and they were curt or rude? (Hard-core New Yorkers, of course, are typically excluded from this generalization. Even among them, though, rejection can often be deflected with proper knowledge of context, leading to appropriate rephrasing, such as: "Excuse me, do you know the way to Grand Central Station, or should I just go screw myself?")

3. *Listen carefully enough to offer honest validation.* Try hard to see it from their perspective, no matter how foreign it is to your own.

That effort fulfills the second principle of the Code, and its emphasis here should be reassuring, because it reveals how simple, consistent, and congruent all of this really is.

Looking beyond your own borders will also broaden your horizons. Validating isn't agreeing; it's just understanding, and understanding different perspectives enriches you intellectually, emotionally, and even spiritually.

4. Don't overthink a conversation or enter one with a set of memorized lines.

The rationale for this is illustrated by a Marine Corps maxim I've mentioned many times: When the first round goes down range, the fog of war sets in, and all hell breaks loose. In a conversation, your first round is your first question. Everything after that, executed properly, is a follow-up question.

A great conversation, therefore, is more about reacting than acting.

If you insist on being rigid about moving the conversation in a linear, predictable manner, you may arrive where you want to—but you'll never know if you could have arrived somewhere better. Even worse, you probably won't fully connect. People know when you're taking them on a verbal ride of your own choosing, and it's never very comfortable.

Connection comes from spontaneity—the spark of unforeseen revelation that penetrates defensive postures and conventional thinking.

Soldiers, surrounded by the *literal* fog of war, pierce the fog with effective, back-and-forth, give-and-take communication. In the figurative fog, that's also your best bet.

5. Check your own stories at the door. It's the hardest thing you can do, because you *love* those stories. They reveal your insights and prove the fitness of your character. Fine. But who are they about? You. So leave them at home.

Have you ever shared something important with someone, only to have them launch their own story a nanosecond later? How did it make you feel? Listened to? Or did you feel like a repository for their own tales of glory?

6. Don't preempt a criticism with a caveat. You won't always agree with people, and it's okay to tell them you don't. But a critically important element of active listening is responding properly to a statement you don't agree with. If you do it wrong, people will feel invalidated, misunderstood, and judged.

One of the least effective ways to respond to is, unfortunately, one of the most common: introducing your criticism with a disclaimer that's intended to let you off the hook.

People typically say something like, "I don't mean to be critical in any possible way, but . . ." What's the next thing out of their mouth? A criticism.

Did they spare your feelings, or even soften the blow? No, usually not. Negative is negative, no matter what.

The social engineering phrase for trying to soften an insult is *"negating the frame,"* which implies an even more egregious act than the insult itself: the negation of someone's *right to feel insulted*.

It's tempting to *negate the frame*. We've all done it. It's never worked. It never will.

If you need to be negative—and sometimes you do—keep your verbal frame positive, as in: "What you think is very reasonable, and I think I know another aspect of it." Or: "Overall, I like your idea, and here are my only suggestions, which may or may not help." When you find points of agreement, always be specific about what they are, or your affirmation might just sound like a line. Also, always ask them about *their* opinion of your response.

This is more than just a polite way to be critical. It's a way to help people discover their own truth, through nonjudgmental exploration, expressed with understanding questions.

And one of those people is you.

7. *Keep listening after you fully understand.* That's because people change their minds, sometimes in the midst of a conversation, or even the middle of a sentence. That degree of Semper-Gumby flexibility is a sign of intelligence. It means somebody never stops thinking, and never stops learning.

If you don't recognize their about-face, they'll know the exact moment you quit listening.

Remember that every connection—with old allies or new—is a new connection. If you get a call from someone with whom you have a warm relationship, don't just A-S-S-U-M-E that it's going to be a warm call, and go on autopilot.

Also, situations change even faster and more often than people do. Keep that in mind.

Treat every call with the same unbounded courtesy of a cold call. When you treat all calls as cold calls, relationships stay in real time, and usually remain warm.

8. *Leave no doubt that you're listening.* Some people think they're active listeners when they know they're paying attention, but that's not enough. You've got to let the other person know you're paying attention, every step of the way.

Several simple techniques convey it:

- **Minimal encouragers.** These include encouraging words or verbal cues that show you're listening, such as, "Oh, really?" and "Uh-huh," and nonverbal cues, such as nodding, smiling, or raising your eyebrows. Skillful use of minimal encouragers contributes to the rhythm, tone, and quality of a conversation.

For good examples of it, watch excellent interviewers on television. With hardly a word, they keep the conversations flowing.

- **Paraphrasing.** Show the person who's talking that you get their point by putting it in your own words—succinctly enough to let them continue controlling the flow of the conversation. Examples might be: "You were *really* lost." This also helps you recall the conversation later, because you're laying down not only an auditory memory (from hearing) but also what's known as a productive-effect memory (from speaking).
- **Reflective questions.** If you paraphrase what someone says—but in the form of a question, such as: "You really *were* lost?"—it prompts them to add more information. This often elicits the brain reward that people get when they teach someone.

- **Conversational threads.** When you want to change the topic without appearing bored or manipulative, thread it toward a different subject that's on the same parallel as the current subject. For example, if you want to move away from a conversation about skydiving to something more personal, you might say, "Skydiving sounds like something for people who don't have many fears. Is that true of you?" It keeps the focus on them, without making it sound like you're tired of what they're talking about.
- **Anchor questions.** These are typically open-ended questions that help you find out how deep your conversation is. They can elicit either a surface response, or a deep one. For example, you might ask, "What do you think the most important element of love is?" If the answer is, "Love usually feels kinda good," you know you're not very deep. If the answer is, "Love is finding the best version of yourself in another person," you know that someone is opening up to you, and that you're creating a genuine connection.

As the conversation progresses, anchor questions often provoke deeper answers. If they don't, you know that either you're not asking the right questions, or that the person you're talking to just doesn't want to reveal themselves. Either way, you at least know where you stand.

Don't make the mistake, if the answers stay on the surface, of assuming that you're just talking to a shallow person. No person on earth is truly shallow. We all know deep truths. The question is: are you *reaching* those truths when you talk to them?

- **Emotional recognition.** The only thing that's more important than knowing what people think is knowing how they feel—and letting them know. Emotions and logic aren't always on the same page. It's human nature, so don't fight that reality. You'll lose.

You probably remember the YouTube video I mentioned that's entitled, "It's Not About the Nail." When did the guy get the reaction he *wanted*? When he showed her that he knew how she *felt*.

Sometimes the best way to connect is just to say, "Tough day?" It's hard to resist somebody who knows how you feel. Call it empathy, emotional intelligence, or whatever: just show that you know.

- **Summarizing questions.** When you paraphrase someone's main point at the *end* of a conversation, you not only let them know that you understood it, but you usually find out that you missed one or two things.

Learning those final facts is gratifying for both parties, because it ties up loose ends, and creates a strong sense of connection.

It's especially valuable if the conversation included any favors that were asked, or commitments that were made—because it helps you remember them, and gives you a great place to start the next conversation.

9. *Limit your use of absolutes.* The primary goal of active listening, as you know, is to make people feel understood, and thereby validated—but people almost never feel understood if you not only have a different perspective, but are overbearing about it, by using words referred to as absolutes, such as *"never," "always,"* or *"everything."*

Many people don't realize that they're coming on too strong, though, when they make the mistake of stating their difference by using all-encompassing absolutes.

For many people, that's a very frequent habit.

However, these words—used without modifiers, and devoid of nuance—can obliterate somebody's feeling of being understood.

They're such hot-button adjectives that they're just fodder for a fight.

It's a fight you'll almost never win, because absolutes—especially when applied to human behavior, or personality—are rarely true.

That's part of the reason they almost never achieve their presumed effect, which is to make a strong statement. Saying something like, "You never compliment me," is far less likely to prompt a compliment than it is a defensive truism, such as: "Never? That's ridiculous!" (Even if the last compliment was a year ago.)

Even if it *was* never, *you* might remember that, but they probably don't—and won't believe you. You end up arguing context.

Absolutes are the ultimate exaggeration, and almost every time you exaggerate, you lose credibility. That's reasonable, because exaggeration is simply a form of lying, even though some people don't seem to realize that.

If you want to keep people from nitpicking, and attacking your language instead of your essential idea, avoid absolutes almost entirely. Even when you make reasonable generalities, it's wise to pepper your language with limiting modifiers, including: *rarely, usually, sometimes, occasionally, often, frequently, from time to time, almost, practically, commonly, probably, almost few, many, nearly, hardly, generally, typically, rather, as a rule, allegedly, apparently,* and *seemingly.*

Some people call these weasel words, but they're commonly used in legal proceedings simply because they preserve *accuracy.* You'll note that this book is rich with modifiers, because that helps keep readers focused on the message instead of its delivery system. It honors reason.

Sometimes you can even make your point *most* effectively by using reverse exaggeration. For example, if someone was late to work every day last week, and is aware that you know it, you might want to say, "You were late several times last week." That sends two messages: (1) you're being generous in your interpretation, and (2) even several times is too many. Compare that to: "You're *always* late."

If your goal in a conversation is just to vent, go ahead and make irrational, confrontational statements, studded with absolutes. If you want to achieve your goal of effective communication, stick with the truth, leavened with a little generosity.

An even *better* version of the prior example is: "I noticed you were late a few times last week, which is really unusual for you. Is anything going on that I could give you a hand with?"

Using modifiers can seem awkward at first, but you'll be surprised at how natural it can become. The immediate payoff will be
a notable lack of disagreements that go offtrack simply because of
sloppy, self-serving language.

10. Don't use debating tactics. This is another poison pill for
active listening. If you use manipulative *tricks* to indicate your
perspective, or to steer the direction of the conversation, people
will know that you don't really want to hear what they have
to say.

Most people will consider your crude disdain for logic and reason to be an insult to their intelligence.

Unfortunately, many news programs now employ a debate-style
format, so the use of debating tactics in casual conversation, and
even in business, seems more common than ever.

Among the most common are:

- **Name-calling.**
- **Putting words in people's mouths.**
- **Avoiding questions by changing the subject.**
- **Scapegoating.**
- **Labeling, instead of defining.**
- **Playing on fears and prejudices.**
- **Misrepresenting someone's position.**
- **Using intimidation and insults.**
- **Employing insinuation and innuendo.**
- **Calling facts opinions, and calling opinions facts.**
- **Being sarcastic, mocking, or dismissive.**

The list goes on—up to almost one hundred offenses, in some
compilations of the dirty tricks of communication—but the whole
repertoire can be wiped out with a single commandment: be true to
the Code of Trust.

If you suspend your ego, remain nonjudgmental, validate people
and their ideas, honor reason, and act generously, you'll not only
avoid these treacherous tools, but never *need* them.

No one has ever come to a greater understanding of another person through manipulation or bullying.

11. Don't apologize by accusing. When you hurt someone, or even when someone just *thinks* you that hurt them, it's hard *not* to be defensive, and deny blame. Leaders rise above that.

Leaders say one of the first things—and most powerful things— your parents ever taught you. They say, "I'm sorry."

In an English language of over a million words, there's a reason only three are colloquially designated as magic: *sorry, please,* and *thanks.*

As you've seen by now, those three words—and the values they convey—embody the very essence of trust building: it's all about them.

What *follows* "I'm sorry" is just as important.

If the first word after "I'm sorry" is "but," you've blown it.

"But" is inevitably followed by excuses, or denials—often ones that put the blame back on the accuser: "I'm sorry I yelled at you, but when you do x-y-z, it makes me mad." In short: the *accuser* is the villain—most often, in a situation in which they are no more the villain than you.

As a rule, the only prize for winning the Blame Game is being crowned Most Insecure Player.

It's not only futile, but fuels the fires of retribution. Therefore, if your apology starts with a *but,* you're the butt.

I know it's hard to apologize and then keep your mouth shut. But it creates a golden moment for connection to occur.

Most people have a deep-seated feeling that if they don't defend themselves, they'll decline in the eyes of others. The opposite happens.

When you proactively accept the blame and take the pain, your stature grows in the eyes of others, and people trust you more than ever—whether you really *deserve* the blame, or not.

They're far more likely at that point to do what you'd hoped for when you dropped the "but bomb" on them: they'll accept some of the blame themselves, or they'll tell you it's okay.

When you do legitimately owe someone an apology, it's wise, and kind, to make it clear that you know exactly why.

A great way to help somebody to unconditionally accept your apology is to put yourself in their position, and tell them *why* you think your actions hurt them. That validates their feeling, without necessarily endorsing it.

If your presumption about the cause of their pain is wrong, they'll usually correct you in a conciliatory way, and you'll gain the priceless insight that only reality offers. Sometimes that insight will be the best-case scenario: the hurt they felt wasn't as bad as you feared.

It often makes abundant sense to apologize for something you didn't even do, particularly if it's very trivial. Does that make you the loser? Or does it make you the leader, who just rose above a petty grievance, and took another step toward his or her ultimate goal?

That's the kind of leadership that alleviates the pain of the people around you—at no cost to you whatsoever. Why wouldn't a leader be *anxious* for those opportunities to occur?

However, if the accusation is not only totally inaccurate, but something you can't reasonably accept, you'll need to set the record straight, without adding to the conflict. That's more difficult, but there's a good system for doing it.

First, keep the conversation focused on the other person's feelings by saying, "I'm sorry you feel that way. I understand. I'd feel the same." Pause for a moment, and let that mollifying phrase warm the atmosphere.

Then offer your excuse or your denial *purely as information*. To act at the level of a true leader, frame it around them, as in: *It's all about them*. Ask for their thoughts and opinions about how they would have acted in a similar situation. Don't ask defensively, but as a student of human behavior. This will inspire them to *want* to listen to what you're telling them.

Pause again—applying the power of silence—as they decide if it's an *acceptable* excuse, or denial. Why not? They'll decide on their

own anyway—and when their acceptance comes of their own voli-
tion, they'll embrace it.

Long after the incident, they'll remember how well you handled
it when you were falsely accused.

If somebody consistently clings to conflicts, though, and insists
on winning minor battles, or finding a scapegoat—instead of staying focused on their own ultimate goal—you'll at least learn enough
about them to limit the linkage of your missions.

Because good apologies are relatively rare, they often bring
people to no conflict at all, just by clearing the air.

12. Put away your damn cell phone. I learned this one from Agent
Youngblood. Here's how:

He made a solid connection with Dr. Rhee, and they started having lunch at the same cheap restaurant every Tuesday.

At this point, Youngblood was obsessed with the relationship.
Rhee's desire to return to North Korea had changed everything.

Dr. Rhee was no longer just a potential source. He was, in effect, a potential defector to an avowed enemy of America, and he
had enough intellectual property in just the left side of his frontal
lobe to shift the international political climate.

But Youngblood, getting smarter by the day, didn't allow the shift
in context to ruin the relationship.

Oddly, they bonded over the L.A. Clippers. They both loved star
power forward Blake Griffin.

One day, while Youngblood was glancing at his phone on the
tablecloth, he asked Dr. Rhee what he liked least about America—
probing for the underlying reasons for his desire for repatriation.

"Americans seem quite friendly," he said, "but it seems an im-
possibility for them to put away their damn cell phones."

Youngblood picked up his phone, cradled it in his palm, and
hoisted it in front of him. "Blake from deep!" he announced, and
arched a long, perfectly back-spinning shot (according to *Youngblood*) at an open trashcan, that landed softly and silently. "Nut-
hin' but trash!" Youngblood crowed.

He later retrieved it, of course, because it had sensitive information—but the point was made.

Rhee gave him a high five—and started to open up unreservedly, for the first time.

After Youngblood mentioned this, I asked a few of my most trusted sources if the same cell-phone thing bothered them. All but one said yes. They were accustomed to people doing it, but when it occurred within the context of them making a sacrifice for their country, it made them feel marginalized.

One of the sad ironies of the technological revolution is that the communication devices that were created to expand personal connections are now often contracting them.

Most people yearn for connection, but the solution to isolation is not to have a list of virtual friends, whose communications are usually limited by the length of a tweet, the expressiveness of a string of abbreviations and emoticons, or a selfie that's programmed to self-destruct.

You just can't connect without keeping it real, and that includes really *being with* someone, without engaging in what childhood psychologists call parallel play, in which toddlers play next to one another, with different toys, and minimal interaction.

Dr. Rhee Answers the Question

I'd briefed Youngblood extensively on the power of asking and active listening—the same lessons I've just described to you—and he'd become an expert at divining the message behind the message, and excavating the hidden truths that lie within people.

Up until the cell-phone shot—a brilliant, street-theater show of respect—Rhee had insisted that he wanted to go back home as a matter of geopolitical principle.

His concept made sense—on a grand, historic level. But Youngblood didn't buy the story, and neither did I.

It all boiled down to a simple matter of calculating a risk/reward ratio—and the math in this one was being calculated ass-backwards: *by a mathematician.*

Until the turning point, it had been inadvisable for Young-blood to poke holes in the fabric of Dr. Rhee's story, because it would risk offending him, and ending the relationship forever.

But this was the time to try.

What Youngblood learned that afternoon was—as typically happens—scarier than the surface story.

With a sigh, Dr. Rhee said, "Here is why I must return. My parents were confined to house arrest shortly before I left, for a very petty offense, by a very petty local party official. That became my primary motivation to seek freedom. I remained one of the privileged, but my parents' loss made the privileges hateful to me."

Rhee said that if he sought voluntary repatriation, the government might relax the sanction against his parents—if, of course, their punishment hadn't been ratcheted up to imprisonment, or worse.

Rhee's true motivation—one far deeper than philosophy—was personal in the most compelling sense: it was a matter of family— the strongest of all contexts.

"I have come to trust you enough," Dr. Rhee said, "to ask if you could at least ascertain their . . . status."

"I don't see how. We have no diplomatic relations."

Rhee acted as if he hadn't heard. "And if they are still being, shall we say . . . harassed . . . perhaps you can help me return."

"That I cannot do."

When Youngblood told me about the encounter, I gave him what you may now regard as obvious advice. "Stay friends," I said. "Keep his trust. Ask the questions that will help him see that his plan is flawed, and very dangerous. And let him know you *understand how he feels.*"

"Right. But now he's more than just a potential source of HUMINT."

"Yeah, it's too bad. He's a good man."

"Better than me," Youngblood said.

The young agent had learned one of the bitterest, but redeeming, lessons of life: humility is reality. That alone would make him a better agent—from that day forth. "When I see Dr. Rhee now," Youngblood said. "it's just kind of sad. He acts like he doesn't hear me."

"Yeah, but keep smiling. He needs that."

"How will I know if I ever get through?"

"He'll smile back."

Communication Technique #3
Decode Nonverbal Communication

Here is the Top Secret FBI Method for connecting with somebody.

Make them smile.

A genuine smile is the gold standard of connection.

It sits at the top of the pyramid of successful nonverbal communication—the third method for completing a connection of trust.

Projecting your message in a physically positive way can occasionally be as important as having a positive message. If your message is positive but your physical delivery is negative, it creates an incongruity that kills trust.

I learned to decipher nonverbal communication from one of its masters, my former FBI colleague Joe Navarro, who helped define body language as a science, and has written about it extensively.

One of the first things I learned from Joe is that nonverbal communication is the sharpest skill when you don't overthink it, but stand back and let its revelations flow into you.

To master it, I put myself back into the mind-set I adopted as a Marine Series Commander at Parris Island. Back then, I'd walk into the barracks and see a bunch of recruits sitting on their lockers, shining their boots or whatever, and through an esoteric blend of intuition and sensory input—tapping into my Spiderman Senses, if you will—I'd get a visceral hit of what was going on. If it didn't feel right, I'd go to the in-barracks office of somebody like Sergeant Howell and say something like, "I don't know what the hell your guys are up to, but knock it off. And he'd say: 'How did you know, Lieutenant?' and I'd say, "My Spidey senses are tingling."

To break it down to hard-core basics: look for smiles, or look for frowns. Those are the classic signs of comfort, and discomfort: the two most primal moods that govern connection.

Each mood has its own set of tells.

The essential signals of comfort include:
- Positive facial expressions.
- Body posture that is slightly angled, rather than full facing, or evasive.
- A significant display of what behavioral scientists call the ventral surfaces: the most vulnerable parts of the body, including the abdomen, chest, shins, palms, groin, shins, and soles.
- Display, in particular, of the abdominal cavity, housing the major organs, which can be critically injured during a physical attack.

The essential signals of discomfort include:
- Negative facial expressions.
- Body postures that are aimed directly at you, or completely away from you.
- Actions that block or protect the ventral surfaces, such as crossing your arms, or legs.

Here are some signals you've seen many times. In the future, try to incorporate awareness of them into your attempts to connect.

Common Specific Displays of Comfort
- Smiling.
- Raising your eyebrows.
- Standing closely, without crowding.
- Tilting your head to one side.
- Standing at a 45-degree angle.
- Touching your hair or face calmly and gently.

- Moving in a graceful, relaxed way.
- Letting your hand linger slightly when you touch someone.
- Holding eye contact without staring.
- Narrowing your eyes slightly when focusing on someone's words.
- Putting one hand on your hip.
- Leaning back while sitting, then leaning forward to show interest.
- Keeping your shoulders, neck, and jaw loose and relaxed.
- Using a low or husky tone of voice, or speaking softly.
- Displaying animated expressions, including surprise.
- Talking at a relatively slow pace.
- Keeping your elbows slightly away from your body.
- Standing straight.
- Keeping you legs and arms more often apart than together.
- Nodding your head, as if in agreement or understanding.

Common Specific Displays of Discomfort

- Frowning, biting your lip, or clenching your teeth.
- Compressing or clenching your eyebrows, lips, forehead, or hands.
- Tensing your shoulders, neck, or jaw.
- Jutting your jaw out.
- Folding your arms tightly across your chest, or crossing your legs.
- Turning away 90 degrees; or completely; or facing head-on.
- Moving in a jerky, stiff, or sudden manner.
- Keeping your palms down, or otherwise unexposed.
- Putting both hands on your hips.
- Positioning yourself so close to someone that they pull back.
- Narrowing your eyes very tightly.
- Staring, avoiding eye contact, or rolling your eyes.
- Tilting your head down at someone, and looking down your nose.
- Looking somebody up and down.

- Holding your chin up at an exaggerated angle.
- Raising your upper lip while your lower remains in place.
- Speaking loudly, very quickly, or in very measured, clipped tones.
- Shaking your head, as if in disagreement or disbelief.

These mannerisms tend to come in clusters that combine facial expressions, postures, and actions. Most behaviorists develop their greatest skills in decoding one particular element of the cluster, such as facial expressions.

Facial expressions have always been my forte—probably because I'm so focused on what people are saying. For me, and many others, facial expressions are the most revealing. I'm always looking at lips, head angle, and eyebrows. I find them to be especially valuable for spotting inconsistencies between what people are saying and what they're probably really thinking.

If I can get someone to smile—even if it's a sad or ironic smile—I usually believe that they're being open and honest, and are experiencing a sense of rapport with me.

When I walk into a room of people, I'm invariably drawn to the group where most of the people are smiling. They're usually the most eager to talk, and to accept a new person into the group. When I'm in that group, I usually try to invite others into it, and get them to smile, too.

Similarly to other elements of connection, it's very important to *individualize* your perception of these nonverbal communicators, because some people have unique expressions, postures, actions, and tones—and can be easily misunderstood.

Because of this, it's very helpful to determine the baseline of someone's nonverbal style, when they're reacting in a neutral way. Then you can more accurately note how they change when different topics are introduced.

For example, in some of my training sessions, I show a revealing video I happened to make when my son was in first grade, and was trying to hide a problem he had. I'd heard that he wasn't getting along with a boy on the school bus, and I wanted to know if it was a real problem.

I started by asking him neutral questions, then questions about things he liked, such as *Star Wars,* or playing with blocks. He showed baseline physical characteristics to the neutral questions, and positive ones to the topic of *Star Wars.*

Then I said, "So, Kevin, tell me about your bus ride." All of a sudden his tempo and tone went from sprightly and animated to turgid and monotone. His verbal communication stayed positive, but his nonverbal communication told me that here was a serious problem I needed to solve.

If I'd asked about the bus first—as we often do when we're concerned—I might have been misled.

As you've probably noticed in crime dramas, polygraph examiners use this same technique. They ask some neutral questions first— like, Where do you live?—*then* they ask where the body's buried.

One of the nonverbal communication techniques that's in vogue these days is to create rapport with a technique called "matching and mirroring": using the same basic body language of the person you're talking to. I think it's too manipulative, because it's not grounded in truth. You need to be *you*—and, ideally, the *best* you: the one who puts others first, and offers them nonjudgmental validation.

It's not wise to fake *any* positive nonverbal technique, because it's too easy to look phony.

Fake smiles are so obvious that photographers usually need to tell people to say "*cheese*" to get rid of them. When you smile, make sure you're smiling on the inside.

If your *message* is positive, you won't need to fake. Focus on that.

Try to eliminate your negative nonverbals that are simply a matter of habit, such as folding your arms, or furrowing your brow.

In the final analysis, no one ever forged a lasting relationship of trust that's based on tricks. That's why this chapter began by showing you that the Code of Trust is also the Code of Communication.

The three techniques of connection just let other people know that your really *do* deserve their trust.

That's *very* important, though, because sometimes trustworthy people do sabotage the gift they're offering by putting it in the wrong package.

When I first met Agent Youngblood, he did that. But he learned not to. He kept asking me the right questions, and really listened.

In a world where connections can be so hard to make, and easy to break, one simple formula is often all it takes to set the stage for a happy ending.

The Happy Ending

The next time that Youngblood met with Dr. Rhee, the engineer was already sitting at their favorite table, with what Youngblood told me was the saddest smile he'd ever seen.

When Youngblood saw it, his Spidey Senses told him that the crisis of possible repatriation was over. And even so, it still made him sad.

"What is it?" he asked Youngblood.

"I cannot go home," Rhee said. "The variables it would create are endless, and the preponderance of them end in situations far worse than the status quo. For everyone. I believe I was deluding myself."

Youngblood touched his friend's shoulder. "You're very wise," he said, "and I'm very sorry."

"I am intelligent. But I am not wise."

"But you reached the right decision."

"It was because of you," said Dr. Rhee. He reached over, and put his hand on Youngblood's.

Youngblood didn't know what to say, so he said nothing, which in certain situations is the only right thing there is to say.

They ate lunch in almost complete silence. It was the comfortable silence of trust.

Seven months later: they met again, and when Dr. Rhee saw Youngblood's beaming face, he knew his friend must surely have very good news.

Youngblood had reached out to a college friend who worked in the State Department. That person tapped a back-channel relationship with an academic who had connections to North Korea. Dr. Rhee's parents had been free from house arrest for more than a year. They were safe, untroubled, and had learned enough about their son's current activities to be very proud of him, and even happy that he was not with them.

This very quiet, anonymous diplomacy was of no value whatsoever to Youngblood's career.

He asked me to not speak about it with him again, and to allow his own identity to remain anonymous in any discussions I ever had about it.

Putting other people first does not always result in moving you closer to your own ultimate goal.

Sometimes—with luck, and partnership with the right person—it results in something far more precious.

That something, or somewhere, lies beyond even the reach of the Fourth Step to Trust, in a part of the human heart that some might consider imaginary, but the wisest among us consider home. It is the place where trust abounds, dreams almost too fine to dream become real, colleagues become friends, and friends stay friends forever.

It is a place I hope you find.

If you do, one of my dreams will be real.

PART III

WIELDING THE POWER OF TRUST

TRUST IN THE DIGITAL AGE

The Power of Trust in the Real World

THE REAL WORLD IS NOW often a virtual world—a labyrinth of electronic communication that is frequently far more treacherous to navigate than the world of direct, personal contact.

The relatively new phenomenon of widespread depersonalization is a prime driver of our society's lack of trust in corporate America, government, the media, and even social relationships.

Political administrations, companies, careers, friendships, marriages, and families—all implicitly dependent upon trust—are now routinely undermined, and often obliterated, by mistakes made in the complex and often faulty mechanisms of the e-world.

These e-disasters occur with almost equal regularity among people who represent a wide variety of contexts.

They include:

- Younger people, who sometimes understand electronic devices better than human behavior, and are vulnerable to making people errors without the benefit of immediate feedback, no matter how sensitive they try to be.

- Older people, whose people skills often outstrip their tech skills. They get in trouble by underestimating the power of digital interaction, or by ignoring it altogether.
- Men and women? Let's just say (as per chapter three), that it's not about the nail. Or is it? This is an enduring gulf that widens in the relatively more sterile, non-tactile environs of e-communication.
- Task-Oriented types, who are sometimes too abrupt in their digital communications, and offend people without knowing it happened.
- People-Oriented types, who are equal-opportunity offenders, by dint of being *overly* personal, at the expense of the issue at hand. These people also sometimes get in trouble for their occasionally careless posts in social media.

Danger lies in every direction: primarily because contact in the digital era—minus in-person, real-time feedback, with the nuance of actual conversation—magnifies the differences that lie between us.

There has never before been a world like this. The power of digital media, in and of itself, can literally offer someone a new persona. Anyone can almost instantly rise to the status of a veritable celebrity, or an opinion maker—and fall just as fast. People tweet their daily activity as if it were breaking news, and establish a presence in the media that, in volume, is sometimes equal to the press coverage of movie stars.

We're also able to disseminate our ideas and opinions to such vast audiences that some of us become as influential as politicians or pundits—and create similar firestorms of reaction and overreaction.

This is almost certainly a version of the real world that will endure, though, because it's natural for people, in an increasingly impersonal, anonymous world, to revel in this spotlight—even if they shine the light themselves, without being able to fully control its consequences, or even escape the attention when they try.

Bona-fide celebrities have always called fame a double-edged sword, and not out of false modesty. Celebrity status confers the difficult demand of upholding the standards that created the fame in the first place: hard work, talent, intelligence, good looks, and charisma.

Now these same demands can fall upon anyone, even if their only fame lies within their own family, company, or sphere of friends.

Most people, even when they're just trying to be positive about themselves, have a hard time living up to the lofty self-portraits that they present in social media, and when they fail, even their strongest supporters can pile on. At this strange time in world history, we all face a phenomenon that's been endured eternally by genuine celebrities: being hoisted up, only to be battered down.

Our society enjoys that spectacle, because it's human nature to hunger for the drama of rise and fall—and often as not, this hunger creates a downfall where none is deserved at all.

In addition to the ability of digital communication to endow people with impossible expectations, it spreads these expectations outward in so many concentric, cross-pollinating circles that their proliferation becomes exponential. At that point, living up to your reputation can be impossible.

It's now equally impossible to escape your foibles, and get a do-over. The secret video you shared with one friend today can go viral on YouTube tomorrow, and the irate email you sent two years ago can become *your very identity* in an influential business blog.

In Greek mythology, Daedalus—the master craftsman who created a complex labyrinth to keep his king safe from the Minotaur—cautioned his son, Icarus, to refrain from flying too close to the sun on wings that Daedalus crafted with wax. The fall of Icarus—due to a combination of his own hubris and the natural limitations of imperfect engineering—has remained a cautionary tale for thousands of years, due to one central reason: *We never learn.* Each generation holds not only itself, but also its technological advances, in such high regard that some of their technology's destructive elements—when paired with human nature—go unrecognized, and become lethal. It's a short hop from nuclear power to nuclear destruction, and from expanded communication to utter humiliation.

When your personal communications do appear in a highly public venue, don't expect them to be in context, accurately portrayed, intelligently critiqued—or ephemeral.

The e-era ushered in a threat that in the pre-digital days was just a bluff inflicted upon young, gullible students: the specter of a "permanent record." Now there really is one.

One nasty remark, committed to the permanent record of digital communication, can haunt you forever, and one opinion you no longer even hold can be a yoke around your neck. This was previously the bane of mostly just politicians, but the blogosphere has made *all* of us politicians.

That's why you need to confine as much of your electronic self-portrayal as you can to the principles of the Code of Trust. And know this: every word you write, even when you don't mention yourself, is a self-portrayal.

You can not only avoid disaster—but also elevate your reputation enormously—by expressing yourself electronically with the principles of the Code: (1) humility, (2) nonjudgmentalism, (3) validation, (4) reason, and (5) generosity.

Thus, the Code reconstructs itself once again, into a Code of Digital Conduct.

So let's start with the first principle—humility, or suspending your ego—and flash at e-speed toward the end.

The Code of Digital Conduct

Digital Principle #1: Suspend Your Ego.

Being humble in digital forums will not only demonstrate your greatness (Zen again—it never ends!), but will also add about twenty points to your IQ.

Writing, even in the truncated text form, brings out self-consciousness as surely as the sun brings out shadows—and self-consciousness inevitably dumbs us down. Writing is far less natural than speaking, and brings out the feared Red Pencil of our inner English teacher. When we write—almost helplessly over-aware of how we look and sound—it can become practically impossible to refrain from, to put it mildly, showing our best side. Less mildly: We tend to make ourselves the subject of every sentence, bask in our own attention, preen, and pontificate—all of which, at the time, seems as natural as smiling for a photo. But in doing so, we skew reality, oversimplify, shade the truth, shun self-deprecation, and leave little space for the one important subject that all readers really want to hear about: themselves.

If you ever happen to write a book, you'll find that when you mention it to people, many of them will tell you that *they've* got a book *they'd* like to write, and the hero of their book is: guess who? (One clue: it's not you.)

If you want to write a book that readers will actually read, make it about *the readers*. Know exactly who your audience is, address them directly, talk about their problems and how to solve them, use your highest intuitive powers to divine how they feel about the subjects you address, rely upon archetypal concepts and character traits, and strain your sense of empathy to the breaking point.

To further expand your audience, use a persona to reflect their journey through life that's flawed, comical, struggling and foolish: named *you*.

One way to practice this principle is to write emails, texts, tweets, and posts that don't include the word "*I*." Good luck. It's hard. But once you've mastered that simple form, people will tell you that you're a great communicator.

When you do discuss yourself, build yourself up by putting yourself down. Don't worry—the reader won't take your self-deprecation at face value. As a rule, that mistake is made only by the writer.

The more foolish you present yourself, the wiser you'll look.

These, of course, are also the reasons that most people *don't* write books.

Digital Principle #2: Be Nonjudgmental.

When you demonstrate acceptance of other people, you're hard to attack. People may disagree with you, but the difference between disagreement and attack is the difference between democracy and dictatorship. Accepting the views of those who disagree with you makes both people equal members of a forum—and equality, by its very nature, is the most fertile ground for accord. That concept was encapsulated by the motto of the French Revolution, which created Europe's first democracy: "Liberty, Equality, Fraternity."

The single most important aspect of accepting people without judgment is, as I've said: Don't argue context. That's the fast path to conflict, because you're basically saying, "What you *are*—personally!—is wrong, and if you'd just *be more like me*, you'd see that I'm right."

A woman who works on my floor at HQ was recently in an e-squabble with a guy in her department. It was memorialized by a mounting string of emails in which he accused her of betraying his trust, and jeopardizing his career, by telling somebody a secret he'd told her.

She came to me for advice, and offered powerful evidence that it hadn't been her who'd blabbed. She'd shown the same evidence to the guy, but he'd discounted it, and was fixated on the harm the secret could cause.

Near the end of the thread, his malice peaked to the point of his questioning whether she was even fit to be an agent.

I knew that he was insecure, and sometimes overreacted to perceived grievances, but this situation was strange even by his standards. The secret was trivial, and couldn't possibly hurt someone's career, or even be a realistic source of embarrassment.

When she saw that she couldn't conclusively prove she was innocent, she tried to convince him of the same impression that I had: The secret was insignificant, and his real problem was worrying when he didn't need to. Both of which were true, extremely relevant to the woman and to me—and completely irrelevant to him.

His context was: *I'm hurt, and it's your fault*—and nothing was going to change that.

I asked her what her goal with this guy was, and she said it was just to be a friendly coworker. She was a serious careerist, and her ultimate goal was to have the kind of healthy relationships within the Bureau that would keep her work process rational, and career path open.

I gave advice to her I've already given to you: don't become the collateral damage in another person's insecurities.

I told her: Try telling him what a *great agent* he is: *sincerely,* and with specific details. If nothing else, I said, it would be a great opportunity for building her muscle-memory skills at recognizing the greatness in others.

I cautioned her to make it crystal clear that his concerns were entirely understandable, and that she was sorry this happened.

She did.

He emailed her back almost instantly, saying, in effect: "No problem! I know you didn't mean any harm, and I'm sorry I overreacted. Thanks for the compliments, and let's have lunch."

It never came up again.

A lot of people might think: She gave him *ammunition!* She virtually *admitted* that she'd done it!

I don't see it that way. He already had the ammunition: his context of what had happened. All she gave him was a reason not to fire it.

Unless your back is against the wall in a court issue, or some other legally governed action, don't hang on to your utter innocence in every dispute. As often as not, you just can't resolve a problem by changing people into better versions of themselves. Nor can you *talk* them out of how they feel. And if you can't talk them out of it, you certainly can't email them out of it.

I know that letting people go off on their own petty, little witch-hunts can be difficult—especially for us Type-A hard chargers—but if you're truly ambitious, you'll accept people as they are, work within their context, keep your eye on the big picture, and go for your ultimate goal.

Especially when the whole thing is in writing!

Do you really want some supervisor, jury, family member, or friend to some day read what you've written, and try to sort fact from fiction? What if they're having a bad day, or are too busy to sort it out?

And even if they're not, do you still want to risk your reputation, and possibly fate, with a permanent record of a battle of wills?

Leaders have bigger fish to fry: Aligning their goals with the goals of others, and putting their goals ahead of their day-to-day moods. That's why they *are* leaders.

Digital Principle #3: Validate Others.

Validating somebody, by simply understanding them, requires empathy—but that emotional trait can be hard to convey in print.

The first and most immediately visible step to validating some-body in an e-communication is to respect the limitations of their time, and be brief. They'll notice that in one second, because noth-ing is more obvious than length.

If your message is a letter to your grandmother, you *want* it to look long—to show your consideration—but in all business com-munications, and even most social ones, it's much more considerate to be brief.

Brevity, in the age of information overload, is a gift.

But brevity is also the curse of modern communication, because so much nuance is lost, so shoot for *brevity with clarity*.

Edit every message you send, and cut the wasted words.

Be particularly careful not to add needless details if you're try-ing to justify or explain your actions. People usually do that just to make *themselves* feel safer. In effect, they're self-medicating with words—on somebody else's time. Ideally, every sentence should be about them, not you.

One of the modern masters of digital communication is my friend and colleague Chris Hadnagy, a social engineer, security consultant, and bestselling author, who has helped me to understand the art of writing compelling emails.

He's also enlisted my help in enabling companies to decipher phishing scams, because inspiring trust is the central goal of a phishing expedition.

He and I recently gave a seminar to a major corporation on phishing, and he used the following sample of a successful phishing scam, which references a completely bogus event:

"Dear (recipient's first name). As you know, the next board meeting is coming up soon. We have placed an agenda with some new items for discussion on a secure server. Please log in to the portal by going to the link below, and entering your (Company Name) credentials." It was signed, "College Board of Directors."

It used one of the most potent manipulative tools—curiosity—and it didn't make any specific commands, which are often seen as red flags. It also implied safety, with the reference to the "secure server."

The email achieved an excellent 35 percent log-in rate.

Then Chris and I added three elements. We inserted a subject line—"Your Updated Agenda"—which made it specifically about the recipients. In the sentence about "new items," we added "specific to you"—reinforcing the focus on them. Then we told them to log in only if they currently planned to attend—empowering them with choice.

Success rate: 100 percent.

Object lesson: Beware of manipulators who know at least *some* of the principles that I've included in the Code of Trust. They are powerful concepts, and it's even possible that some scammers will use the information in this book against you. That's just life in the new real world.

Bottom line: When you're trying to decode a suspicious-looking email, don't settle for just the right words: Look for the actions behind them. If you can't connect the email to a valid entity in your life, don't respond to it.

On the flip side: To write effectively, repurpose the phishing tactics I just showed you, and employ them in an honorable pursuit. Make your emails and other messages *all about them*. Be *humble*. *Validate* people, and empower them with choice. Be rational, and tell people exactly who you are and what you want. Be generous: offer them something, even if it's just a compliment, or the gift of brevity.

Even so, as I've said before, trust is a moving target, and we never fully learn all of its lessons. Let me tell you about a scam that even I recently fell for. I got a Facebook notification from my daughter on my iPad. I clicked on it—immediately. And immediately saw that I'd been scammed. I spent the next half hour changing every password I have.

Okay, I *know*, I'm Mr. FBI Superspy—*and they had me at "daughter."* Manipulators come at you through the people and groups that you trust and love. (So to scam me, and other dads, don't bother with humility, validation, or generosity. Just email: "Daddy, will you please transfer your entire 401 (k) to my new account in the Caymans this afternoon? It's *important*!")

On the flip side again, to inspire genuine trust in an email, ask about someone's family. You'll elicit the same sense of trust, and biochemical brain reward, that scammers do, but will be using your powers in the service of empathy and consideration.

Validation is often even more important in purely social communication, because that venue often revolves around emotions, which are much harder to express in writing than in person.

For example, a friend of mine was recently trying to break up with his girlfriend by email, *Ding! Ding! Ding!* (Sorry for the interruption: those words triggered a program I downloaded from DangerousBehavior.com), and he was getting *nowhere*, because all of her replies were needy, bewildered pleas for him to reconsider.

He came to me, and said that the problem was that he was "a horrible communicator."

"Own that," I told him. "Just admit that you've caused a lot of stress in her life by being such a bad communicator, and say nice things that validate not only her communication skills, but her worth as a great person."

Next day: "Rob! She wants to just be friends!"

Code words for *dump him*? Not in this case. Turns out, she'd wanted to break up, too—but had felt attacked—and really *did* want to be friends. When he owned up to his realistic fault, and reminded her that she had absolutely nothing to be insecure about, she was able to let go of the romance without letting go of her self-esteem.

A note of caution: If you employ this method, be *way* more creative than to say, "It's not you, it's me," which now means: It's *you*. Be genuinely validating, and state the specific actions and traits that make *you* responsible for the failure of a relationship.

Validating others has a magical effect: it brings out the best in everybody.

What better message to someone could you ever put in writing?

Digital Principle #4: Honor Reason.

One of the great advantages of digital communication is that it offers us the time and resources to be accurate and honest. Equal to this advantage, of course, is the responsibility.

As I've mentioned, trust collapses without honesty, and honesty rests upon our ability to tell the truth. Most people think that telling the truth is essentially just a moral issue—but it's far more complicated than that.

"*Right and wrong*" are interesting words, because they have two distinct meanings: "moral and immoral," and "correct and incorrect."

It's often harder to be moral than it is correct.

Distinguishing what's moral from what's immoral is often *easier* than sifting fact from fiction, and what's real from what you *hope* is real, but that's something we all need to do.

It's so important that it's not enough to just give it a try. If you just *think* you know the facts—but are wrong—you *can not* tell the truth. It's not logically possible.

Some people believe, "If I *thought* it was true, that's good enough." But that's the kind of immature excuse that we expect to hear from children, along the same lines as, "I didn't *mean* to do that."

One of the better parental responses to that common childhood reasoning is: "You need to mean *not* to do it."

To inspire trust, you have an obligation to know *what's true,* and—even harder—to convey it accurately.

You can't always be certain of what's true, but when you're not, it's still easy to be honest by just stating the uncertainty. That's the purpose of the modifiers that I've previously mentioned, such as: *almost always, usually, often, sometimes, rarely,* and *almost never.* There are thousands of them in this book alone.

Use them freely, and your writing will become markedly more truthful.

The good news: digital communication can actually make it easier to be honest, because when we write something, we usually have the time and information we need to sort out fact, fiction, probability, and mystery—and to convey them properly.

The bad news: everybody *knows* you have the time and resources to get things right.

Some situations do unfold too fast for that to apply, but most of the time we're up against a higher standard of credibility—due mostly to the Net—than has ever before existed.

The best news: The principle of honoring reason will greatly soften that circumstance. If you state things reasonably and rationally, you'll send an implicit message that—even if you make an honest mistake—you are someone who is thoughtful and truthful, and deserve the benefit of the doubt.

The best news *ever:* If you adjust to the new reality of scrutiny, and double-check your main points for accuracy and clarity, you'll soon establish a permanent record of honesty, dependability, and *trustworthiness.* This record will be, very literally, written truth that will follow you throughout life. No prior era offered this lasting, widespread form of endorsement.

The last filter to apply in your expression of the truth is the context of the other person. You can't, in effect, explain anything to anyone in a language they don't know.

A classic example of this would be a person with the glass-half-full outlook sticking solely to that philosophy when speaking to a glass-half-empty person.

Every word you say needs to be tempered by empathy.

A bittersweet parallel to that truth is that empathy for others springs most naturally from similar suffering. Too often, our ability to help people exists in direct relation to how badly we've been hurt. That's sad, but it's not tragic. Tragedy exists when you've been hurt, but are unable—for one reason or another—to mint value from your pain by helping someone else.

Sadness is a quality that can deepen and enrich your acts and attitudes, without destroying you.

Digital Principle #5: Be Generous.

In the digital era, and particularly within the burgeoning realm of social media, it's incumbent upon you to conform to the code of diplomatic, statesmanlike behavior that has previously been expected primarily of just public figures: because we're almost *all* public figures now.

One of the most critical elements of this is to *rise above* attacks upon you in various media. These assaults most commonly occur in comments that appear in social media, email threads, in-house corporate communications, customer reviews of small businesses, and blurbs or articles in online or print media.

Sometimes these are demonstrably false and defamatory, and sometimes they're uncomfortably accurate. Either way, ask yourself: what would a diplomat do?

As a rule, the most statesmanlike of statesmen would reply, in effect: "Thank you, sir—may I have another?"

With that ultra-diplomatic approach, you'll achieve two things:

(1) **By refusing to engage, you will deprive your antagonists of what they were seeking: a chance to get a rise out of you.**

> Some detractors just want to bleed off some of their own, internalized anger, and if they can concoct a dependable, predictable forum for it, they'll keep attacking, and you'll stay on their hit list.
>
> (2) By politely refusing to get caught up in the game, you'll elevate your public presence and amplify your aura of strength and goodwill. People admire those who can take a hit, and shrug it off.

Because I'm someone who represents the Big-Bad Government, and am also an author and consultant, you might assume that I've been involved in many negative exchanges, but I haven't. I generally defuse the attack after their first shot goes downrange, by saying something like, "That's an interesting point of view. Thanks for sharing it, because I've never thought of it quite like that before." Then—poof!—the antagonists waft off into the ether.

We're conditioned by insecurity to want to have the last word in an angry exchange—but that's not what leaders want. They generally want the last word—inevitably a corrosive one that lingers unpleasantly in the listener's ear—to be in the voice of the attacker.

But what if that person is totally anonymous, as happens so often these days? This is an unprecedented phenomenon, due to the Net, that brings out the worst in many people.

Once again, the Code comes to the rescue. It can, in a very realistic way, pierce the veil of anonymity, because it acts upon primal, inalienable human drives, traits, and neurological functions. When you address someone's most basic inner elements, you don't need to know their name to get through to them.

This is especially true of messages delivered to the proverbial better angels of our nature.

When I respond to an anonymous attack in accord with the benign principles of the Code, it not only deprives the attacker of venting vitriol, but—even more powerfully—it gives them what they *really* want: which is *not* simply to be a jerk.

Like virtually every other person on earth, their core desire—

even if it is haunted by frank personality disorder—is to satisfy the universal human need to be accepted, understood, validated, and treated with reason and generosity.

In the near term, those glorious gifts give people the dopamine-driven brain rush that makes them want to see you again. In the long term, it can rescue them from a life of self-perpetuating isolation.

In my own experience, certain anonymous attackers have abandoned not only their animosity, but their anonymity, and established a casual but cordial online relationship with me.

Manipulative people might call that "killing people with kindness," but I don't. I call it treating people with good manners.

Good manners—which were ancient long before the Age of Chivalry—hold magic.

Unfortunately, good manners have taken a hard blow from the depersonalized aspects of the digital era—including the mechanized manners of modern communication, such as automated birthday greetings.

However, it's your choice to approach the current dearth of manners as a problem or as an opportunity.

It's a fact of physics that nature abhors a vacuum—just as it is a law of human behavior that every deficit provides the chance of a reward for those who can fulfill it. Therefore, if you are the one person in the chat room or the email thread with impeccable manners, you'll stand out. If you're the one person who calls someone on their birthday, instead of connecting with a tweet or text, you'll be the one whose consideration is remembered, and rewarded with trust.

As you've noticed, gift giving—in the figurative sense of the phrase—is an integral element of the fourth principle of the Code: Be Generous. Like many figurative phrases, though, it holds its highest power in its most literal sense. People love to get gifts, even if they're just tokens. They especially love it when you can encapsulate or reflect the nature of your relationship with them through the gift.

Therefore, something I try to apply in every gift I give is the element of thoughfulness, because there's a reason why "it's the thought that counts" is a cliché. As a rule—one of many I'll propose in the final chapter, "Trust Training Manual: 15 Drills"—I try to avoid giving gift cards to people. When you give them something that shows your understanding of them—and thus your implicit acceptance—magic happens.

Technology has unquestionably shifted the direction of modern behavior. However, as a wise man once said, the more people change, the more they remain insane—or something to that effect—meaning: we'll never perfect the art of human interaction, no matter how much technical support we get. That grand achievement will remain forever out of reach, because we're innately flawed beings. Even so, we'll never stop striving, because we are *human* beings, and *that's human nature.*

Modern digital technology, used properly, can help close the gap between striving to connect, and achieving it.

But it's just a tool—far less life changing than the invention of the wheel, or the advent of electricity—and it has even more innate flaws and flat-out inabilities than all of humankind's imperfections combined.

In the pursuit of leadership, don't leave the hard work to the robots.

Trust is not a product that can be made by machines.

— 10 —

TRUST IN A TOXIC ENVIRONMENT

Trust creates power. It simply does, whether you want it to or not.

I'm sorry.

Power is a burden. It is a grave responsibility that trust-based leaders do not love, and accept only when it's clear that they can wield the power more positively than anyone else.

Wielding power is, without doubt, the hardest single action of a great leader.

Trusted leaders perceive power differently than do many people, who see it as the old Roman Emperor thumbs-up/thumbs-down exercise of privilege. That archaic expression of power—which is still common—never flowers naturally, grows exponentially, or lasts indefinitely.

Trust-based leaders take no pleasure in their own power because their deepest interest and investment is in other people.

They know that when they do achieve power from their acts of helping others, it will often be an exhausting process, with a primary payoff of only making life better for those around them.

Even so, they never stop trying to help the people they care about—and even those they've never met, but love in the abstract, as human beings—because they know that help is love brought to life.

In return, those who are helped offer their sacred trust, adding one by one to the leader's ever-expanding tribe of trust, and fund of mutually shared resources.

In contrast, people who seek power for power's sake—or to assuage their own fears of inadequacy—rarely achieve it, because their sole focus is upon themselves. People limited by that outlook, as you well know, are never really trusted. Even when these people think they have power, they usually have only its gaudy and hollow illusion: the grandiose pipe dream of control.

In reality, the only thing we can really control is our own context: our view of the world.

However, power-hungry people often deceive themselves into thinking that they truly control those within their sphere—whether their domain is an entire nation, a company, or a family—but their control is rarely more than the cold, soulless reflection of their own fear, cruelly displaced upon those they manipulate.

Manipulative leaders often bask in this fear, confusing it with respect and adoration, and believe that if they're sufficiently manipulative, it will last forever.

It doesn't. The fear that's enforced by manipulation is ephemeral, because it's a toxic feeling—a learned response, never natural—that is absolutely contrary to human nature. It's in us—but it's not us.

Fear—and it's social component: distrust—are among the most common feelings that human beings have, but neither is universal nor endemic. No one was ever born feeling afraid, or distrustful.

Conversely, even as infants, we settled into contentment in the arms of whomever happened to hold us, feeling even before we could think that all embraces are an embodiment of help, caring, affection, and security.

Love, then, lies within the deepest, newborn heart of human life.

Fear can lie near the heart of human life, but never within it— just as cancer cells can invade the human body, but never function as part of it.

Even when fear lies close to the human core, though, courage begins to grow, since courage by definition is a response to fear.

Because fear is wholly unnatural—nothing but a crude reaction to repeated harm and betrayal—those who are purposefully manipulated by fear, year after year, inevitably rebel. Grievances build, courage grows, and people explode, sometimes in vain, but again and again—even at the cost of their comfort, fortune, freedom, and lives—to serve the dream that somehow, someday they will alchemize freedom from fear for those who survive.

At each tyrant's inevitable tipping point—their Waterloo, or Appomattox, or Berlin Wall—fear-driven power falters, then fails, and those who wield it fall.

This is not a dream, nor even idealism, but a constant law of human history, and an utterly predictable formula for the future.

Fear and love remain the only two primal emotions in life—polar opposites, with many faces—and they continually shift and swirl. When fear gets the upper hand, it feels as if it'll forever rule the world. But love always prevails—not necessarily in a single lifetime, but certainly within the eventuality of human experience—for the simplest of reasons: it's what we prefer, because it's part of what we are.

With its arrival comes a natural linkage of missions—with new friends and old, former strangers, and even foes—because the binding force of trust always travels in the wake of love, just as love springs spontaneously from trust.

Trust and love are not just feelings. They are actions that commonly chart, and steer, the course of life.

This is one of the great secrets of trust that hides each day in plain sight.

Even so, it's an enigma that is utterly transparent to all trust-based leaders, who know that the only measure of trust that is true is not how you feel, but what you do.

Fighting Fire with Water

Tough people fight fire with fire.

Wise people fight fire with water.

Shrewd people keep their friends close, and their enemies closer.
Wise people keep their enemies close, and their friends closer.

When you're wise, you don't have to be so tough and shrewd. It's no longer necessary to extinguish one fire after another, or to stay one step ahead of your enemies. Fires in the world of the wise are few and far between, and the number of enemies is negligible.

When this serendipity descends, peace reigns, wisdom is reinforced, trust blooms, and leadership naturally beckons.

If nothing else, living in this state of grace will save you an incalculable amount of time.

Because your time on this earth is your life, this wise, trust-driven approach to human interaction can virtually save your life, one day at a time.

It can vault you into the stratosphere of those who create new value—financially, emotionally, and socially—instead of just managing what existed in the first place.

When you're no longer compelled to fight the innumerable, shape-shifting wars commonly and endlessly waged by the tough and shrewd, you have time to seek a newer world.

You can rise above the grim task of managing the flawed and self-defeating elements of your own financial enterprises, personal psyche, or set of social and family relationships, and float in the heavenly stratosphere that exists far beyond our usual state of earth-bound stress.

One of the most potent affirmative-defense mechanisms built into the the Code of Trust is that it simply will not accommodate your participation in—and perpetuation of—a toxic, destructive environment. It not only enables you—but compels you—to shield yourself from the unhealthy aspects of your environment, or to fix them, or to escape them.

After any one of those three actions, you're free to create a world that reflects the better angels of your nature, populated by positive people who will make you feel rich not just in friendship and support, but—better yet—in expanded opportunities to help those within your circle of trust.

The world you create will fulfill your vision of the best possible reality, and will inevitably reflect your own ultimate goal, temperament, and philosophy.

It will be a world in which sharing your resources with those who trust you becomes a source of satisfaction that is at least equal to the unavoidable burden of doing your absolute best for other people. This satisfaction is arguably your greatest reward for climbing out of the world of conflict and drama.

The courageous new world that the Code offers has abundant room for the creation of wealth, personal pleasure, altruistic endeavors, and nurturance of the people and the earth around us. When human behavior is at its best, all of these wondrous elements function in concert and confluence.

To me, when the Code is functioning at its highest level, it allows you to become a glorious conduit of resources. The more resources that flow in, the more that flow out, creating the opposite of a vicious cycle: a virtuous cycle, in which abundance suddenly seems to be everywhere.

This joyous sharing of resources can flow seamlessly from your initial goals, to your means goals, to your ultimate goal—and beyond.

Tough, shrewd people often doubt that such a world even exists—except in the movies—because they think that the so-called real world is an unforgiving, fickle realm, dominated by the traumatized and hardened survivors who cling to the deep-seated, antisocial urges of self-interest, manipulation, greed, and vanity.

Ask yourself honestly: is that your world—or is that the one that you mostly just see in the movies?

Because you are a person who has read almost all of this book, I have to assume that your world comfortably accommodates a vision of hope and goodwill—even in hard times, and among the toughest and shrewdest of people.

Even so, here's a heartbreaking fact of real life in the real world: trust, for some, is simply out of reach. Some people have been bullied and beaten to such an extent that they've lost sight of how sane and kind that others can be. Asking them to summon a vision of a new world, governed by trust, is like telling a person with impaired eyesight that they could see if only they'd look more carefully. Sometimes this opportunity to find a new world is suspended all the way to the end of the lives of those who yearn for it.

Even so, I love chatting with people who feel like this, because many of them can be reached, with the right approach. I ask them about their ultimate goal, and means goals, and we try to see if what they're doing furthers those goals. More often than not, they take heart, and try harder.

I don't believe in the concept of doom. Where there's life, there's hope.

Even those of us who've been pushed to our limits still have the necessary reserves of will and optimism to rise above the life we see, and seek the world that we know can be.

When people find it—and they usually do, given the resilience of the human heart—it's a world that's largely inhabited by people who are good, deals that are fair, and relationships based on respect and affection.

In that world, trust is the coin of the realm.

Even in the fabled cold, cruel world, most people do their best to be kind and fair, and when they fail, and fall into the behaviors that bring them shame, it's mostly due to desperation. No one's childhood dream was to be a jerk, and even people with hard lives rarely wake up wondering who they can hurt that day, and how badly.

Desperation, though, is common. People can easily become desperate after they lose almost everything they have, after a lifetime of saving. That sad story was a cliché in the Great Recession, and its wake is still upon us, in a world of vanished assets, more work for less money, and more geopolitical turmoil despite terrible sacrifices.

Other people lose those they love—life's most devastating and unavoidable tragedy—and will do almost anything to fill the deep hole of that loss. Sometimes their desperation seduces them into partnering with people who aren't worthy of them, and sometimes it goads them to numb their pain with whatever anesthetic seems to work.

Millions of others live each day with chronic pain, loneliness, disability, or disfigurement, and are tempted each day to shift some of that suffering to those around them.

Countless others are desperate because their minds have become a muddled soup of remembered abuse, or skewed brain chemistry, and they sometimes succumb to a life bereft of action, replaced only by reaction: rarely appropriate.

Cold, cruel worlds do exist.

Most distressing of all, our cold, cruel worlds can start with an outside force, but become so ingrained upon our thoughts and behavior that after time they continue to exist mostly because of us.

I love to inspire people to see new possibilities, and one of my dreams is that I can help you to create a world in which you feel safe, are understood, and can gain the trust of so many people that you never feel truly alone.

That world is not too much to expect.

It's become the earth that I walk, because of the grace and good luck of being surrounded by the best possible people for me, and because I've worked hard to achieve what has become my ultimate goal—my wellspring from which all else flows: the ideal of having healthy, happy relationships with the people around me.

For the vast majority of us—including most of those who have suffered—this is the real real world.

I think that in a free society—devoid, at least in the moment, of natural disasters and unforeseen tragedy—it can be yours for the taking.

You may think—even at this late stage of our virtual relationship—that I'm being naïve. That's reasonable. I didn't accept the philosophy that I'm offering to you after reading just one book about it, and I don't expect you to.

I don't think that this world will enter the core of your being until you've made it become real in your own world, through your own acts.

You might even fail to fully accept it until you see others around you adopt the Code, or an ethic much like it, and succeed with their own global re-creation.

When that happens, each day brings greater peace, calm, influence, and leadership.

Even then, you might have reservations. The source most likely to feed your fears will almost certainly be the flawed behavior of those around you.

I'll try to help you with that in this chapter.

It's about implementing a trust-based system in our individual microcosms of distrust and dysfunction, populated by people who are quite different from you, and resistant to change.

It's absolutely possible that this is the world you're living in now, because it is so utterly common.

This century's financial turmoil and political upheaval—magnified by the attendant stress of global competition and destabilization—brought out the worst in many desperate people. Our current era has marked such a historic drop in trust that entire organizations, governments, and cultures have become poisoned with cynicism and self-involvement.

There is a way out of this spiral of distrust, but it takes courage.

The surest escape route is, most simply: when people behave badly, don't fight fire with fire by throwing their bad behavior back in their faces.

The trust-based leaders who fight fire with water have far greater power over these myriad and multiplying inflammatory situations, which consume the lives of so many people.

This approach takes discipline, but it works. It cools off hotheads, and it raises the bar of good behavior for everyone involved.

If you react to people with the same negative qualities that they display, you're just playing their game. Toxic people feed on the fearful and angry reactions they evoke, and they're generally better at the game of attack/retaliate than emotionally healthy people.

That game is more than just a waste of time. It's a soul-destroying descent into destruction and self-destruction. It's not even a game you'd want to win, because that means you played it—and once you play it, it never ends.

Every person you beat will soon be out to beat you. The only way out of the game is to rise above it.

It's inevitable that you'll meet toxic, desperate people in your career and personal life who poison the environments around them.

You already know some of these people, because the fear-based behaviors that define toxicity are all too common: narcissism, paranoia, ruthlessness, arrogance, obsession with control, bullying, volatility, rigidity, authoritarianism, and passive-aggressive behavior.

It's vitally important to implement the Code of Trust in the face of this barrage of dysfunction, blame, and impossible expectation. Your only unassailable protection from people who seem to like problems is to be true to the Code's ethic, and let common decency and common sense serve as your shield.

The Code is so powerful that it's not only a survival tool for people trapped in toxic environments, but can also be a curative mechanism for their entire microcosm.

Surviving and reversing toxic behavior is a two-step process.

Step One: Put Out the Fire

Your first action is hardest. You need to give toxic people what they need. That's difficult, because these people will almost always try to coerce you into giving them not what they need, but what they want: more drama, with you as a pawn in their play.

They want that because they've lost touch with what they really need: respect and love—delivered with humility, nonjudgmental validation, reason, and generosity.

Those elements of the Code are the universal gifts that allow us to internalize the warm feelings that others have for us. They help us feel good about ourselves, and believe that we can largely control our own destinies.

Most toxic people once sought the simple, primal need for self-esteem and control over their own lives, but were thwarted, usually so early in life that the trauma from that failure devastated them, or entered their psyche so deeply it's stayed ever since.

As a rule, when people grow up with this deficit, it's so overwhelming that it prompts them to launch a life of acting out their needs for approval and self-determination, in one drama after another.

To succeed with these people, you sometimes need to go back to their own square one, and offer them what they've always needed but never gotten.

Even though they may be dreadfully toxic in the ways that they relate to you, the only way to create a sane relationship is to—like it or not—make it all about them. You need to sublimate your ego to theirs, learn their context, speak to them in the language that breaks down barriers, and carefully craft your various encounters with them.

Try to understand what their ultimate goal is, and try to help them reach it. Many people who behave badly have reasonable goals, but have unreasonable and unhealthy methods of trying to attain them. When you show toxic people that you recognize their goal, and have made it one of your own, they have vastly less reason to launch their usual forms of attack.

By this point, I doubt that this sounds complicated to you—but if it does, just think of it as treating people who are hurting with human kindness.

To make these concessions to their bruised egos palatable, try to rid yourself of the insecurities that a dysfunctional person might prey upon. If you refuse to allow them to undermine your own sense of self-worth, you'll be far less likely to take their attacks personally—and then respond inappropriately.

Corollary to the central principle of the Code—It's All About Them—is: It's not about me. That nugget of wisdom comes in handy when people are trying to convince you that they only have one problem in life: you. When you see through that folly, their barbs and jabs will seem more comical than hurtful.

Use that escape from your own distress to make them feel more secure: by showing them the real real world, with your actions as well as your words—which should always be congruent. As you do, you'll understand them better, and they will understand you better. As your mutual understanding increases, so will your tolerance of one another—and, trust me, they'll initially find it just as hard to tolerate you, as you will to tolerate them.

It's also very helpful to simply adhere to good manners, and abide by the universally agreed upon standards of etiquette. A mere "please" or "thank you"—and their multitude of variations—can at least temporarily tame the savage beasts that people can become.

These words are especially effective when lit by the glow of a sincere smile. It can't be a phony smile, which is the kiss of death—but it needn't be. Even when people are brutal, you can usually think of at least one positive thing to say to them. (For example, if you have the misfortune to to someday meet Satan, just say, "You look good in red!" You'll have a friend for eternity—although I guess that's a negative in this case.)

When you adhere to the simple philosophy of repaying bad with good, you'll experience a transcendental ascension, buoyed by the power of the highest ideals of humankind.

Step Two: Rebuild In the Rubble
In the wake of a toxic person's scorched-earth policy, you need to repair the damage that's been done.

An ideal way to do this, which will also help prevent future fires, is to build positive, productive relationships with the people who work directly with the toxic person. This builds the best possible social support system for your own problems, since there is a majesty in joining forces with others who experience the same problem. This act of power also isolates unacceptable behavior, and makes its toxicity more obvious.

When even just one person opts out of a sick game, entire groups often stop fighting fire with fire—and sometimes gradually stop reacting at all.

When toxic people can no longer get the reactions that they're trying to provoke, their tactics frequently become obsolete, and are abandoned. Even before that, their behavior starts to stick out like a sore thumb, and diminishes them even in their own eyes.

That reality check, of course, can hurt their feelings. If you're doing it for that retaliatory reason, though, you're still playing their game, and that will sabotage your opportunity to rebuild your environment.

If you do it for the right reasons—sincere concern for the well-being of the offenders, and those around them—many toxic people will begin to get glimpses of the real real world, and may well be grateful for the wake-up call.

If your environment is limited in scope—such as that of a family, a group of friends, or a small business—it can be relatively easy to heal a group culture.

If you've expanded your world to include an entire division, company, organization, or government entity, it will be harder, but still possible. You'll need to patiently spread the Code of Trust in concentric circles, which will grow ever larger, until finally—with luck and work—they become the reigning philosophy.

In addition to these personal, self-actuated methods of dealing with toxic people in the workplace, you can also implement certain protective mechanisms created by your own company. Most companies now have strict policies in place to deal with emotional abuse. Use them. Don't be a victim. Sometimes this causes so much initial turmoil that people regret initiating their complaints, but in the long run it's almost always worth the risk and effort.

If nothing else, it will be your message to yourself that you deserve respect, and that you refuse to be the collateral damage in another person's insecurities.

There are also periodic training sessions at many companies, in which employees learn what forms of behavior are unacceptable, how they can address them, and what they can do if the problems can't be solved through direct communication.

If your company doesn't have any mechanism to protect its own people, try to help create one.

Despite the laxity of workplace protection in the past, you now exist in a time and place in which these transgressions are no longer considered normal.

After all, this is your life—but it's not yours if you cede the direction of it to people who may not have your best interests at heart. It's only your life if you live it.

The demand for fair treatment is often harder for young people to voice than older people, many of whom have already paid the price of repeated abuse, and don't intend to pay it again.

Your journey through your career will without question expose you to people who do not have your best interests in mind, but if you're proactive, your fate will largely rest in your own hands.

On this often treacherous journey, here are some of the archetypal toxic people that you will meet.

The Bad Guys

Realistically, there are no bad guys—just fearful people who are trapped in their own problems and illusions.

As always, if you judge them—good/bad, right/wrong—you'll just drive them further down the road they're on, and they'll try to hijack you into accompanying them.

Though it may be painful to admit it, you probable do understand these people, because there's at least a small piece of them in all of us.

Here's a lineup of the Six Usual Suspects. Note how virtually all of their problems are fear driven.

The Six Most Common Types of Toxic People
1. Control freaks. Think back upon the wise words of my trust guru, Jesse Thorne, who said that the phrase "control freak" is an oxymoron, because people with this trait are clearly out of control.

They typically try to micromanage, because they never feel safe enough to place even a small part of their fate in the hands of others.

That's a mistake on even just an operational level, because others are going to influence their fate whether they like it or not.

Sometimes the only thing that control freaks accomplish is to rob others of their own creativity and motivation, and drive away people who have a strong sense of independence.

There is an effective method for dealing with them, and you'll soon see that the same general approach is applicable to most of the six most common types of dysfunctional people. I've already summarized that approach: adherence to the principles of the Code.

One of these methods, as I mentioned, is simply to help give these people what they obviously don't have: a sense of self-respect and security, which usually just means—in the simplest terms—helping them to feel as if have enough, and are good enough.

For example, you can't correct the self-defeating behavior of control freaks by depriving them of control. The "water" that extinguishes their fire is the assurance that they do have control. If you give them that, they'll cede control—true to the Zen of trust. This doesn't always work—but also that's the nature of Zen: the only reason it usually works is because sometimes it doesn't. (Unravel that, Grasshopper.)

Many people who are obsessed with control have other obsessive-compulsive urges—all driven by fear—which are expressed by everything from overthinking problems to excessive hand-washing. If you can identify that broad trait in them, it will make it easier for you to see that their problems are not your fault, and will keep you from becoming their collateral damage.

2. Hotheads. This category includes volatile people, hyper-emotional people, and hyperactive people.

Hot-headed behavior is often associated with biochemical imbalance, but can also be caused by excessive, recurring trauma. As a rule, it's reinforced by unavoidably tense environments, including those governed by strict deadlines, intense scrutiny, and the trademark of stress: high-demand, low-control situations.

Biologically, this trait reflects lack of control by the thought-centered frontal lobes, which manage impulse control through the mechanism known as executive function. This control, unfortunately, is ceded to the more primitive areas of the brain, including the part of the reptilian brain that I mentioned in the chapter on the chemistry of trust—your neurological fear center: the amygdala.

People sometimes develop what's colloquially called a hot amygdala from experiencing too much trauma, but it's more commonly the result of imbalanced brain biochemistry. The biochemical causes can now actually be easier to deal with in many people, because several classes of medication, including antidepressants, can successfully ameliorate the problematic imbalances.

This behavior is characterized by people lashing out without even knowing that they're being inappropriate, or working frantically on something that doesn't need to be done. Sometimes it's expressed by a tendency to go off on dramatic tangents.

The common behavioral cure for the hot amygdala—one you can apply yourself—is to just help these people calm down. That's easier said than done, but we've all had to deal with that type of situation many times, and it's not rocket science.

If you do try to help these people feel better, be careful to not become entangled in their endless string of faux crises, or to respond to their outburst with one of your own. That's often what they want you to do—because it seems to justify their behavior—but it's not what they need. They need reassurance: a gentle reality check delivered with logic and empathy.

In many dysfunctional organizations, this kind of overt bad behavior is actually lauded, due to the still-surviving myth that force is more dependable than inspiration.

Even in the face of this institutional enablement, though, it often takes only one courageous person to change a broad culture by insisting upon respect—calmly and compassionately—without sinking to the level of the offender, or taking the bait to join their drama.

Your best behavior in a maelstrom of bad temper is to demonstrate your dignity, show some empathy, cut some slack, remind yourself that it's not about you, and focus intently upon your ultimate goal.

Try to get others around you to do the same. People who aren't in full control of themselves often respond remarkably well to a nurturing community of coworkers, friends, and family members.

Rest assured that their dream in life was never to be the resident troublemaker.

3. Passive-aggressive people. Not everybody has the prerogative of being able to act like a hot-headed jerk when they feel like it, but even most powerless of people are usually sly enough to make life miserable for everyone around them without even saying a word.

They rule their worlds with the hurt look, the dismissive grunt, the left-handed compliment, the cold shrug or half smile, self-pity, smoldering resentment, and the eternal aura of being disappointed, while pretending to pretend not to be. Unravel that quadruple negative— or quintuple, since "pretend" is intrinsically self-negating! When you've gotten to the twisted crux of that verbal puzzle, you'll have a better understanding of what passes for logic in the world of passive aggression.

As a rule, this trait is more common among mid-management or lower-level employees, because most C-suite executives have the leverage to get away with losing their tempers. At the mid-management level, workers can be equally adept at sending their internal pain up the hierarchy, or down.

Because these people specialize in sneak attacks and subtle destruction, document most of the efforts you make on their behalf, and keep other people in the loop on what you're doing. You may occasionally need that evidence to reinsert reality.

Many passive-aggressive people grew up in a family in which freedom of expression was forbidden, and they later locked themselves into that same self-censoring cell by means of a bad marriage, powerless job, or obsequious personality.

As with other members of the usual suspects, don't try to beat these people at their own game. They're a pro, and you're an amateur (hopefully).

Be reasonable. Be generous. Don't take their pouting personally. Because most of our worst behaviors come from desperation—

in this case the desperation of having anger that can't be openly expressed—validate the feelings that lie beneath the behaviors of passive-aggressive people.

Encourage them to be themselves. Let them vent. Let them be politically incorrect. Allow them to elaborate on their endless loops of double-bind situations. Hold their hand—literally or figuratively. Be the kind of person they've spent their lifetime seeking—but in the wrong way.

You'll often find that when they see you as part of the solution, instead of part of the problem, you'll get special treatment.

Your own problems with them will subside long before those of the people who can't get past the cold shrug, half smile, or hurt look, because they're sure that it's all about them.

4. Egomaniacs. These people can be almost impossible to deal with, because far too often, they're the boss. Large corporations, or any depersonalized institution, tends to reward narcissistic ego freaks—partly just because they excel at grabbing rewards. They invariably look good on paper—unless you look closely, in which case you often find misrepresentations.

These people present themselves as preternaturally confident, but of course that's the opposite of what they really are. If you're really confident, you act it, instead of advertise it.

Because egomaniacs have deep-seated insecurities, they almost never feel content, and look at every achievement as merely a stepping-stone to the next. They glorify their ethic of discontent, with the presumption that it paints them as a brave pioneer of ultra-accomplishment. They often have no idea what their ultimate goal is—because they don't want one. It would unmask the depth of their bottomless pit.

For that reason alone, they lack the self-censoring rudder that keeps those of us with ultimate goals on track.

Because their journey has no destination, they dart in and out of jobs, projects, professions, friendships, and even conventions as sacred and grounding as parenthood and marriage.

They have a notable lack of empathy, mostly because they have an infinite ignorance of their own core self. If they knew themselves better, they'd be capable of knowing others.

They don't lack the brain power to know themselves, but the courage, because their secret fear is that they're ultimately unlovable. Many of them, sadly, were saddled with this opinion by the most influential people of their formative years, most commonly, those who should have loved them most: their parents.

When this self-loathing is paired with innate intelligence, charisma, good looks, and drive, it often leaves people with bright-shiny shells, and nothing inside.

As counterintuitive as it may sound, build them up. Praise what they've done, and even more important, who they are. It's common for them to be the type of person who can't take a compliment, so be specific, be lavish, and praise the person behind the achievement, instead of just the achievement. Be genuine in your validation, or it will have the opposite of the intended effect.

When egomanicacs start to feel that you're the one person in the world who appreciates them, their growth can begin.

If you're just one of the many who try to take them down a notch, guess who will get taken down?

Does expanding their sense of worth make you the suck-up in this situation? No: not if you're doing it for their sake, instead of yours. It makes you the person with wisdom, and compassion.

Over time, this generous approach might help make you a leader, because narcissists often block the door to others' ascension. If you're one of their favored few—or, ideally, the person who helped them grow—that won't happen.

Not all egomaniacs respond to the principles of the Code, of course. Many wounds never heal, and the first cut is the deepest. But these are people with multiple resources—brains, energy, and charm—and if you give them a chance, most of them can finally grow up.

5. Bullies. This type of person is often a hardened amalgam of many negative traits: narcissism, anger, impulsivity, hyper-

emotionalism, obsession, and repression. As always, the glue that holds these unsavory behaviors together is fear.

Almost all bullies were bullied themselves. That fact, in and of itself, should inspire the compassion in you that these people need, even though they often repel it.

The scariest thing about bullies is that they're survivors. That's self-evident, since they survived bullying themselves, and rose to the level where they could reverse the role. They're artful at dominating the weak and being submissive to the strong, hiding their abusiveness, keeping everyone off balance by hurting the best people, pursuing power for its own sake, and operating free from the constraints of remorse.

They see the world solely in terms of short-term power differentials, and often lack any kind of cohesive, long-range plan. In place of plans, they apply strategies, and deceive themselves into believing that stopgap measures can be endlessly applied.

Lacking not only a comprehensive plan, but an integrated self, they are infinitely compartmentalized—but therein lies your opportunity.

The way that you can learn to sincerely like a bully is to break down their various compartments, and find the shards of them that are unsullied by the cruel forces that first created their bullying behavior. When you locate the elements of their personality that respond to humility, reason, and generosity, you can become a positive force in their life—and at least keep them from being a negative force in yours.

Often these compartments lie in the realm of sentimentality: a first cousin to love, without love's messy necessities of help and commitment.

If those of us in the international intelligence community learned anything from the training films of the Austin Powers series, it's that even Dr. Evil had sentimental weaknesses for Mini-Me, as well as his hairless cat, Mr. Bigglesworth, and even Mini-Me's cat, Mini-Mr. Bigglesworth. These small windows of sentimentality opened

Evil to vulnerability—which could have become his touchstone of healing, if not for the crushing pressure for more sequels.

Think about adopting the role of Mini-Me—not as a sycophant or accomplice, but solely as someone who looks for goodness that others, in their general repugnance, choose not to see. Through this difficult discipline, you can often establish contact with an otherwise impenetrable person.

Being nonjudgmental to a person who is constantly judged is not only an excellent exercise in tolerance, but an illuminating exploration into the neurological heart of darkness, where fear and anger intersect.

Bullies almost welcome judgmentalism, because they are accustomed to contempt, and develop a perverse taste for it. Exploiting contempt is, in effect, their own version of Muhammad Ali's brilliant rope-a-dope strategy. When you stop punching them as hard as everyone else does, you not only deprive them of their strategic sustenance, but break their toxic pattern of learned responses.

In those moments, you have an opportunity to find the person within the person, and free them, if only momentarily.

Moments add up.

Bullies are usually bright enough to know that each day they sow the seeds of their own demise, creating an endgame they often court, because it's mostly themselves that they despise. When you infiltrate their defenses with subversive but genuine affiliation with whatever tenderness in them that you can find, you disable the process of their self-destruction.

At that point, you can begin to shine light on the needlessness of their addiction to self-destruction.

Similarly to propping up the bruised egos of narcissists, your efforts to subordinate your ego to a bully may be misunderstood by those around you. It might seem to some that you just punked out. So keep your channels of communication open with the others who are bullied, so that they see that your courageous efforts are on behalf of all of those who suffer: including the bully.

This is very important, because if you're perceived as someone who is currying favor for their own selfish interests, the sacrifices you make will be turned against you.

As with your efforts to unravel the toxic behavior of each of the six primary types of problematic people, manage your expectations.

Realize that not everyone responds to even your best efforts, and that sometimes the wisest action is to remove yourself from the situation entirely. When that's possible and practical, it's often the smart move.

6. People with Disorders. This is a large, varied class of people who fall into two essential categories: people with mood or mental disorders, and people with substance disorders.

People with these issues can manifest their bad behavior in many of the forms I already mentioned—ranging from bullying to pouting—and when they do, the disturbing traits are often quite pronounced, because they're exaggerated by the underlying disorders.

Paradoxically, this magnification can sometimes make the disordered person's problem easier to confront: it becomes the proverbial elephant in the room.

The most common mood and mental disorders that create toxic behavior are depression, bipolar disorder, posttraumatic stress disorder, generalized anxiety disorder, obsessive-compulsive disorder, ADHD, Asperger's, and mild, manageable schizoaffective disorders, including those characterized by paranoia.

Each problem has its own manifestations, with numerous subsets of unhealthy behaviors.

The most common substance disorder is alcohol abuse, followed by the growing problem of prescription drug abuse, which can include stimulants, or narcotics. Even moderately benign drugs, such as marijuana or insomnia medications, can sometimes disturb mood and cognitive function.

Substance abuse problems are sometimes more insidious than mind and mood disorders, because of the bifurcation of the person with the problem: their sober self, and their intoxicated self. Those two elements of personality invariably combine with that of a third party: the substance itself. A substance as powerful as alcohol has an agenda of its own, and that agenda is: drink me!

Even though some people cling to denial, most people who have these problems know that they do. The disorders have probably been diagnosed, and it's quite possible that these people are already being treated.

What do these people need? The same things everyone does: understanding without judgment, compassion, a rational perspective on the problem, and real-world, real-time help.

It's a misconception that people with chronic problems typically reject offers of assistance. Even an offer that is not acted upon is still accepted as an offer of caring.

It's also a misconception that people will typically react belligerently if you bring up the subject of treatment. In our relatively sophisticated era of disorder management, most people are comfortable talking about their medications and ancillary treatments, such as counseling or nutritional therapy.

The best possible way to approach these conversations is with humility, and zero judgment. Nobody likes condescension, especially when it's delivered in the guise of concern. If you can't discuss someone's problem within the context of having plenty of problems of your own, don't bother. You'll sound preachy, and disconnected.

In dealing with these people, I'm often reminded of what my wife, Kim, says: "We're all working on something."

Like you, I've known innumerable people whose lives were made harder by various substance-related disorders, and every one of them also had amazing skills and virtues. To reach these people, cite those fine qualities—very specifically—because the single greatest fear of many of these people is judgmentalism.

The issues of disorder or addiction, like so many others, are also wisely broached through the format of questions, instead of statements. Such as: Do you feel like you're drinking is starting to be a problem, or does it seem to be pretty much under control? Or: Are you taking any meds for your depression, or have any interest in trying that?

If you want to keep people talking to you, take their answers at face value, because rhetorical questions aren't really questions.

I've done this countless times, without drama. If you've tried something similar, without success, try it again, as you apply the principles of the Code. This time, it might work better.

To Seek a Newer World

The bane of the modern world is the ubiquity of toxicity—environmental, as well as social—which are often linked, in our increasingly frayed human biochemistry, and in our flawed institutions, beset by forces never before experienced.

In your journey to a life of healthy, happy relationships, the toughest test of your ability to inspire trust will come from confronting various victims of fear—scarred early in their lives—who made the terrible transition to the role of victimizer, in their desperate attempts to survive.

The challenges we face will never change. Nor should they, since that would signal the last step of social evolution itself.

What can change is your own role in this journey toward peace of mind, and the achievement of prosperity—as well as the far greater achievement of helping many, many others to achieve peace and prosperity.

This is the archetypal journey of humankind—one made noble and epic only by its difficulty—and it is typically too hard to be undertaken alone.

The best hope for its regular and predictable culmination comes from the combined power of many: knit together by the thread of love, and love's most powerful social expression, trust.

Far too few accept the totality of this challenge, and those who do must still be led, even if the burden of leadership must be passed from one to another—freely and without desire—as the finest animation of love made real in this world.

One of humanity's greatest renditions of this journey is the myth of Odysseus, and his epic ten-year journey home to his wife, and to his life as the king of Ithaca, after ten years of fighting the Trojan War. Odysseus was overwhelmed with betrayal—by his enemies, friends, gods, and fate itself, with tricks as bold as the Trojan Horse, monsters as fierce as the Cyclops, and temptations as seductive as the Sirens. But his trust for his wife and the legitimacy of his life never wavered. Nor did the love of his wife for him—and the trust that flowed from that love—as she faced trials as perilous as his.

The strength of each came from the only thing greater than their own moral character: the power of their trust in one another.

This was the power that created a new world, when Ulysses returned, and assumed his throne.

Centuries later, Alfred Tennyson wrote his own version of the epic journey of Ulysses, and it became an instant classic. His poem Ulysses ends:

One equal temper of heroic hearts,
Made weak by time and fate, but strong in will
To strive, to seek, to find, and not to yield.

The young Tennyson wrote this celebration of the human spirit not in the triumph of his own youthful power, but in response to the wreckage of his life. He wrote it when he had to return home, after his father died, to accept the responsibility of helping his mother and ten siblings, three of whom were mentally ill.

In so doing, Tennyson created not only a world in which his family could survive, but an inspiring vision of possibility, for himself, for others, and for millions to come, not yet alive.

The vision is there, and to see it, all you need to do is look.

A new world can be yours.

No matter the obstacles that exist, no matter the lateness of the day, never stop believing that one simple fact.

Within you lies a wondrous power, one you've worked and suffered to find: people can trust you.

If ever we should meet, I will trust you.

That is my last lesson for you, and my best.

I will end our long exploration in the next chapter, with a final story that encapsulates the role that trust has played in my own journey—from childhood, to the Naval Academy, to the Marines, to the FBI, and to the chapter ahead, where mystery lies.

It's a story of a life of lasting leadership—and an old world made new—and it can be the story of your life, and your journey, too.

Let this, then, be the anthem of our shared quest:

The lights begin to twinkle from the rocks;
The long day wanes; the slow moon climbs; the deep
Moans 'round with many voices. Come, my friends.
'Tis not to late to seek a newer world.

— 11 —

THE LIFE OF LASTING LEADERSHIP

Quantico
June 6

I was on an important call with a prominent official from another three-letter government agency, but when my caller ID indicated that someone even more important was trying to get through, I got off fast. The caller was in my tribe of trust. Those calls come first.

It was Lyla Khoury—the agent I mentioned in chapter five who worked with me on a Mideast case, during the same time that she was regaining the lost trust of her daughter.

These days, I remember more about her once-wayward daughter than the case. The human brain's preference for prioritizing memories of people over events is a near constant, and is one of the fiercest guardians of our finest instincts.

"Lyla! How's your daughter?"

"*Expensive!*"

"Great!" It meant that Amira—whose goal had once been to be a hairdresser—and as different from her hard-driving, Type-A mother as humanly possible—had been accepted by the prestigious design school she'd applied to.

"I feel your pain," I said. That meant, as Lyla knew, that my daughter had just been accepted by her own dream school, George Mason University.

"Congratulations, Robin! I *guess*. Won't that be kind of steep for a jobless guy?" She was teasing me about my imminent retirement from the FBI, after twenty-one years of service there, plus nine more in the Naval Academy and Marines.

Then she got down to business, and when she was done, I went straight home, to make sure everybody was fine, and that we hadn't had any unexpected visits.

It's a small world, even in clandestine international operations—or, at its highest levels, *especially* in spy ops—but you never know how small it is until you have to deal with people who don't trust you. When that happens, it seems as if everybody knows everybody, and trusts *nobody*. If there's anything that's more contagious than trust, it's distrust.

I'm still shocked at how malignant distrust is. At this moment in history, it has metastasized into one of the greatest societal demons we face—not just in government, foreign affairs, business, and media—but even among people in our personal lives, including those we once trusted implicitly. By every measure of behavioral psychology, lack of trust is at record heights, and is shrinking our world into a stage populated by adversaries who seem to be everywhere.

By this time in your life, you've probably faced some of the same trials of trust that most of us have, and they've probably shaken your faith in people, and even made you question your ability to chart the course of your own destiny.

When distrust invades our lives, we never know what's next—and no matter how often it happens, we're always surprised.

Life's predictable occurrences, of course, tend to be the ones we planned, but the surprises usually come from people who have their *own* plans for us—and sometimes come from fate itself, which has an agenda of its own.

That's why I rely so much on systems.

The systems that I've designed to create and convey trust constantly expand the borders of safety—for me and others—and provide a buffer between the linear paths of our goals, and the meandering chaos that descends when our actions are implemented in the real world, in real time.

When you're working within a trust-based system—which organically creates a tribe of trusted associates—you have immeasurably more influence over what happens, far greater powers of prediction, and a team behind you when things go south.

Best of all, you can control your own *reactions* to life's shocking twists and turns, and that alone is gold. *Panic attacks.* That's not just a condition, but an unavoidable phenomenon that befalls those who face their problems alone, with no principles to protect them, and no tribe of trust to turn to.

By the time I got home, I'd settled down, and was ready to activate my systems, alert my tribe of trust, and solve one more problem on my way to retirement.

Hopefully.

Lyla's message: The operative from the former Soviet-bloc nation that I told you about in chapter one was back in play, more than twenty years later. Lyla had been tasked with tracking his moves, and they all pointed toward infiltration of America's privatized defense system.

She said he was bitter and angry.

And was looking for me.

That happens. People take things personally. Always.

Long ago, I'd hit him hard, and neutralized him, curtailing his career and killing the kick-back income he'd gotten from his own country's defense contractors, who were grateful for the technologies he'd pilfered from American companies.

His life after that was grim.

Complicating the situation: To find him before he found me, and keep the upper hand, I needed the help of the tech wizard I told you about in the second chapter, who, as you probably remember, blew me off, because he didn't trust me. His antipathy for me, I thought, might be even greater than that of the intelligence agent. At least the spy and I were in the same game.

The techie, a math student when I met him and now CEO of a security firm, had known the operative back in the olden days—when geopolitical life seemed little more complicated than sorting capitalists from communists. Now they were in touch again.

Back then, the technologist had been clean. He probably still was, because he had FBI connections. But who knew? If life was simple, we wouldn't need spies, or even systems for creating trust.

After all these years, I still regretted how I treated him. I'd been tone deaf to his own goals, context, and communications style, and had compartmentalized him in my mind as the geeky second banana in a movie—"Best Friend" of the leading man—as you may recall.

After one meeting, I was dead to him.

Not a day goes by when I don't think about the people I've hurt. If there really are ghosts in this world, those are mine.

But now I have an ultimate goal, and it's my greatest source of strength. It's the dream that guides my days, and lets me sleep at night.

My ultimate goal now is just to have healthy, happy relationships.

It's that simple. That hard. And that majestic.

Los Angeles
June 7

I took a deep breath and followed an executive secretary into the plush corner office of the man I once dismissively called Best Friend: Frank Hale, now president of a powerful big-data security firm that focuses on the defense industry.

I felt queasy, because I really needed his help, and thought he might snub me, just to even the score—or that he might even be working with the operative, *against* me.

"Robin Dreeke!" Frank boomed, as he stood and reached out his hand. "The only guy in New York who thought Wayne Gretzky was a first baseman!"

I knew immediately that all was well. One of the most valuable benefits of learning how to be trusted is gaining the ability to recognize trustworthiness in others, sometimes almost instantly.

"Ohhhh." I did a parody of shame, but it wasn't much a stretch.

"Lyla told me you'd be calling," he said. "I've helped her with a few different things, and this is really on her radar. Mostly because of you. She speaks highly of you."

"The feeling's mutual. She said you might have some insights, since you knew him during his first deployment."

"He plays his hand close to the vest. But when he mentions you, there's a *hell* of an edge to his voice."

"Lyla thinks he's building a new network within the defense industry. She's tracked his travel to D.C., Orlando, St. Pete, Huntsville, and Colorado Springs."

"All the hot spots for aerospace. That's what he wanted to pick my brain about."

"Any idea if he's still on the take?"

"Doubt it. He spent too much time in his country's version of Siberia. After he met *you*."

"I thought his country's version of Siberia *was* Siberia."

"No. Colder." He chuckled. Frank had changed. We both had. "The last time I talked to him," Frank said, "he asked if I had a secure line to you, and when I said I didn't, he asked about a home phone or address—which is maybe what he wanted all along."

That gave me a chill.

"If I had to guess," Frank said, "I'd say that he'll show up at the SMD Symposium later this week in Rocket City." He meant the Space and Missile Defense Symposium in Huntsville, Alabama—home of the U.S. Space and Rocket Center, and once a focal point for the Apollo moon program.

"I'll try to intercept him there," I said. "Thank you so much, Frank. I've always felt bad about how I treated you. In fact, I'm writing a book about how to treat people, and I put my meeting with you in it, as an example of what *not* to do. But I disguised you—as a Columbia University student."

"Col-*ummm*-bia? Is that the best you could do? Not MIT? *Berkeley*, even?"

"Oh, no, I've offended you again!"

He grinned. A ghost was gone and life was good. My tribe of trust felt stronger than ever, and each time that happens, you have less fear.

Even so, sometimes that security is an illusion. You never know. Usually, though, the real illusion is fear.

Washington, D.C.
June 8

I picked up my phone from the Georgetown restaurant's royal-blue tablecloth and checked the caller ID.

"Hey, Lyla!"

"Rob, did you get a call from Paul—you know, Joe College? He's got info on our target."

"I'm with him right now."

"*Good!* Let me say hi and I'll leave you alone."

I handed the phone to my old friend from the Marines—the guy who was best buddies with the kid whose money got stolen. As I mentioned, he'd become CEO of his own cryptography company, and these days we have lunch every other week.

While they chatted I felt increasingly comfortable. As I built my own tribe of trust over the years, I created a system for integrating it with others. I call it the Hub and Spoke Method, after a flight technique, in which a pilot focuses on a central instrument, or hub, then glances at the instruments that surround it, one by one, always returning to the hub.

Each person who is in a tribe of trust is always at the hub of their own tribe, with the other people they trust as their spokes. The other people may or may not know each other.

Because each person has his or her own spokes, multiple tribes become linked.

This creates powerful, interlocked webs of people who share a single, common element: *trust*. No other element in human life—not money, intellect, interests, position, nor physical proximity—creates such potent power.

When each hub wields this power in the interests of all of the respective spokes—and they do the same—influence and resources expand exponentially.

Joe College got off the phone and said, "Lyla wants me to get to the point, and tell you that our subject is on the move, and headed for Huntsville."

"Who told her that?"

"*I* did. I checked the guy out. That's why you're paying for lunch. For all three of us."

"Three?"

"*Sarge* is coming."

In the intersection of our tribes, that could only mean one person. "Sergeant *Howell*?" He nodded. "I haven't seen Howell since he locked horns with the Company Commander! Remember that—when Howell took up the collection for the kid who got ripped-off?"

"You mean *my man:* Shane Frink—the Mayor of Fallujah!"

"Yeah, *Shane!* I thought Howell was still down at CENTCOM."

"I made him an offer he couldn't refuse."

"He works for *you*?"

"*With* me. Sarge doesn't work *for* anybody."

In the glow of that moment—of fond remembrance, and confident anticipation—I forgot all about my problem.

The most wondrous quality of a tribe of trust is the magic sense of safety that it can create in such an uncertain world.

That night, though, I still felt unsettled. I had one loose end: what in *hell* was I going to *say* to the subject?

But I knew who to ask. Before I went to bed, I made a call, and arranged a meeting the next day in New York.

Wall Street
June 9

As my train arrived in New York, I got a text from Jesse Thorne, my old trust guru: *"Meet me in Battery Park."*

Jesse was at the World Trade Center, giving a seminar on trust to hedge-fund managers. When I'd called him the previous evening, he said that the Wall Street One-Percenters couldn't understand why their clients, after the Great Recession, were demanding more transparency. The hedge-fund guys, he said, apparently thought that a spy handler could help them sell their clients on the need for *more* secrecy, not less.

"They don't get the Zen thing," he'd said. "People love secrets, but only when they're *in* on them. Which means the secret isn't a secret anymore. Which means that people *don't* love them. They just fear them. And fear doesn't attract money."

Jesse said his presentation was about "spilling your guts, grabbing your balls, and letting nature take its course—which is gonna happen *anyway*."

At the park, I saw Jesse from a distance, on a wrought-iron bench with a view of the Statue of Liberty—and even before I got there, somebody had buttonholed him, and was sitting down for a chat. It reminded me of the last time he and I had been here, just before September 11, 2001, when widespread trust among Americans took its last figurative breath.

Trust in our country and its major institutions—declining for twenty years before 9/11—spiked dramatically for a few months after the attacks, then plummeted, and never recovered.

And yet—there was Jesse, an unremarkable, aging man, alone on a bench in the wealthiest, most cynical microcosm of America— where people were *proud* to call themselves sharks—attracting strangers as if he were handing out hundred-dollar bills.

The last time we'd been here, he was helping me teach six FBI trainees the skills that inspire trust in strangers. The drill was for me to take the trainees to the park, one at a time, and have them approach a "stranger" that I pointed out—Jesse—and strike up a conversation. Then he would tell me how well they'd done.

After I steered the last one over, I huddled with Jesse, but he was confused. "I couldn't tell which ones were the students, he said. "So *many* people sat down to talk."

That was the day I realized that some people have *it*: an intangible force that draws others in—and Jesse was one of them.

I now call that force the Beacon, equating it to the beam from a lighthouse that offers safety and direction. Jesse was born with the Beacon.

I wasn't. But I taught myself how to create that quality, using the Code and the Steps.

You can create it, too, and become the Beacon for your family, your neighborhood, your office, your company, or your country—and accept the majestic burden of leadership.

When Jesse saw me coming, he called out, "Rob-on-the-Job! Don't you *ever* take a day off?"

"What about *you*," I said to Jesse, "working today, when you don't even *have* to?"

"I'm keeping America safe for hedge-fund managers. Excuse me, I meant *from*. You should be out flying with your little boy on a day like this."

"Not so little, now. He just won a statewide engineering contest." Jesse was still a colleague—but, family, too. Trust can morph through countless forms and phases.

To my surprise, Jesse said, "I hear you're getting a blast from the past."

"Who told you that?"

"Three different people. Two from HQ, plus some newbie in Berzekeley, California, who says he knows ninety languages. A lot of people seem to care what happens to you, for some reason."

"There's no accounting for taste."

"Robin Dreeke: *modest*! Strange new world!"

"Here's my problem, Jesse. I know this guy is pissed at me. But I don't know what he wants, or how to find out."

He shrugged. "Just ask him. And if what he wants is reasonable, do it."

I waited for him to continue, but he didn't. When I realized he was done—and that his simple advice was perfect—I felt like an idiot.

I kept my composure, but Jesse could see inside me. He put his hand on my shoulder. "It's okay. You've done *well*, Robin. You've made a *difference*."

I didn't know what to say. Jesse was one of a scant few agents who'd received two Director's Awards, and I felt like I'd just gotten my version of one.

At that moment, I realized this, and I hope you know it already: You'll never be perfect—but you're good enough now.

Jesse Thorne shook my hand, knotted his tie, and headed back to Freedom Tower.

Rocket City: Huntsville, Alabama
June 10

My God! He looked so much older. I watched him work his way down the hotel dining-room's buffet line, waiting to intercept him at the coffee station, with my own cup conspicuously empty.

The decades had left many marks on him—reflections of time spent in far crueler environments than my own, due to his station assignments in the years since I had neutralized him, beginning on the sugary white sands of Miami Beach.

My first volley—my opening remark—was poised for release the first second he saw me. It was, "You must have many questions for me!"

I was hoping that would lead to what he wanted, and that I could give it to him.

When that shot went downrange, of course, all hell would break loose. But, the Code! It's so comforting. Immersion in a trust-based way of life leaves you with such strong situational awareness that life's inevitable conflagrations play out in what seems like slow motion, and surprise becomes manageable. It comes from the lack of fear. When your goals rise above those of fulfilling your own needs, it's much harder to worry.

From ten feet away, we locked eyes, and he seemed to recognize me. I was surprised at his lack of surprise and, as usual, once again—despite all my philosophies and the best-laid plans of mice and men—all hell broke loose: hello darkness, my old friend.

He studied my name tag: Robin Dark, the same pseudonym I'd used about twenty years ago, when we'd met at the kayak rental station on South Beach.

"I remember you," he said calmly.

I bladed my body at a nonthreatening 45-degree angle, tilted my head, maintained eye contact, and smiled.

I made a point of studying his name tag, which no longer said Terrence Bonney, but had a far more Eastern European flavor. "Was it . . . kayaks?" I said. "At an aerospace convention? A long time ago?"

"*Very* long. But I am not really a *kayaker*. Nor was I ever." He was almost instantly revealing reality, and that, too, was surprising. He meant that he was a foreign operative—seeking either classified, or open-source information—and that I knew it, and that he knew I knew it.

"You must have many questions for me!" I said.

He shrugged. "No." He filled his cup, turned his back, and started to walk away.

He stopped and looked over his shoulder at me "You are the one who neutered me," he said flatly, his jaw squared and jutting.

"You mean, *neutralized*?" This was not going *at all* as planned.

"No. I used the correct word. *Neutered*. My lengthy station assignment after our brief encounter was not suitable for wives."

He nodded toward the nearest table and we both sat down.

"I'm sorry," I said. I meant it.

The memories of the hurt that we inflict as young people, even as they recede with time, grow sharper in focus.

"Nor was it hospitable for families," he said, twisting the knife.

"I am very sorry." I couldn't imagine being without my kids. "I hope that you reunited."

"I did. With nothing to hide or regret. My wife had great faith in me, and her belief in me enabled me to fulfill that faith."

He was giving me good reasons to be afraid. Clearly he was bitter, and placed blame on me. And the only reason I was here, I realized, was because he wanted me to be.

"It sounds as if I blame you, and I do not," he said, and again I was shocked, because it was as if he, like Jesse, had seen inside me.

Or maybe he and Jesse just recognized some very obvious things about human nature that those of us with the sin of pride—that we call ambition—are blind to.

"I do have one question for you," he said. "As you will see, it is not a proper question to pose in a coffee line. It is this, Robin *Dark. . . .*" He paused over the pseudonym, mocking not just its falsity, but the callous arrogance that had once informed my belief that I was a top-secret, film-noir *force*, fighting evil, at whatever cost. "Do you wish to punish me?"

"Punish you?"

"Yes."

"*No.*"

"In the more brutal world in which I matured, it was common to seek not only justice, but inflict punishment. You would call it a 'a deterrent action.' Or 'an ounce of prevention.'"

"Why would you suspect me of that?"

"Because when you *neu-tra-lized* me," he said, drawing out the word to its full effect, "I believe you took a certain degree of satisfaction from it. A sense of pleasure. I have been concerned, since I have returned to America, that you might wish to continue your activities against me, for reasons known best to you. More correctly, *only* to you."

I was stunned. No one had ever spoken to me like that.

Maybe someone should have. Over time, though, I had learned to talk to myself like that, and it had been a bitter, saving grace.

He stayed quiet and so did I.

Finally I said, "I recall being proud of keeping my country safe."

"And?"

"It felt good."

"Your country and it's *economy*?" he said.

"Yes."

He nodded his head, almost amiably, and some of the tension left him. "I can understand that. I had those feelings, and others much less noble. We both came from what historians now call the Bloody Century. We both tried to make it less so."

"I think I finally understand what I did to you," I said. "So, thank you" . . . he tilted his head back, and looked skeptically down his nose and chin at me . . . "no, *really*, thank you! For letting me see that."

His posture straightened. "That is my pleasure."

"I can't change it," I said. "So. What can I do for you? Now."

"Tell me without equivocation that there is no, what do you call it, grudge match. No hidden agenda. No secret indictment. No special treatment based upon what has been."

"Absolutely not." I made it personal again: "And I confess that I was cold-hearted about the pain I caused you. And I am sincere when I ask you what I can do for you."

His face softened. "*I* caused most of what happened to me. By trying to make money. Those were the charges against me. Not failure of duty.

"And now I serve my country faithfully, and more honestly. Yes, I am here to learn what Americans know, but through open-source information, with no subterfuge, nor any illegality. Our nations are allies now, and mine is becoming a nation of free people, finally."

That was true—in comparison to his country's far more repressive past. "How close to retirement are you?" I asked.

"Next year."

"Me, too."

He reached out his coffee cup, and we toasted our mutual freedom from a lifetime of constant responsibility: a goal that is primal and universal—arguably the most common, timeless dream of humankind.

"You could continue to serve your country by becoming a consultant. For us."

"A spy?"

"A consultant. You would tell us what you think is in the best interests of your country. And only that."

One more huge surprise: he did not look surprised.

"At one of my stations," he said, "we had very little to do at night other than watch films in a cafeteria, mostly American films, many of them classics, and I saw things in them—ideas, principles—that I do not see on the streets of America every day. America has greatness that even Americans fail to see."

I knew exactly what he meant, and in that instant we were the most unlikely brothers imaginable in the vast tribe of American patriots.

"So you'll consider it?" I said.

"I will put it this way: Robin Dreeke, this could be the beginning of a beautiful friendship."

He smiled, and as his face lit, it left behind the scarred marks of an old man. Even one moment of connection in this world can change you.

I raised my cup to him. "Here's lookin' at you, kid!"

We touched cups again, as my life as an American spy drew closer to its end.

Trust in the Streets of New York
A Midsummer Night

Tough town, New York. As I said at the beginning of this book: if you can learn trust there, you can learn it anywhere.

I was back where I started—in Manhattan—learning one last lesson about trust: arguably the most important yet.

New Yorkers have big hearts, but they don't hand out trust like penny candy, because the city is too full of manipulators: everybody from the hand-out artists on the sidewalks, to the guys in ten-thousand-dollar suits who walk right past them—and past other fine people, momentarily down on their luck, who are looking for a hand up—treating each category with equal contempt.

But that toughness was nowhere in sight on this meaningful night, as Kim and I wandered around a dazzling ballroom, ablaze with color from crystal chandeliers, party dresses, and the formal uniforms of military and law enforcement agents from a multitude of branches.

It was a retirement ceremony for one of my heroes, the Jedi Master that I mentioned previously—Vern Schrader, now a thirty-seven-year FBI veteran—who first told me that the sole secret of trust is to put others first.

The ceremony reminded me of my own upcoming retirement, and I was edgy—unsatisfied with my quickly waning FBI career, and uncertain about what lay ahead.

When we're young, our hearts are on fire with dreams of glory, as we revel in small victories and agonize over every defeat. But even as the flames still blaze, we glimpse the beginning of the end, and our glories recede so deeply into the past that only their dim memories constitute what's left of our dreams.

In those moments, we wonder: Was it worth it? All that sacrifice? Those years of feeling tight and wired every morning and every night?

Looking around me, though, at a vastly larger crowd than any I'd seen at similar ceremonies, it was clear that something grand had been created by the career of Vern Schrader, the Vietnam Vet and FBI crime-scene photographer who'd revolutionized his profession.

As the din around me grew, I slipped into a reverie of the old days, remembering the only time I was able to repay Vern's mountain of wisdom with a kernel of my own. At the time, he was worried about his youngest daughter, who was developmentally disabled—adorable, but childlike. He was afraid she'd never be able to support herself.

I empathized completely, but had a heartfelt epiphany.

"I'll always love my own daughter as much as I do now," I said, "while she's still in that innocent stage of constantly wanting to hug me and say, 'I love you, daddy.' But the day will come when the hugs won't be so often, or innocent—and she might never call me 'daddy' again."

He was so visibly moved that I could almost see his context concerning his daughter shift, and from that time on, it was never quite the same. He valued the gift that accompanied his pain.

Even then, I had an inkling of the lessons I'd later learn. As I've said, I am not a born leader. What I haven't said, because it might sound vain, is that I was born with the heart of a leader, unformed and unfinished.

So were you. So is everyone.

I was lucky enough to have the right people to help me find it. My wife. My kids. My mentors. My colleagues. My friends. Without them, I'd have been lost.

If you're still struggling to lead, find the people who can take you to your leader's heart.

You know most of them already.

"Robin!" It was Kim, tugging at my hand. "Look who's here."

"Vern!" I grabbed his hand.

"Robin, there was no *way* I was going to miss seeing *you* tonight!" Pulling me close, so I could hear clearly, Vern said, "So many of the people I've talked to tonight say that things have really changed, mostly in your end of the Bureau."

"Yeah, because of Director Comey! He teaches some of the same things *you* taught me."

"I meant because of *you*, Robin."

I didn't know what to say.

If anything could ever lift me out of my malaise, that was it.

But it didn't. Vern slapped me on the back and headed to the podium.

The speeches began, so I went on autopilot, to tune out the bureaucrats and their clichés. But something incredible happened. Everybody who spoke was funny, emotional, wise, and genuine.

They were all channeling their inner Vern Schrader, who was allergic to posturing, and playing it safe. I was shocked to see how much one person could inspire the attitudes of so many.

Police chiefs, mayors, congressmen, and agents from the FBI, Justice, Homeland, and the CIA didn't even mention Vern's game-changing innovations, but reveled in him as a person: how he'd drop anything on a moment's notice, come out on holidays with a smile on his face, and always do the right thing, regardless of the pressures or the people involved.

I'd never heard anything like it.

I bent closely toward Kim's ear. "Next year," I said urgently, "is this what they'll be saying about me? Or just that I did a *good job*? I hurt too many people, Kim, back when I was out for myself. I didn't even trust the people who trusted me. Is *that* what they'll remember?"

"Nahhh!" She looked at me like I was crazy. Kim can convey more truth in a word than most people can in a speech.

I looked around, and saw a different world. So many friends! Such an amazing evening!

Vern's wife spoke for a moment, and so did his two older daughters—very accomplished women, who talked about Vern being their best friend. That put a lump in my throat.

I thought about my own kids. They were keeping me close, at an age when so many kids push their parents away. They were my heroes.

Vern's youngest daughter rose, and ambled shyly toward the podium. "When I needed my daddy," she said haltingly, squinting at her notes, "he was there for me. Every single time. I was the most important person in the world to him. Now he's the most important person in the world to me." She stopped abruptly, crumpled her notes, hurried over to Vern, and threw her arms around him. "I love you, daddy."

Vern rocked her, and kept his composure—though I don't know how. He didn't look self-conscious, and neither did his daughter. They looked as if they didn't have a care in the world. The room was quiet with peace.

My eyes glassed up. I felt Kim squeeze my hand, looked at her, and saw that her pretty eyes were shiny with tears, too.

I was ready for my retirement.
I was ready for my new life.
I was ready.

What you do in this world is the single best reflection of who you are—but it's still just one more look in the mirror. What actually defines you—the only thing you can fully control, safe from the forces of fate, and the acts of others—is what lies inside.

That's why it's so important for the inner you—the real you—to focus with absolute intensity on the sacred values, embraced universally, that can make the *true you* the person you dream of being.

The Code of Trust—created on the fly, during difficult days, in the real world, in real time—is only one expression of those values. But it was a work of love, took a lifetime, and has already changed many lives. It once was just mine, and now it's ours.

The Code can give you the strength to re-create yourself, and rise above ordinary realities. With it, you can reach the plane of ideals inhabited only by the better angels of our nature, where finally you'll feel at home among all you meet.

In the eyes of the world, you may falter and fail, overcome by the forces that dwarf personal power. But if you can just be a person who puts others first, your inner world will be rich, your heart will be full, your friends will be everywhere, and all the problems you once considered so dreadful will fade gradually and gracefully into the realm of irrelevance.

The power of putting others first will place you in such a state of grace that all of these gifts will arrive without effort, as naturally and sequentially as the changing face of nature itself.

That's the lesson I learned from Vern in the last hours of his last day on the job. He wasn't even trying to teach me. He was just living his life, the only way he knew.

It's also my last lesson for you: At some point in your life of putting others first, you won't even have to try. Your acts will simply embody the real you—and everyone who knows you will trust you.

If you live this life, we will someday, somehow meet—in person or online, directly or indirectly, literally or figuratively—and we will feel as if we've known each other forever.

Until then, my friend. . . .

Wherever You Are Now

Now that your lessons of trust are done, you will—as do all who work hard and study well—become a teacher.

I trust you implicitly to teach these lessons properly. I have no fear that you will use them for the opposite of their intended purpose, as tools for selfish gain.

You've learned that in the pursuit of the loftiest goals, there is no such a thing as self-centered, long-term gain, since selfishness invariably self-destructs, and leads to loss, and feeling alone.

Whatever fantasies you may once have had about being an army of one are over.

Trust takes two. And those two are just the beginning.

As your tribe of trust grows, you'll teach *yourself* new lessons every day. The Code is a philosophy, but like all viable philosophies, it's lessons are best learned in the field, from the only person who sees the whole picture: oneself.

As trust elevates you to leadership, you'll often be afraid that you'll fail to fully share the lessons of trust with those you love most.

Don't worry.

Here is your first lesson as a fellow teacher.

As you spread the Code of Trust among those you hold most dear—your closest colleagues, your friends, and your family—it will instantly become clear that you can't go wrong: because those to whom you've given your heart, and entrusted your life, have been *your* teachers of trust—your tribe—all along.

— 12 —

THE TRUST TRAINING MANUAL: 15 DRILLS

Y OU DON'T HAVE TO READ this chapter right now—at least not the whole thing. You have to *do* it. Soon, and for the rest of your life!

(Sorry—I was channeling the *Casablanca* references from the last chapter. How about: *pretty* soon, and *fairly often*?)

Now that you've learned the lessons of inspiring trust, you need to enact them—repetitively, consistently, and in the field of real life, in real time.

To become a true artist of trust inspiration, you will need to *practice* the Code and the Steps—thinking on your feet, and staying flexible once your proverbial first shot goes downrange.

It's Semper Gumby time!

You'll probably discover that even though you've learned the Code and Steps cognitively, you still haven't internalized them so deeply that you know them kinesthetically: as muscle memory, so deeply embedded that they're virtually instinctual.

Don't be discouraged by the fact that you still need to think about them. On occasion, that applies to everybody, including me. This way of living isn't always easy. For me, that's especially true when I'm at the peak of relaxation—among those, ironically, who deserve my very best behavior: my closest friends and family.

These exercises will help solve that. I recommend that you practice at least one of them every week. As a rule, the opportunities to practice them will arise spontaneously, but you can also proactively apply them in situations that you create yourself, with people you know, and even with complete strangers.

It's common for people, however, to resist practice—in any field of acquired skills, from sports to music to business management— because training is just not as exciting as real life. In the real world, though, the absolute masters—the Michael Jordans, Mick Jaggers, Warren Buffets, and Meryl Streeps—are invariably the first to arrive at practice and preparation sessions, and the last to leave. Practice isn't the only reason that the most accomplished people make it to the top, but it is the primary reason they stay there.

When I give seminars on the Code of Trust, I wait until the last day, when most people think they've mastered my system, and ask them to do a simple exercise.

I suggest that you do this, too—right now—as the very first of your trust-building drills.

(1) **Write your name, twice.**
(2) **Put your pen in your other hand, and write it again, twice.**
(3) **Compare signatures.**

Without doubt, the ones written in your usual hand are better, and even if the others are close, you needed more time and effort to achieve that. It's not just because you're naturally right handed or left handed. It's because you've practiced your entire life with one hand, which far outweighs any genetic predisposition. Many people, for example, lose the ability to use their dominant hand—due to arthritis, injury, or other factors—and yet, with practice, they learn to do so well with the other hand that it eventually feels natural.

Sometimes it's harder for Type-A hard chargers than others to learn skills that don't come naturally, because go-getters are accustomed to succeeding with their own methodologies. In the nuanced, delicate science of trust, though, the blunt-force drive, charisma, and intellect of Type-A people can actually be a handicap.

Because I'm a Type-A guy myself, who was not a born leader, I desperately needed the muscle memory of trust inspiration that only practice can endow.

Here's a credo we often cite in the FBI: the time to practice interviewing is *not* when you're knocking on the door.

The same principle applied to the Marine's firearms proficiency practice. We were required to qualify with our firearms every three months, not because we forgot how to shoot, but to retain and continue to develop muscle memory, so that if the day ever came when we were in a firefight, the necessary skills would be natural.

War is not the place to ruminate—nor is the boardroom, closing time in a sales call, nor during a delicate moment in a deep conversation.

When I ran the Behavioral Team, I instilled the beauty of practice in everyone, and we typically trained in the same way that your trust-muscle drills are now presented: as interactive, two-person role play. It's the only form that allows people to both say and *hear* the words they'll use in real life, which adds a huge dimension of reality. That's why people practice speeches out loud. It's also allows you to note the other person's reactions, and quickly evaluate the vast number of variables that appear when the fog of war descends.

Another element I added was switching roles, which adds another layer of learning. Reversing roles, even in an artificial setting, gives you a sense of how it feels to be on the other end.

One of the primary lessons from being on the receiving end of a trust-building drill is experiencing how quickly your *perception of the other person* dwindles to just one of two key impressions: genuine, or creepy.

When people approach you, it's natural to be wary, and if their demeanor doesn't quickly relieve that wariness, they come off as creepy.

That common, instantaneous response is one of the reasons the

Code and the Steps are so valuable. The two systems *powerfully project* altruism, and acceptance.

Warning: The mannerisms of altruism and acceptance—if *not delivered skillfully*—come off as *ultra*-creepy. That's another reason practice is so important. Your most laudable intentions can be misinterpreted if you don't express them with crystal clarity.

There's a magic bullet, though, for not looking creepy, and it's one of the easiest methods to practice. As you may have guessed, that elixir is a distillation of the Code's central thesis: To inspire trust, put others first. When you approach someone, focus intently on putting their needs first, and they'll almost always feel good about engaging with you.

Be careful, though. If you say the right words, but secretly cling to your own agenda, you'll come off as *mega*-ultra-creepy.

Therefore, even as drills, these training techniques are not just for your *own* benefit. When you perform them with excellence, you will benefit the world around you.

Let's move out, My Team! One more hill to climb!

See the hill. Take the hill.

15 Drills to Build Your Trust Muscles

Drill #1: Establish a time constraint.

The first one is easy and important—and will, like all the exercises, draw upon principles that you already know.

Establishing a time constraint is an excellent opener for almost any conversation, even with someone you know. Remember: Just knowing someone doesn't mean they deserve less than your best. Their time is just as valuable as that of a stranger.

Use one of the many different phrases I taught you: "Do you have a second or two?" "I've got to catch a bus in a minute, but. . . ." "Could you please give me a quick opinion about something?" "I have to get back to my ____, but. . . . ."

One of the best is simply to ask, "How are you doing for time?"

That makes it so much easier for them to disengage. Of course, you may not want them to disengage, but it's not about you.

You can also use a nonverbal: check your watch, put on your hat, rise out of your seat, or remain standing, instead of sitting down.

The goal is to engage them in conversation for at least a few moments, and the ultimate goal is to make them feel so comfortable that they extend the conversation themselves.

The great motivating value of this is that you'll achieve an extremely high positive response rate, and it will encourage you to do some of the harder drills.

Drill #2: Use the third-party reference technique.

Your goal is to connect with a total stranger, by talking about something immediately at hand. Find a person who is engaged with some thing or activity, which serves as the "third party" that you will refer to. The third party can be a book in a bookstore, carrots at a supermarket, or a sports team on TV.

It's easier if the "third party" is generic, or neutral, and not very personal. It also helps to find someone who's just browsing or meandering, rather than hurrying through some task.

Approach the subject and make a reference to the neutral issue at hand: the book, the carrots, or the team.

Empower them by seeking their thoughts and opinions on the neutral issue: "Do you know if these are GMO carrots?" Or, "My wife just read that book, and I want to buy her another by the same author. Any suggestions?"

You may have noticed that I mentioned a spouse. That makes it clear that you're not trying to pick somebody up, which is a relatively common reason for a stranger to strike up a random conversation, which can be annoying, or even threatening.

Don't rush your speech. Keep your nonverbals inviting: blade your body, tilt your head, make friendly eye contact, and smile.

After you break the ice, stick to the Code: suspend your ego, be nonjudgmental, validate the other person, honor reason, and be generous.

The ultimate success is moving from the neutral subject to something more personal.

Best sign of success: the subject doesn't seem interested in breaking off the conversation until you offer that cue yourself.

Drill #3: Speak at the speed of trust.

The speed of trust is a speech velocity that's relatively slow, devoid of rushing.

This drill might feel awkward if you naturally have a fast rate of speech, or are in a locale in which people tend to speak quickly—such as, counterintuitively, Oregon, which a study recently cited as the state with the fastest talkers. (An Oregonian I know assures me it's because so many New Yorkers recently moved there, and quickly took over. But, given that they talk so fast, who can trust an Oregonian?) Although innumerable trustworthy people speak quickly, there's a good reason that people who aren't trusted are colloquially referred to as fast-talkers: some people purposefully accelerate their speech when they want to hide something or confuse you because it gives you less time to think about what they're saying. It's the verbal equivalent of fine print. Consider, for example, the speech rate of a carnival barker or a bad salesperson.

You can apply this to people you know, but it's an even better challenge if you use it with a stranger.

Pick a topic that fits your listener and warrants an extension of the conversation. Speak about it notably more slowly than usual, but focus on sounding thoughtful and meaningful—as if you're trying to communicate emphasis. Don't just slow down mechanically or arbitrarily because you might sound creepy.

To gauge your success, keep track of eye contact. If they're losing interest, it will show.

For contrast, do the same thing while talking faster than usual. You can even do it in the same conversation.

You're almost certain to see notable results.

Drill #4: Bridge generational context.

The goal of this drill is to relate to someone from a different generation, and overcome the natural barriers that separate various age groups. The ultimate goal is to relate to them so effectively that they forget that you're from a different generation.

The drill: Approach someone from a different generation, and therefore different context. The more they look emblematic of their generation—based on their clothing, mannerisms, or the setting—the better.

This exercise can be done with an acquaintance or a stranger. The acquaintance will be able to give you immediate, honest feedback, but the drill will be somewhat less real world. The encounter with a stranger will be more realistic, but you'll need to infer much of the feedback, based upon the reactions you get.

One of the best strategies for connecting is, as I mentioned in chapter seven, to make a reference to their generation's version of various aspects of life that are important to most people, including: political events, other major events, movies, TV shows, books, songs, technologies, sports, board games, or cultural heroes. Other dependable subjects are personal aspects of the subjects life—such as retirement if you're talking to a Traditionalist, or parenting if you're talking to a member of Generation X. It's easiest to connect over something that may have occurred in your subject's most impressionable years, generally from age seven to nineteen.

Don't pretend to know a great deal about the subject at hand. Just focus on what they have to say about it.

It's also important to address them according to their generation's general attitudes and philosophies. Suspend your own as you focus on theirs.

The key to bridging generations is to never judge, but simply to seek comprehension of the qualities and preferences of each generation. As I've said before, validation doesn't mean agreement—it means being able to see things from an alternate perspective.

For every generation, all of the cultural touchstones are threaded together with a person's basic context, communications style, priorities, and problems, and give you an insight into who they really are.

Talking about someone else's generational topics naturally validates the person you approach, and creates an opportunity for you to dig deeper—into the *individual*—without sounding like you're from another planet.

So, for extra points, after your subject feels understood—and lowers their shields—move into more personal, multigenerational topics, and try to engage them human to human, as if generations are largely irrelevant to the totality of human interaction.

In this latter phase of the drill, I often ask people about their favorite memories, or their best friends, or their biggest dreams. These individualized, nonthreatening avenues of discussion tend to reveal the unique personalities of people.

When I understand someone's essential personality type, I'm able to address them within their full psychodynamic context, and use their preferred style of communication.

Often as not, that's when the real conversation starts.

For the detailed description of generational differences, see the material in chapter seven, under the heading "The 5 Ws."

Drill #5: Employ the assistance technique.

You probably recall that a tenet of evolutionary psychology is that people are hard wired to enjoy offering assistance—as not only a mechanism to receive assistance themselves, but also to satisfy the innate human drive for altruism.

Here's the drill: Connect with a stranger—or someone you know—by asking for assistance. This bonding exercise often feels more profound when you do it with a stranger, but it's of more practical value when you do it with someone you already know, because you're more likely to see them again.

This technique is one of the few tried-and-true ways to not only establish cordial contact with a stranger or casual acquaintance, but to actually make a friend, since people tend to like those people whom they help, as I mentioned when I told you about the Ben Franklin effect.

Like so many of these exercises, this one is most easily enacted when you combine it with other techniques, such as establishing a time constraint, speaking relatively slowly, and focusing on a neutral issue.

Choose a topic of need that fits your personality and context, and then approach the subject, establish a time constraint, speak slowly, keep your nonverbals friendly, and empower them by asking for assistance.

As I've mentioned, if you approach somebody who might be suspicious that you're hitting on them, mention your significant other, to dispel that concern.

You've probably already done this many times already—because we all need help from time to time, even from strangers—so it will feel natural, and you're almost certain to succeed. Therefore, don't focus on a mere pass/fail, but upon your ability to deepen the encounter into something meaningful, such as engaging in a more substantial conversation after they address your need.

A more substantial conversation could include prompting the person to reveal something about themselves, or connecting so well that it becomes obvious that they feel better because they met you.

When you ask for help, keep it short, and get to the point. Your opening line can be as simple as: "Excuse me, if you have a second, do you know if there's WiFi in this building, and if there is, do you need a password?"

Very few people will just blow you off.

But equally few will suddenly embrace your presence.

What happens next is up to you.

Drill #6: Empower others.
This is a big-picture drill, and it tests one of the primary tenets of inspiring trust. It's something you can do almost every day, as a normal course of conduct.

The best single way to empower others—and not only elicit their best qualities, but also make them want to be part of your tribe of trust—is to suspend your ego when you're with them.

Although I consider virtually all people to be on the same level as human beings, society generally assigns different levels of status, based upon external factors, such as money, beauty, and professional achievement. Because of that, this drill will elicit different reactions, based upon how people perceive the context of their own status.

If you and your subject are both at the same essential level of status, as dictated by society, suspending your ego will give those people the biological brain rewards that make them want to be around you. If you are at a higher level than they are in the proverbial pecking order, they will not only appreciate this mode of conduct, but will admire you for it.

The drill: approach someone—a stranger or a person you already know—and have a conversation that's solely about their needs, wants, challenges, and opinions.

Keep your own ideas to yourself, no matter how tempted you are to offer them.

If you have good stories that relate directly to the issue at hand, forget about them.

Pay such careful attention to them that they begin to offer you equal attention.

Do absolutely nothing that indicates that you have a relatively higher rank in the status hierarchy than they do—because in the context of a trust-based relationship, whatever title or position you have is irrelevant to them. All they care about is being treated with nonjudgmental validation, understanding, rationality, and generosity. The goal: make them feel so comfortable that they speak with animation and pleasure, and seem somewhat reluctant to end the conversation.

Best-case scenario: They will act as if they want to talk to you again. If they are a stranger, and offer you contact information, you will know that you succeeded admirably.

Drill #7: Don't agree to disagree.
This is one of the hardest exercises, especially for opinionated, well-informed people.

The drill: bring up a controversial topic, particularly one that you think your subject feels differently about than you do—and don't disagree with them, no matter what they say.

Express genuine curiosity about why they feel the way they do, and tell them you appreciate seeing their interesting perspective. Encourage them to elaborate. Do not correct them if they say something that you think, or even know, is false.

Don't try to change their mind, or to "enlighten" them in any way. Allow them full freedom of thought.

Attempt to see the topic so clearly from their perspective that you actually begin to tweak certain elements of your own opinions.

The goal: make them feel so safe in your presence that they share their opinions with total candor.

Bonus points: Actually change *your* opinion. If that happens, don't consider it a loss. Consider it a victory. There's a word for altering one of your opinions: *learning.*

The current political climate that condemns politicians for changing their opinions—labeling it as flip-flopping, to pander to current public opinion—is often nonsense. That's frequently just an illogical debating tactic intended only to discredit someone, with no regard for their sincere change of opinion.

Changing your mind on an issue can be one of the smartest things you ever do. It shows that you're open to new ideas, and that you listen to other people's opinions.

Good listeners are good learners, and good learners are smart.

Drill #8: Never argue context.

You've seen this advice many times in the book, and now it's time for you to practice it.

This drill is somewhat similar to the prior one, about not disagreeing, no matter how tempted you are. In this drill, though, it is acceptable to disagree—rationally, generously, and respectfully—but not to disagree due to differing *contexts.*

Hence—despite my antipathy for absolutes: *Never* argue context. If your goal is to have healthy, happy relationships, arguing context is a choice with predictably negative results.

If you're a Yankee fan and they're a Red Sox fan, don't try to change that. It's their context. Besides, they're *right*. (For the first time in this book: Just kidding! You can't be too careful about Boston fans.)

That doesn't mean that you can't take them to a Yankees game. Just don't expect them to cheer at the same time you do.

The drill: Bring up a controversial subject, similarly to the initial action in Drill #7. Seek their opinion first, and don't offer your own unless they ask for it.

If they do ask for your opinion, you can offer it, but remain respectful of how they feel, and tell them you're interested in their opinion, but haven't had time to fully consider it. This generous, rational behavior will give them a panoply of brain rewards that will make them want to keep talking to you, and hearing what you have to say.

When you do offer your opinion, don't offer even a hint of criticism about who or what they are, or question why they can't be more like you.

Try to understand their context—but from their perspective, not yours. Start this process by systematically learning about their context, guided by the information I gave you in chapter six. Discern their communications style, demography, generational attitudes, and personality type.

Again, as in Drill #7, don't be surprised if you change their point of view—and don't be surprised if they change yours.

After approximately twenty years of working with people from a variety of nationalities, ethnicities, political affiliations, and philosophies, I've developed a broad appreciation of what each person has to offer. I've found that the broader my own context becomes, the harder it is for me to be judgmental.

A terrible deficit in our current culture is the lack of the civil give-and-take that has expanded individual and societal intelligence for thousands of years.

Don't expect this drill to be easy. But if you can master the art of not judging others, there is no element of human interaction that will be beyond your abilities.

Drill #9: Manage your expectations.

It's ideal to have no expectations at all—but that's not always possible, and sometimes it isn't practical.

For example, if you expect someone to finish a project by its due date, and they've assured you that they will, it makes sense to expect them to complete it on time.

Just don't bet the farm on it. Things happen.

One thing that often prevents people from delivering what they promise is simple optimism. That's a common personality trait among Type-A hard chargers—and it's usually helpful. But not always.

Also, many people make unrealistic promises just because they're afraid to disappoint others, or to prevent others from pressuring them.

Difficulties arise when you expect everything to match your highest hopes. That's asking for disappointment.

Similarly, it's wise to have reasonable expectations of yourself.

The drill: Think about something you wish to achieve, and jot down your expectations about how well you'll do it, and how soon. Then manage your expectations of yourself, by jotting down a shorthand version of your Plan B—and C, and D.

Realize that the goals you set are moving targets. Know that just dreaming something doesn't make it real—no matter how many movies you've seen to the contrary.

Then do the hard part: manage your expectation of others. Make a few notes about ways they might fall short, and how you can give them a hand, or prevent it from happening.

The powers that animate this action are patience and flexibility. When you feel your expectations rising, summon all of the patience and flexibility you have, and let the Code do the rest. With the right kind of attention to its principles, you can almost feel its majestic forces working.

Then review your goal again, in this more realistic light.

If you do, you'll sleep better at night, and get along better with the people on your various projects.

Managing expectations requires Gumby super powers—but it's well within your capabilities.

Drill #10: Craft an encounter.

You probably starting doing this as soon as you read the chapter about it. If not, start now.

You'll probably meet someone today, even if it's just the co-workers you see every day, or your spouse at the end of the day. Instead of your typical non-preparation, craft that encounter, within the limited parameters afforded you.

Prepare to engage! Think about the environment in which you'd most like to meet: your office, their office, the lunchroom, your living room, or your kitchen. If possible, optimize the time of the encounter. Think about what they will want, need, and expect. Present yourself properly—from *their* perspective: a suit, a sweater, a limo?

Plan your opening remark—your first shot downrange—and let it be guided by the Code.

Prepare for the various responses to that remark, using the who-what-when-where-why system in chapter seven.

Engage!

Then review how well it went, and compare it to meetings that were not crafted at all. As a rule, the ones you craft are inordinately more satisfying for all parties involved.

Drill #11: Speak according to the Code of Communication.

The drill: spend an entire day, or at least a day at work, speaking only in a manner that's consistent with the trust-inspiring Code of Communication.

As you may recall, the Code of Communication—like so many of the procedural aspects of my system—is an absolutely direct reflection of the Code of Trust, and consists of these five Code qualities: 1. Suspend your ego. 2. Be nonjudgmental. 3. Validate others. 4. Honor reason. 5. Be generous.

As you may recall from chapter eight, the Code of Communication employs three essential techniques: 1. Direct the course of a conversation with questions. 2. Influence the outcome of a conversation with active listening. 3. Decode nonverbal communication.

Various tips: Keep your opinions to yourself. Check your own stories at the door. Keep you nonverbals consistent with your verbals. Don't criticize, even with caveats. Use occasional encouraging remarks, paraphrase what people say, limit your use of absolutes, and leave your debating tactics back in high school, where they belong.

Each time you stray from that form, try to catch yourself, and correct course. Don't even try to be perfect. Won't happen.

Here's a promise: for once, when you talk the talk, without always walking the walk, it will still pay enormous dividends.

Drill #12: Tap the power of apology.

Great leaders apologize more often than most people. It's not because they're wrong more often. It's because they're humble enough to offer apologies without feeling personally demeaned, and know that nothing signifies concern and respect for others better than an apology.

It's also because leaders are almost constantly involved in efforts that require the sacrifice of team members' individual needs and goals—and when team members offer that, they deserve more than just "Thanks." They also sometimes deserve: "I'm sorry."

A positive aspect of a leader's frequent need to apologize is that it's typically easier for them. That's because they've got their eyes on the prize—their ultimate goal—which greatly softens the blow of having to apologize.

It's worth it. Their only real concern is: will the words out of my mouth move me closer to my ultimate goal, or not?

Leaders also know that apologizing is nothing more than assuming at least a degree of responsibility for whatever went wrong. That's simple honesty, based on the reality that nobody's perfect, and honesty is a cardinal character trait of the Code.

The drill: Apologize to somebody today. Don't worry about finding the opportunity. If you're a leader, it will find you. You may need to ask for sacrifice, which is the very essence of teamwork, or some plan may fail that you played a part in.

I guarantee that many of the times you need to make an apology will be when you least feel like it. Those will be during times of conflict, when the devil on your shoulder will be quoting Benjamin Disraeli: "Never apologize! Never explain!"—while the angel on the other shoulder says, "If Disreali was so smart, how come I don't know who he is?"

You may even need to apologize to someone who made a serious mistake. If that happens, realize that in one way or another you may have helped cause—or failed to prevent—the mistake.

Take accountability for whatever role you may have played, no matter how small. Realize that if you played only a minor role in the problem, you may have been the straw that broke the camel's back. Also, even a minor concession will greatly improve the morale of the person who primarily caused the problem, and make them far less defensive about taking responsibility for their own role. Plus, they'll never forget that when they screwed up, you stepped forward and shared some of the blame.

As always, never argue context.

Be patient.

Know that when your goal is to have healthy relationships and honest communication, this is one of the important, difficult actions that achieves that. If you realize this, even something as ostensibly painful as apologizing can feel good, in and of itself.

Don't think about just the reaction of the person you're apologizing to, but also the reactions of everyone who will witness or hear about the fact that you made amends with someone. Apologies have a benign snowballing effect, and the lack of apologies can create a virtual avalanche of discord.

There are many ways to craft an apology, so find one that suits your personality.

The only inviolable rule: If your apology includes the word *but,* you're the butt.

Drill #13: Remove the poison from a toxic person.

For your sake, I hope you don't meet a venomous person anytime soon. But you probably will. When it happens, be ready to work the Code and turn a potentially devastating encounter into a positive one.

If you're one of the lucky few who rarely meet troubled, insecure people, you'll still benefit by role-playing this with someone because it can't help but strengthen your sense of empathy, a golden quality.

As in so many instances, your saving grace in dealing with a toxic person will be knowing your ultimate goal: the long-awaited destination that makes the difficult travel bearable. The moment you encounter a toxic person, shift your focus to that goal.

The single most important strategy is to rise above the troubling behavior of the other person, instead of responding in kind. It's hard. But it works. Many people fight fire with fire—but wise people fight fire with water.

Ask yourself, What can I do to quench this inflammatory behavior? Don't take the attack personally and get emotionally hijacked. That's usually what a toxic person wants, because conflict is often a form of sport to them. For the most part, they've abandoned hope that reason, empathy, and generosity will serve their needs, and have retreated into their own dark world of head games and war games.

Instead of giving them what they want, give them what they need: validation, understanding, generosity, rationality, and inclusion.

Those universally desired qualities can fill the deep holes of hurt in almost anyone.

Don't expect it to work immediately.

But expect it to work.

When it does, expect to have a person in your life who feels that when others vilified them, you looked within them, and found their hidden heart. Expect to have a new member in your tribe of trust who will be proud to follow your lead forever.

Drill #14: Reprimand without rancor.

No matter how well you manage your expectations, there will be times when you'll need to tell people that they must do things differently.

In any project of significance—from having a happy family vacation, to restructuring a division in a corporation—the need for requesting different behavior is inevitable. That's just a fact of daily life for most managers, parents, and team members.

Some managers, of course, believe they need to kick asses to keep groups motivated, but that's just old-fashioned, fear-based management, and its efficacy has severe limitations. Whoever you are trying to intimidate already has fears of their own, and won't—in the long run, without harboring resentment—respond positively to a gratuitous increase in their anxiety.

In fact, the best way to turn a subordinate into a backstabber is to first stab them in the front.

Nobody ever went to work in the morning, or came home from work at night, with the goal of being the resident screw-up, or ass.

The drill: identify a challenge that someone is having, and instead of being notably critical, help them solve it, to your mutual satisfaction, without even letting them know that they are being reprimanded.

That can be easier than it sounds, since many people don't even realize they've made a mistake—partly because they didn't *intend* to be a screw-up, and did what they thought was right. In that situation, the mistake was simply part of their context, and there's no point in arguing about it.

If your goal is to have them recognize *your* context, and do things the way you want them done, ask yourself: Why should they? The correct answer is not: "Because I'm the boss"—or, "Because I know best."

The reason is because your way is the right way. It's not because the right way is *your* way.

Approach them from the perspective of their context, with nonjudgmental validation, and start by mentioning various things they've done that you really like—not to butter them up, or to show what a great person you are, but to show them what *you* consider success, from *your* context.

Then help them see the problem from your perspective. Use a non-accusatory line of questioning, along the lines of: I never saw this done in quite this way before. What made you do it this way? What are the advantages? What challenges are you having?

If they don't seem to understand your observations, ask them if they're curious about what you observed.

Be sincere, not patronizing.

Sometimes you'll see that their way really is best, and sometimes they'll start to see that there are better ways to do it. Either way, they will lower their shields, and: Shields Down, Information In!

Seek their thoughts and opinions about the larger scope of their work. Ask them if they're moving successfully toward their goals.

Speak in the language of trust, don't personalize your dissatisfaction, and don't become collateral damage in their own defensive insecurities.

Above all, solve the *problem*—not the person.

This will take a little longer than something along the lines of: You screwed up—now fix it! It will be time well spent.

The solutions to the person's shortcomings—if they exist—are up to *them*. Solving problems, one by one, is the best way for you to help them discover their own challenges, and fix them.

When you fix their problems, they'll have the same problem again.

When they fix their own problems, the problems will stay fixed.

Drill #15: Build your tribe of trust.

As I indicated in chapter eleven—in the section about building a network of trust with the Hub and Spoke Method—there is no finite limit to the size of a tribe of trust.

Every person in the tribe is not only a spoke in your tribe, but also the hub of their own tribe—resulting in a limitless network of affiliations.

The reach of these connected tribes can be truly astonishing.

Here's the drill: make a simple Hub-and-Spoke diagram of your own tribe of trust, with yourself in the center, and those who trust you, and are trusted by you, as spokes.

Make a few brief notations, in your own style, of the special qualities that exist among those in your tribe. For example, if someone is your most trusted associate, write their name larger, underline it, or place them closer to you in your system of spokes. If someone has a particular power or an ultimate goal, make a note of it by their name.

Then enlarge your diagram, to the best of your ability, by making each of the people who are your spokes into hubs of their own, with their own spokes. As your diagram grows into a web of connection, it will resemble the overlapping circles of a Venn diagram.

Last, make a list, perhaps in the margins, of people who might be valuable members of not only your own tribe of trust, but also the tribes of those who are your spokes.

If some of those people seem eminently well suited to be spokes in your diagram (and hubs of their own), put them in the appropriate places, with an indicator that signifies the desirability of their inclusion.

Step back. See your diagram as your own universe of trust.

Keep the diagram.

Add to it. Improve it. Watch it grow.

Look at it from time to time, and stand in awe of all that you've learned; of all of the amazing people who surround you; and of all the vast, unnumbered possibilities that your life now holds.

Stop. Celebrate these possibilities.

Then begin again.

APPENDIX

YOUR USERS GUIDE TO *THE CODE OF TRUST* WITH A GLOSSARY

The Primary Points in *The Code of Trust*

1. The Mission of *The Code of Trust*

The purpose of the book is to teach a consistent, replicable system for becoming trustworthy, and conveying that trustworthiness to others. This will naturally confer leadership, and better relationships with most people.

2. *The Code of Trust*'s Central Assertion

Long-term, unimpeachable leadership is absolutely dependent upon inspiring the trust of those one wishes to lead. Leading through trust is the one strategy for leadership that is almost universally effective—for virtually all leaders, in practically every situation—and is the only one that endures.

3. The Theme of *The Code of Trust*

To inspire trust, put others first.

4. The Power Point of *The Code of Trust*

Trust has become the single most powerful element in achieving success, personally and professionally. In our current era, widely dubbed

The Age of Distrust, every form of fraud is routinely exposed by the Internet, the explosion of traditional media, and the ubiquity of social media. Manipulation, as a major motivating force, is dead.

5. The Methodology Presented in *The Code of Trust*

To become trustworthy, follow the five-rule system designated as the Code of Trust. To inspire others to recognize your trustworthiness, follow the four-point system designated as the Four Steps to Trust.

6. The Setting of *The Code of Trust*

The book is set in the Federal Bureau of Investigation's Counterintelligence Behavioral Analysis Program, with a national and international reach.

The Program is part of the FBI's Counterintelligence Division, which is part of the FBI's National Security Branch, tasked with defending the United States against terrorist and foreign intelligence threats.

The mission of the Behavioral Analysis Program is to attain the highest levels of understanding of human behavior, including the behavioral traits that inspire trust.

The Program consists of a team of expert FBI Counterintelligence Special Agents who—through their training, backgrounds, and experiences—have mastered the act of inspiring trust, often using the systematic program described in this book.

7. The Narrator of *The Code of Trust*

Special Agent Robin Dreeke—whose life experiences and concepts compose the core of the book—is a former head of the FBI's Behavioral Analysis Program, a graduate of the U.S. Naval Academy, a former captain in the United States Marines, and a consultant to businesses, universities, law enforcement agencies, and other institutions.

The Systems of Trust

1. THE CODE OF TRUST
The Five Rules to Gain Trust and Be a Leader

Rule # 1: *Suspend your ego.* Inspiring trust requires putting the needs, wants, dreams, and desires of the other people ahead of your own. If you put others first, there is no reason for them not to follow you. If you're just thinking about yourself, why should they? The single most compelling trait of trust is simple humility.

Rule #2: *Be nonjudgmental.* Respect the opinions, attitudes, ideas, and perspectives of all people—no matter how foreign, or even opposed to your own. Respect doesn't mean approval. It means understanding.

Rule #3: *Validate others.* Recognize the human decency that resides in at least a small part of virtually every human being on earth, and try to understand people from that perspective. Validation, like respect, doesn't mean approval. It means understanding.

Rule #4: *Honor reason.* Be honest, and resist all forms of manipulation—from flattery, to coercion. Only those who rely on reason, reflected by honesty, can create the foundation of rational, shared self-interest that all enduring trust rests upon.

Rule #5: *Be generous.* People do not allow themselves to trust those who create one-sided relationships. Selfishness repels. Generosity attracts.

2. THE FOUR STEPS:
The Action Plan for Inspiring Trust

1. *Align Your Goals!* Determine your own ultimate goal, and align it with those of others, making their goals part of yours. You will achieve the power of combined forces.

2. Apply the Power of Context! People only trust those who know them, so learn the traits, desires, demographics, and ideas of others: their context. You cannot deal with people effectively unless you know how they see the world.

3. Craft Your Encounters! To inspire trust, a meeting needs to proceed almost perfectly, from the beginning remark until the final decision to link missions. Achieving this requires strategic evaluation of the people, their primary motivations, the place, the time, and the precise subject matter. A carefully crafted meeting is a work of art, and the setting for success.

4. Connect! Every connection culminates with two people speaking the "language of trust." This language is founded in a philosophy of reason, respect, and consideration. It consists of a vocabulary of power words that evoke trust and eliminate the natural wariness that almost all people bring to their encounters with others. The person who is the first to use the language of trust is usually the one who drives the meeting and secures the lasting linkage of missions that only trust can deliver. The most succinct way to describe the language of trust is: it's all about them.

3. OPENING REMARKS:
The Seven-Point System

1. Establish a time limit. It shows respect and limits defensiveness.

2. Ask for assistance. We are all biologically programmed to help others, and to believe that those whom we help deserve it and are worthy of our attention.

3. Offer something. Offering is as powerful as asking in the formation of a personal bond. It prompts reciprocal gift-giving and can begin a cascade of mutual benefit.

4. Stick to the subject: them. If you have stories of your own, keep them to yourself, and people will consider you a great conversationalist.

5. Empower and validate people. Making friends is not about how you make people feel about you. It's how you make them feel about themselves. People crave your understanding even more than your approval.

6. *Manage your expectations.* The more you think about what you hope to get from people, the less likely you'll be to get it. The more you think about what you can give, the more you'll get.

7. *Explain yourself skillfully.* It's not enough for your heart to be in the right place. Your head needs to be there, too. Be rational, speak slowly, use positive language, and forget every manipulative trick you ever learned.

4. THE COMMUNICATIONS STYLE INVENTORY: A Four-Part System for Effective Interaction

To inspire trust, speak to people in the way they prefer to be spoken to.

There are four basic types of communicators, based upon the personality traits of being direct or indirect, and people oriented or task oriented.

Direct communicators speak freely, think out loud, like verbal give-and-take, and don't want to be held to everything that pops out of their mouths. They believe that these traits lead to honest, open communication.

Indirect communicators choose words and thoughts carefully, think before they speak, are typically quite rational, and like to be taken seriously when they say something.

These two categories are naturally coupled with the two classic traits of being *people oriented,* or *task oriented.*

Task-oriented types are often go-getters who focus more on the job than the people who do it, can be impatient with people, are often fun, and can burn out fast.

People-oriented types are generally calmer, more careful, patient, have great endurance, and are more focused on how does a job than on the job itself.

These two types of communicators and two types of personalities combine to create four general types of communicators:

1. *Direct, Task-Oriented Communicators.* They like to speak

succinctly, stick strictly to the point, focus on schedules and budgets, and keep humor to a reasonable minimum.

2. *Direct, People-Oriented Communicators.* They're logical and linear, but like to illustrate their points with stories. They're intuitive, and you can speak emotionally with them, but you'll lose credibility if you substitute intuition for critical thinking, and your emotional appeals don't make sense.

3. *Indirect, Task-Oriented Communicators.* Speak clearly and rationally to them, and they'll follow every word. When you veer into emotion and speculation, you've lost them.

4. *Indirect, People-Oriented Communicators.* These people will tolerate a lack of structure and directness in communication, but that doesn't mean they like it. Don't take advantage of the empathy of a people-oriented, indirect types by thinking that their tolerance gives you license to go off on tangents.

5. THE DISC SYSTEM
A Four-Component Personality Type System

Dominance Style. This type of person likes power, prestige, material possessions, and accomplishments. They're efficient, like challenges, and want to know "why" about all issues. To succeed, they need an emphasis on external values, a wide scope of operation, and help with people skills, and pacing.

Influence style. This type of person gravitates toward popularity, public recognition, group activities, and camaraderie. To succeed, they sometimes need to be prodded, and reminded that details matter.

Steady style. This type of person is good at maintaining the status-quo, and having a happy, balanced life. They thrive on security, but are sometimes too slow, and not very creative. They need reassurance, and a sense of being understood.

Conscientious style. This type of person likes limited exposure to risk, teamwork, and lack of change. They are good at helping others, but often need help themselves, particularly with their self-confidence.

5. THE ACTIVE LISTENING SYSTEM
Twelve Commandments

1. Listen for what matters most—*to them.*
2. Keep your opinions to yourself.
3. Listen carefully enough to offer honest validation.
4. Don't overthink a conversation or enter one with a set of memorized lines.
5. Check your own stories at the door.
6. Don't preempt a criticism with a caveat.
7. Keep listening after you fully understand.
8. Leave no doubt that you're listening.
9. Limit your use of absolutes.
10. Don't use debating tactics.
11. Don't apologize by accusing.
12. Put away the damn cell phone.

6. A SYSTEM FOR DIRECTING A CONVERSATION: THE POWER OF ASKING

1. Use questions to create clarity.
2. Influence actions by what you ask.
3. Ask in accord with the Platinum Rule.
4. Ask instead of argue.
5. Ask people about their micro-context.
6. Ask instead of accuse.
7. Ask open-ended questions.
8. Make statements with questions.

GLOSSARY:
THE TERMS OF TRUST

70 WORDS AND PHRASES TO REMEMBER

Access Agent

A term applied to a United States private citizen who is recruited by the FBI, or another federal intelligence agency, to provide information regarding a potential spy, also known as a "subject," or any other person who is a suspected of threatening American security. The citizen is asked to help provide access to the subject, in order to initiate an investigation, or to help with an ongoing investigation.

The Age of Distrust

A phrase now commonly applied to the current era of widespread distrust in America. This age is generally considered to have begun during the turbulent era most significantly characterized by the Vietnam War, and the Watergate scandal. Since then, there has been an increasing lack of faith in basic American institutions, including government, business, education, and medicine. The trust in these fundamental elements of society is now at a record low, according to most studies and polls.

Air Support Control Officer

A U.S. Marine Corps assignment. It is similar to that of an air traffic controller, but applies to combat situations.

Aligning goals

The act of combining the various goals of two or more people, to help each person better achieve his or her own goal. This act typically occurs only in an atmosphere of mutual trust, and the act amplifies this trust. It generally involves finding common interests that will benefit each person. When the goals of at least two people are aligned, each person is almost always better able to reach his or her own goal. Aligning goals is the single most important act in building a network of trust, also referred to, in this book, as a tribe of trust. It can also powerfully enable at least one of the people involved to rise to a position of leadership.

Attaché

A person who is attached to a foreign embassy. That person generally has a specific area of expertise—such as a knowledge of military affairs, in the case of a "military attaché.

Beacon

A term coined in *The Code of Trust* to specifically refer to a person who emanates trustworthiness. Their aura of trustworthiness is the result of the past actions, current behavior, attitudes (particularly the willingness to put others first), and characteristics of the person's verbal and nonverbal communication. This projection of trustworthiness, likened to the beacon of a lighthouse, naturally attracts other people, offering them a sense of security, direction, and empowerment. This quality endows people with the ability to become widely trusted, sometimes even by virtual strangers.

Beans, Bullets, and Band-Aids

A military expression that refers to the three primary support elements that must be present during the chaos of a battle. These support elements are designed and coordinated prior to the battle. *Beans* refers to food, *Bullets* to auxiliary ammunition, and *Band-Aids* to medical care. Robin Dreeke adapted this phrase to apply to the preparation for nonmilitary encounters, particularly those in which a person is seeking to inspire trust. These civilian encounters also often also involve chaos and confusion. For these encounters, various preparatory elements, akin to "Beans, Bullets, and Band-Aids," are designed to meet the multiple variables that may occur.

Ben Franklin Effect

This is a colloquial term for a phenomenon, first described by Benjamin Franklin, that occurs when one person asks another for a favor. Franklin observed that people who ask for a favor, and receive it, generally provoke a feeling of approval from the person who granted the favor. This happens because the person who granted the favor is naturally disposed to feel as if he or she must surely like the person who asked for help, or he or she wouldn't have granted the favor. To feel otherwise would create a sense of inner conflict, referred to as cognitive dissonance. The Ben Franklin effect can be applied as a method for gaining the approval of and affiliation with those in whom one wishes to inspire trust. It is especially helpful for gaining the approval of a stranger, whose opinion of the favor-seeker has been neutral to that point. The favor that one asks for can be very simple and subtle, such as asking for permission to sit, or asking for directions.

Brain Hijacking

A colloquial term that refers to the confusion, and the decrease of the ability to be rational, that can occur during moments of stress or conflict, often resulting in a shift of control of a situation to the person who created a conflict. In this situation, emotions usually overpower reason, creating negative consequences. Brain hijacking can result from an obvious threat or insult, and even from the sense of being subtly manipulated. This common phenomenon interferes significantly with the behaviors that inspire trust, and is one reason that manipulation does not effectively inspire robust, lasting trust. Because of the trust-damaging effects of brain hijacking, one of the five rules of the Code of Trust is: honor reason. This prevents the person who is seeking trust from engaging in manipulation, and it prevents the person whose trust is being sought from overreacting to the perception of manipulation, an insult, or any other form of aggression or coercion. In moments

of brain hijacking, it is very helpful to be guided by a system that focuses on rational, reasonable thought. The system becomes a default
platform for remaining in control of the situation.

Caudate Nucleus

The primary pleasure center of the brain. It is a major site for romantic
attachment, and for other forms of bonding, including the development
of trust. It is primarily influenced by the rewarding, stimulating neurotransmitter known as dopamine. Impaired function of this area of the
brain can significantly reduce one's ability to be trusting. This physical
impairment, and the lack of trust that it triggers, is often present in
people with neurological and psychological disorders. These disorders,
characterized by worry and agitation, include obsessive-compulsive
disorder, PTSD, neurotransmitter imbalance, frank paranoia, and
ADHD. Temporary impairment from mild conditions associated with
these disorders is quite common. It is therefore important to be aware of
the presence of these disorders, even in their subtle forms, in the process
of inspiring trust.

CENTCOM

The acronym for the U.S. Central Command, the single most powerful
military entity in the world. CENTCOM oversees all U.S. military
operations in the Middle East, North Africa, and Central Asia.

The chemistry of trust is all about us.

A phrase, coined in *The Code of Trust,* that refers to the linkage of biochemical and psychological elements of trust inspiration that occurs
during a positive encounter. Although the biochemical elements are
linked to the psychological elements, they are also distinctly different
from the psychological aspects of bonding, which are often colloquially described as "*chemistry.*" These two distinct elements can become
linked when one person invokes the Code of Trust, and begins to inspire trust in another person, using the Code's tenets. This triggers rewarding biochemical reactions in the other person, such as the secretion
of feel-good neurotransmitters. This shift in biochemistry amplifies the

psychological gratification that implementation of the Code imparts. The resulting inspiration of trust often rewards the other person so much that it triggers a shift in their attention from themselves to the person who inspired them, and prompts them to engage in positive behaviors. At that point, both parties experience equally rewarding biochemical and psychological reactions, as the barriers that separate them fall. In effect, "you" and "I" become us—confirming the concept that the chemistry of trust is all about us.

Code of Communication
This five-element code, based directly upon the Code of Trust, is an important part of the Language of Trust, as described in this book. It primarily describes the philosophical elements of the Language of Trust, such as the concepts of putting others first, and offering nonjudgmental validation.

Coercion
This is an act that involves the use of force or threats to motivate action. It is one of the most common tools of manipulation, and is often delivered very subtly. Although it can achieve temporary compliance, it severely undermines trust, as do virtually all acts of manipulation. Despite this, manipulation is still commonly used as a tactic, albeit ineffective, for creating trust.

Communications Style Inventory
This is a system created by Robin Dreeke for addressing people in the specific manner in which they prefer to be addressed, such as in a highly personal manner, or in a more formal, impersonal manner. The Dreeke "CSI" was derived in part from the Marston DISC system (see *DISC*), the first popular system of personality typing. The CSI categorizes people into four general types of communicators: Direct, Task-Oriented Communicators; Direct, People-Oriented Communicators; Indirect, Task-Oriented Communicators; and Indirect, People-Oriented Communicators. Dreeke has demonstrated that addressing people in their preferred style of communication is a major asset in inspiring their trust.

Contentment Neurotransmitters

These are the calming brain chemicals—including serotonin, and GABA (gamma aminobutyric acid)—that carry positive thoughts and emotions, including the feeling of trust. Deficits or functional derangement of these neurotransmitters, which is very common, can critically impair the ability to trust, even when that lack of trust is irrational. A neurotransmitter that is also an important component of positive emotion, and involved in transmitting feelings of trust, is the stimulating, excitatory neurotransmitter dopamine. Hormones that have similar, trust-transmitting qualities include oxytocin and endorphins.

Context

A person's context is their general, overal makeup, including their beliefs, personality traits, behaviors, and demographic characteristics. Each of these elements of their context strongly influences their opinions and goals. To inspire trust, it is important to relate to a person within the framework of their context, rather than to try to change some or all of it, or to superimpose your own context on them. Altering someone's context is almost impossible to do in a short-term situation. Therefore, one of the rules of trust inspiration is, "Never argue context." Approach people as they are, rather than how you want them to be.

Counterintelligence Division

This is a major component of the FBI's National Security Branch, and focuses on threats to America from foreign sources. It is most commonly active in investigating, exposing, and neutralizing foreign spies, and in recruiting American citizens to help gather information about threats to the United States.

Craft your encounters

This phrase is the title of one of the Four Steps to Trust. It refers to the act of engaging in detailed, systematic preparation for meeting someone, particularly if the goal of the meeting is to inspire their trust. It is important in all meetings, but is most important in an initial meeting. It is often essential in overcoming the natural barriers that people erect to keep from being exploited and manipulated.

The Crucible
A difficult final training period for Marine Corps candidates.

DI
A military acronym for Drill Instructor, the trainer of new military personnel. Drill Instructors are charged with changing the attitudes and philosophies of new recruits, away from the realm of self-interest, toward a spirit of unselfishness, teamwork, and camaraderie. Building the trust of individual recruits for one another is a central effort in this reorientation.

Director's Award
The highest award that is presented to agents of the Federal Bureau of Investigation. Its name is a reference to the Director of the agency. It tends to reward selfless, group-oriented achievement even more than individual heroics.

DISC
The first prominent system of personality and behavior typing. It was created in 1928 by William Moulton Marston, and is still widely used. It has inspired several new generations of similar systems, including one created by Robin Dreeke that is described in this book. The acronym stands for four essential types of behaviors: Dominance, Inducement, Submission, and Compliance. Marston also created the modern polygraph machine, and the comic book character Wonder Woman.

Encryption
The use of secret, proprietary coding to send messages. It is commonly used by intelligence agencies in the transmission of classified information. Hostile foreign sources regularly attempt to break encrypted codes, and to recruit, or co-opt, the personnel who have expertise in and access to the codes.

Erewhon

A euphemism—*Nowhere* spelled backward—that is used within the FBI and other intelligence agencies to designate a country anonymously, to avoid revealing its actual name. A similar euphemism is "Centralia."

Evolutionary Psychology

An approach to psychology that ascribes certain human behaviors to the adaptation responses that are governed by the processes of natural selection. Because trust is a learned response, and is subject to changes in situations, various aspects of trust can be evaluated effectively from the perspective of evolutionary psychology.

FBI Bulletin

The *Bulletin* is a publication of the FBI, available to the public online, that reflects emerging strategies in law enforcement and national security. One recurring topic in the publication is the study of the systems designed to foster and maintain trust. Robin Dreeke has authored several articles in the *Bulletin* on the inspiration of trust, and on other issues.

Feed-Forward response

This is an unconscious act in which the body prepares itself for a specific action, when it is spurred by anticipation of the action. For example, anticipating a conflict can cause an increase in heart rate, prior to the actual conflict. The feed-forward response can also perpetuate a thought or emotion, even after the thought or emotion has proved to be no longer valid. For example, a fast heart rate, due to thoughts of fear, can create further thoughts of fear, many of which may no longer be rational. Because this physical response can endow the body with, in effect, "a mind of its own," it is a common barrier to trust. People often remain resistant to trust even after the resistance is no longer rational, simply because of stress-response factors, such as an increase in blood pressure, heart rate, blood vessel constriction, and rate of breathing. To restore the ability of a person to be open to trust, these physical factors often need to be addressed first. For example, people who are agitated are sometimes advised to take a deep breath, to intervene in the stress response. Persuasion and reassurance that is made prior to the cessation of the physical factors of the stress response is often of negligible value.

5 Ws of Crafting an Encounter

The 5 Ws are part of the fourth step to trust, Craft the Encounter. Applying them properly amplifies the opportunity to inspire trust. Each of the 5 Ws refers to an aspect of a person that significantly determines the most effective way in which to address him or her. They include knowing the following: (1) *Who,* in detail, the person is, demographically and personally. (2) *What* the person's external attributes are, including their occupation, preferred style of dress, and conversational style. (3) *When* the most likely time is that they will lower their defensive shields. (4) *Where* the ideal place is for them to lower their defensive shields. (5) *Why* it is in their best interests to meet you, and to align your mutual goals.

Forebrain

The only part of the three primary areas of the human brain that has risen significantly beyond irrational, animalistic instincts. It is situated directly behind the forehead. It was the last of the three areas to develop during evolution and is the last to develop in a human fetus. The forebrain's outer layers—most notably the frontal lobe—are the focal point of human reasoning, and therefore the physical site of trust. Because the forebrain is primarily concerned with logic, reason, and memory, efforts to build trust must be based upon rational thought processes. Building trust strictly through emotion is typically ineffective in the creation of lasting, abundant trust.

Fourth Class Company Commander

A rank among students at the U.S. Naval Academy. It designates responsibility for the other students, or plebes. The rank is often indicative of the ability of a student to inspire trust in his or her peers. As such, the assignment is used as a template to teach trust inspiration in the U.S. military.

Hindbrain

Also referred to as the reptilian brain, this is the rear portion of the brain, nearest the spine. It was the first part of the brain to develop during evolution, and is the first part to develop in a human fetus. It controls basic physical functions, but is incapable of bonding emotions or higher thought. It is involved in the detection of danger, and can be activated by overt acts that negate trust, including threatening body language, or coercive messages. Once its forces are engaged, it can be difficult to overcome them with logic and positive emotion.

Hub and Spoke Method

The method devised by Robin Dreeke for helping to create groups that are linked by mutual trust. His system is named after a flight technique, in which a pilot focuses on a central instrument, or hub, then glances at the instruments that surround it, designated as "spokes." In a tribe of trust, each "spoke" is also the "hub" of his or her own tribe of trust. This can create networks of overlapping tribes, all linked by the quality of mutual trust.

HUMINT

An acronym used by U.S. intelligence agencies that stands for *hum*an sources of *int*elligence. These human sources are people who know facts, or can help determine facts, that relate to matters of national security. It is generally considered the most reliable source of intelligence.

IARPA

The acronym for the Intelligence Advanced Research Projects Activity, a government group, with which Robin Dreeke has worked, that has done extensive research on trust.

IMINT

An acronym used by U.S. intelligence agencies that stands for *Im*agery *Int*elligence. The images reveal facts relevant to intelligence investigations, and are gained through various imaging techniques, including the use of spy satellites.

Isopraxis
A behavioral technique aimed at gaining acceptance and affiliation with a person by essentially adopting that person's style of verbal and non-verbal communication. Although the technique can be effective when it is implemented skillfully, it can become self-defeating when it is used in a clumsy, exaggerated manner.

It's all about them
A phrase that reflects the sentiment of putting others first. The concept is critically important as a method of inspiring trust. It requires an emotional commitment to the best interests of others, as well as a shift in attention from oneself to others. This can initially be difficult for people who are accustomed to seeking advancement through self-promotion, and focus upon their own self-interests.

Language of Trust
A concept, created in *The Code of Trust,* that refers to a specific trust-inspiring style of speaking. The style is based upon a philosophical commitment to humility, reason, respect, and consideration, in contrast to egotism, irrationality, judgmentalism, and selfishness. Various words and phrases compose and animate this language, and others defeat it. Mastering the language is essential to those who seek trust-based leadership.

Manipulation
The commonly used psychological technique that attempts to change the behavior or perception of others by using coercive, dishonest, or irrational tactics. Although it is the polar opposite of the trust-based model, people often try to use it as a technique for creating a genuine sense of trust. Trust created by manipulation is almost always shallow, and short lived. In many cases, any display of manipulation defeats the possibility of inspiring trust. This can occur even among people who can easily benefit from aligning their mutual goals.

Maslow's Hierarchy of Needs

A theory of psychology created by Abraham Maslow in 1943 that espouses the existence of a very limited number of primary human needs. These needs were stated to include: physical well-being; safety; love and belonging; self-esteem, self-actualization; and self-transcendence. This psychological construct, and others related to it or derived from it, can help people decide upon their own ultimate goals. Knowing one's ultimate goal creates the mission that enables people to willingly sacrifice minor, immediate privileges, in pursuit of their ultimate goals.

Midbrain

Also referred to as the mammalian brain, it is the middle portion of the human brain. It was the second part of the three-part human brain to develop during evolution, and is the second part to develop in a human fetus. The midbrain is capable of emotion and various physical functions, but is limited in its ability to access the full range of the intellect, which is governed primarily by the forebrain.

Neurobiology

The science of the nervous system that includes the physical, tangible elements of the nervous system, along with the intangible, psychological elements of thought and emotion. Trust, like most complex behavioral attributes, is influenced by a combination of tangible and intangible factors, and can best be understood within the framework of neurobiology.

Nonjudgmental

A general attitude that is extremely conducive to the inspiration of trust. A nonjudgmental attitude is arguably the single most important element in inspiring trust, because it allows other people to be open and honest about who they are and what they want, without fear of rejection. People who are nonjudgmental are often those who have risen beyond egotism, which invariably creates an aura of superiority that is often interpreted as a judgmental attitude.

Nonverbal Communication

An element of communication commonly referred to as body language. Nonverbal communication, as demonstrated by body language expert Joe Navarro, must be in strict accord with verbal communication. If it is not, it will trigger an immediate suspension of trust. Similarly, nonverbal communication must be presented naturally, rather than mechanically, to avoid creating a sense of distrust. As a rule, the most important nonverbal cues in the inspiration of trust are those that are delivered with facial expressions.

Operative

A person, either a private citizen or professional intelligence agent, who is actively engaged in serving government intelligence efforts. Citizen-operatives, also referred to as co-optees, are typically motivated by a desire to help protect their country's national security. The tasks of a citizen-operative can vary, but often involve providing information about people who are suspected of being spies.

OSINT

An acronym used by U.S. intelligence agencies that stands for Open-Source Intelligence. This source of intelligence is composed of public records, and other nonclassified sources of information, including academic and business information. Many foreign operatives engage primarily in acquiring open-source intelligence. Although obtaining this information is legal, the information is often used to enable foreign companies or governments to violate patents, and to make illegal use of proprietary information.

Platinum Rule

An extension of the "do unto others" Golden Rule. The Platinum Rule advocates treating people not necessarily in the way that you want to be treated, but in the way that they want to be treated, even if that way would not be your own preference. It was created by Dr. Tony Alessandra, and was the subject of the 1996 book *The Platinum Rule*, by Alessandra, and Michael O'Connor, PhD. The philosophy of the Platinum

Rule was adapted by Robin Dreeke to serve as an important element in trust-inspiring behavior.

Principles of Digital Interaction
Five principles that govern effective use of digital communication devices in the inspiration of trust. The five principles are closely associated with, and are another iteration of, the Code of Trust: suspend your ego; be nonjudgmental; validate others; honor reason; and be generous. They are tailored to the nuances, advantages, and limitations of digital communication, and the emerging etiquette of the digital era. The principles are a further indication that the Code of Trust is a fundamental, universal framework for positive human interaction. It is as applicable to matters of electronic relationship-building as it is to spoken communication, but requires some adaptation.

Proprietary Information
Information, such as a trade secret, that is not intended for public dissemination, nor is legally available. Gaining access to this information, which is not open-source information, is a primary activity of foreign operatives. It is typically obtained through bribery, coercion, trickery, and theft. It is particularly destructive to the U.S. technology and manufacturing industries, and is estimated to cost American businesses more than $5 billion per year. The FBI is closely involved in stopping this form of malfeasance, which undermines not only the American economy, but America's national security.

Props
Various articles that create an image or impression, including those used by the FBI and other intelligence agencies to help inspire trust. The props—including clothing, accessories, and other accoutrements—are used to create a sense of kinship and affiliation, and to improve effective communication. These same elements can be used in any environment in which a person is seeking to make a positive impression, or to make others feel comfortable, secure, and trusting. A simple example

of it is to dress in approximately the same general style, tailored to your own tastes, as the person with whom you are meeting.

Quantico

The rural Virginia site of the FBI Academy, as well as the headquarters of the Behavioral Analysis Unit, which sometimes works in conjunction with the Academy. The Academy is a training base for all FBI agents, and numerous American law enforcement agencies. Quantico is also a massive Marine Corps base, known as the Crossroads of the Marine Corps.

Recruiting

A term applied in the intelligence community to finding private citizens who are willing to help professional American intelligence agents. The citizens who are successfully recruited are called operatives, sources, or co-optees. Recruiting, also referred to as co-opting, is a major function of the Behavioral Analysis Unit. Recruiting requires Behavioral Analysis agents to be skillful at establishing trust, often on an almost immediate basis.

Recruit Training

The Marine Corps training period known colloquially as boot camp. During this period, recruits are trained to shift their focus from themselves to others, a process that builds team strength, and begins the process of instilling trust among one another in new Marines.

See the hill, take the hill

A Marine Corps phrase that refers to bold action to achieve a goal, sometimes in the absence of careful planning. This style of action can be appropriate for short-term, aggressive missions, but is not effective for nuanced, human-based missions, such as the inspiration of lasting trust. Creating long-term trust—a process of subtlety, sincerity, and finesse—generally requires adherence to a proven, replicable system.

Semper Gumby!

This is a facetious Marine Corps expression that celebrates flexibility. It is a reference to the flexible, clay-character Gumby, who once appeared in television cartoons. Inspiring trust requires a commitment to flexibility, because the process is dependent upon adjusting to inevitable changes in people and situations. These changes—often unexpected, and seemingly contradictory—can emerge gradually, or suddenly.

Shields Down, Information In!

A phrase that refers to people becoming less defensive when they don't feel attacked. When they feel attacked, they reflexively put up shields, and often refuse to accept information—particularly if it's negative—no matter how true or obvious the information may be. As a rule, the best way to keep people from putting up shields is simply to avoid being critical or judgmental. An open, accepting attitude is very effective for encouraging people to accept information, even when it's not something they want to hear. A nonjudgmental attitude is excellent for inspiring not only the free flow of information, but trust itself.

SMEAC

A widely used military acronym that describes the basic elements of a military encounter, each of which requires intensive preparation. These elements are: Situation, Mission, Execution, Administration and Logistics, and Coordination. Robin Dreeke applied this system of preparation to the third step of inspiring trust: Craft the Encounter. The same basic elements occur in nonmilitary encounters, and preparation for them should be firmly entrenched before the encounter begins. During a systematic phase of preparation, there is still time to address each element carefully, and to explore back-up plans.

Somatic

A term used in anatomy and psychology that refers to a physical entity, even though this physical entity may be expressed through a nonphysical thought or emotion. Many elements of thought and emotion, including the mental and emotional aspects of trust, have strong somatic components. For example, a physical influence as simple as fatigue, or hunger, can impair a person's ability to be trusting.

Soviet bloc

The aggregation of nations that were once dominated by the former Soviet Union. The Soviet bloc, which encompassed most of Eastern Europe, was previously a major source of espionage applied against America, and was a focus of the FBI's Behavioral Analysis Program. Even after the disintegration of the Soviet bloc, climaxing with the fall of the Berlin Wall in 1989, many former Soviet-aligned nations continued to spy on America, with a focus on appropriating military and industrial secrets.

Special Agent in Charge

An elevated FBI rank, abbreviated as SAC, that often refers to the director of a regional FBI division. This rank is above that of a Special Agent, and achieving it generally requires a number of years of outstanding work. The rank is directly above that of an Assistant Special Agent in Charge, abbreviated as ASAC.

Subject

In the field of espionage, a subject is a person under suspicion of major malfeasance, including spying.

Term of Art

A word or phrase that has a specific meaning within a particular field, or profession. Terms of art used in the FBI's Behavioral Analysis Unit include "Craft the Encounter," which refers to analyzing an upcoming meeting with a person so carefully that the meeting is almost certain to conclude successfully. In general, people tend to prepare for meetings relatively casually, and this lax preparation often dooms the encounter to defeat.

Think Tank
A company or organization that generates intellectual property. They offer research, raw data, and advice, and often have government contracts with a wide variety of agencies, including the FBI.

To inspire trust, put others first
This phrase is the primary principle of trust-inspiration that is espoused in *The Code of Trust*. It is the stated theme of the book.

Tribe of trust
A phrase, coined in *The Code of Trust,* that refers to an informal group of people who gather around a trusted figure, and, by extension, trust one another. Frequently, each person in that group is also the center of his or her own group, creating a system of overlapping, interlocked groups. Almost all strong leaders are supported by a tribe of trust, and are frequently supported by many interlocked tribes of trust.

Trust
The formal, widely accepted definition of trust is: A strong belief in the truth, effectiveness, ability, or power of someone or some thing. Trust inspires confidence in, and triggers actions that promote, the person or thing that has inspired the trust.

Ultimate goal
A phrase that refers to a person's long-term, most highly valued ambition, or dream. When people identify and embrace their ultimate goals, they are far more capable of sacrificing the short-term satisfaction of temporary pleasures, and lesser goals. This allows them to put others first, which may slow their immediate progress, but accelerates their long-term progress. Putting others first creates large groups of people who trust them, and often elevates them to positions of leadership. In those elevated positions, with large numbers of people supporting them, the achievement of their ultimate goals becomes far more possible and practical.

Validation

Understanding the beliefs of another person, without necessarily agreeing with them. Validation is often confused with agreement, acceptance, or even admiration, but it is significantly different. Validating people inspires their trust, because validation, or understanding, is all that most people require. It is human nature to know that not everyone will agree with you, and people are typically so pleased with simple understanding that they are prompted to extend their trust.

When the first shot goes downrange, all hell breaks loose

A commonly used military phrase that describes the predictable chaos of battle, sometimes called the fog of war, that begins almost immediately after a battle starts. This chaos invariably interferes with the plans that have been prepared, and must be met with systematic back-up plans, and flexibility. Robin Dreeke adapted the phrase to nonmilitary encounters—particularly those in which the difficult task of inspiring trust is a goal. In those encounters, one's opening remark is equated with the "first shot downrange." After the opening remark, almost anything can happen, so a set of reliable systems needs to be in place, and strategies need to be flexible. The Four Steps to Trust, used in conjunction with the Code of Trust, provides most of this necessary support. The rest comes from adherence to the creed of: Semper Gumby!

ACKNOWLEDGMENTS

Robin Dreeke

My first thanks goes to my coauthor and brother for life, Cam Stauth. From day one Cam was the most inspired partner who put his lifelong experiences into our work with great conviction and mutual admiration. This would never have happened without him.

My heartfelt thanks to Marc Resnick for recognizing the uniqueness and power of the Code of Trust. He has been an amazing and supportive editor who has made the publishing process a joy. His ability to both recognize and draw out the value of individuals with unique backgrounds and tools is a unique and valued gift.

Like Marc, this book would never have been written without Nathaniel Jacks of InkWell Management. Nat heard of my work with trust through an article by Eric Barker (whom I'm also extremely grateful to). Following a few discussions, Nat recommended I team with Cam and the rest is history. Nat's gift for recognizing unique stories, assembling writing teams, and ultimately bringing these ideas to the world is his calling-card strength and I'm extremely grateful for being part of his circle.

I would be derelict and remiss if I didn't give my thanks to a great friend in my life Joe Navarro. I first met Joe many years ago when I was a fresh newbie to our behavioral team and Joe was the senior Jedi Master. From that first meeting Joe has been a part of my life, giving encouragement, guidance, mentorship, and always the most important gift . . . validation. Thank you, Joe, for always encouraging and pushing me to pass valuable information and life skills on to others.

Lastly, I need to thank everyone I have ever had a conversation with, whether you thought it was good or bad. I have reflected on them all and still do, thinking of how I could have communicated better, validated you more, made you feel more comfortable, and ultimately left you feeling better for having chatted. *The Code of Trust* is a compilation of all I have learned and continue to learn from you all. Thank you for allowing me to share a part of your life.

Cameron Stauth

My first, heartfelt thank-you goes to my good friend and coauthor, Robin Dreeke. One of the unsurpassed advantages that I've enjoyed from each of the books that I've written with other people has been the year-long, one-on-one tutelage and mentoring from some of the most accomplished and wisest people in the world. Robin is one of them, and it will be almost impossible for anyone who reads this book to resist envy for what I was lucky enough to enjoy, and benefit from, in my own life.

I'm also grateful to Marc Resnick for recognizing the value of this book, and the revolutionary idea behind it, more fully than anyone else in publishing, and for crafting it to its conclusion. Marc is a "writer's editor," with a gift for language, pacing, storytelling, and above all the primacy of important ideas.

Nathaniel Jacks, of InkWell Management, made my inclusion in this book not only possible, but a joyful experience, and Richard Pine, a partner at InkWell, has made the entirety of my career into an exciting and rewarding adventure. Much of what I know about trust, I learned from him.

Jessica Bodreau, manager of Your Virtual Office, was a virtual godsend in this project and the one before it, due to her extraordinary skills at everything from transcribing to organizing, and her dedication to excellence.

Gabriel Stauth was the project's chief technical associate, as he also was for every book I've written in the past ten years. There's nothing better than working with your son. The counsel of my daughter Adrienne, the wisest member of the family, also proved indispensable in a book about humankind's most powerful and delicate quality.

Camille Cole was very helpful in the final edit of this project, and others, sometimes in difficult circumstances.

The ideas, creativity, courage, and generosity of Lori Brockman, my wife, appear in or behind many of the best pages in the book.

Thank you all.

INDEX

from leaders, 125
to validate, 227, 335
for what matters most, 226–27, 335
locale, as what variable, 190
love, 266, 267
word of, dopamine and serotonin trigger from, 116
lying, exaggeration and, 32–33

Mandela, Nelson, 110
manipulation, 5–6, 25, 40–41, 65, 198, 330
brain hijacking and, 90
error of, 13
flattery and, 61
Marston, William Moulton, 135, 136
matching and mirroring, 244
material, external goals, 36–37
Me Decade, of 1970s, 41
medication, chemistry of trust and, 92
memory
acetylcholine neurotransmitters and, 90
leadership trust-inspiring, 87
of lines, active listening and, 228, 335
methodology, of *The Code of Trust,* 330
micro-context information, in communication technique, 218–19
Millennials, 189
minimal encouragers, in active listening techniques, 230
mission
of *The Code of Trust,* 329
link, as why variable, 198
in SMEAC planning system, 172
modifiers, active listening limiting of, 233, 335
motivations
for C style, *157–58, 158–59*
for D style, *151, 151–53*
for I style, *153, 154–55*
for S style, *155–56, 156–57*

narrator, of *The Code of Trust,* 330
National Academy for Law Enforcement Executives, FBI Counterintelligence Behavioral Analysis Program, 7, 14, 137
Navarro, Joe, 14, 18, 19, 141, 240

needs for success
of C style, *157–58*
of D style, *151*
of I style, *153*
of S style, *155–56*
negativity occurrence, in Personal DISCernment Inventory styles, 164–65
neurochemistry. *See* chemistry of trust
neurological consequences, of stress, 175
neurotransmitters
acetylcholine thought and memory, 90
adrenaline, 91, 144
adrenergic and thyroxine, 144
dopamine, 88, 116, 144, 207–8
GABA, 88, 144
for positive feelings, 87–88
serotonin, 88, 116, 144
nonjudgmental acceptance
in active listening, 227
in Code of Communication, 204
in Code of Digital Conduct, 254–56
from leaders, 58–59
nonverbal head tilt for, 39
nonjudgmental acceptance, in Code of Trust, 10, 13, 30, 40, 45, 49, 82, 331
confessions from, 57–58
course correction and, 60
insecurities and fears difficulty for, 58
nonjudgmental questions, 20, 214
nonverbal communication, 210–12, 240, 245–46
comfort signals and displays, 241–42
to defuse awkwardness, 18
discomfort signals and displays, 241, 242–43
head tilt as nonjudgmental acceptance, 39
I'm-sorry-wave, 52, 53, 54
to make people feel at ease, 34
matching and mirroring, 244
nonverbal style baseline, 243–44
nonverbal language, of trust, 32

open-ended questions, 20, 220–21, 335
opening remarks
ask for assistance, 177–78, 332
for C style, 161–62
Code of Trust reflection of, 174
for D style, 161